Extraordinary Dreams
and
How to Work With Them

SUNY series in Dream Studies
Robert L. Van de Castle, editor

EXTRAORDINARY DREAMS AND HOW TO WORK WITH THEM

Stanley Krippner,
Fariba Bogzaran,
and
André Percia de Carvalho

SUNY PRESS

STATE UNIVERSITY OF NEW YORK PRESS

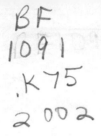
Published by
State University of New York Press, Albany

For information, address State University of New York Press,
90 State Street, Suite 700, Albany, NY 12207

Production by Marilyn P. Semerad
Marketing by Patrick Durocher

Library of Congress Cataloging-in-Publication Data

Krippner, Stanley, 1932–
    Extraordinary dreams and how to work with them / Stanley Krippner,
Fariba Bogzaran, André Percia de Carvalho.
    p. cm. — (SUNY series in dream studies)
    Includes bibliographical references and index.
    ISBN 0-7914-5257-3 (alk. paper) — ISBN 0-7914-5258-1 (pbk. : alk. paper)
    1. Dreams. I. Bogzaran, Fariba, 1958– II. Carvalho, André Percia de, 1969–
III. Title. IV. Series.

BF1091 .K75 2002

                                                              2001042011

10 9 8 7 6 5 4 3 2 1

To extraordinary dreamers
Rita Dwyer
Daniel Deslauriers
Patricia Garfield
Montague Ullman
Robert Van de Castle
and our other pioneering colleagues

Contents

Acknowledgments

The authors would like to express their appreciation to the Chair for the Study of Consciousness at Saybrook Graduate School for partially funding the preparation of this book, and acknowledge the support of the Dream Studies Program at John F. Kennedy University.

We would like to thank Steve Hart for his assistance in locating many reference materials; Marilyn Fowler and Dolores Richards for their invaluable editorial input; and the support of Daniel Kortenkamp, Tara Matheny-Schuster, Caroline Crossfield, Laura Faith, Emily Anderson, and our conscientious production editor, Marilyn P. Semerad.

Unless otherwise noted, all non-cited dream reports in this book were obtained from our students and colleagues. We would like to thank them for their collaboration, without which this book would not have been possible. Some of the material in this book was previously published in *Sonhos Exoticos* by Stanley Krippner and André Percia de Carvalho, Summus Publications, Sao Paulo, Brazil, 1998.

In the World They Call a Dream

These things I have seen
in the world they call
a dream: the swaying
of tall burgundy trees
surrounded by luminous
red auras; twin moons,
milky and full, above
the horizon; a bottomless
canyon where silvery water
rose to fill the void;
yellow stars swirling
in an inky sky.

These things I have done
in the world they call
a dream: stood enraptured
in an empty light-filled
room jutting into the
sea; ridden captive
on a train whose journey
had no end; scuttled
through craggy underground
paths to reach a city of
women; glided over a beach
in search of stones.

These things I have said
in the world they call
a dream: that relationships
ripen like apples, and
sometimes a little worm
gets inside; that people
are used to complex
"truths"; that to take away
our humanity is to take away
our best tool; that we don't
have to prove we can swim
by almost drowning.

—Deborah Hillman

Introduction

*D*olores had just dreamed that someone was banging on the front door of her house in the middle of the night. In the dream, she walked down the hallway and saw a man in an overcoat through the front door, silhouetted by the full moon outside. He had a hat pulled down low over his face. Alarmed, she called out, "What do you want?" He answered brusquely, "I want to sleep here tonight."

Dolores walked back to her bedroom and called the emergency operator. When she explained her concern about the man at the front door, the operator replied, "Oh yes, we know who he is. His name is Nisrock." Perplexed, Dolores asked for the spelling of the odd name. Meanwhile, she could hear the man trying the other doors of her house. They were all well locked. A split second later, she noticed that her telephone was sitting on a large Spanish dresser she had left behind in a move sixteen years earlier. At that moment, she realized that this was a dream and awakened.

Several days later, still reflecting on the dream, Dolores stopped at the local library and found an interesting book about the unconscious. She opened it at random, and, to her amazement, saw a drawing from an old manuscript. The caption read, "Nisrock, the winged Babylonian god who takes the souls of dreamers to the place of the dream."

The remarkable synchronicity first led Dolores to conclude that the dream was precognitive. It seemed to foretell an event, namely the soon-to-be-discovered book with the origin of the name Nisrock. However, as she began to reflect on her life in relation to the dream, she realized that the Nisrock figure was more accurately a representation of the unknown to which she needed to "open" herself. She had recently moved from the United States to another country and was worried about her ability to survive on her own. Her concerns had her "locked in" and she needed the courage to open herself to new experiences. As Dolores worked to more fully understand her dream, she realized that it was helping her psychologically, emotionally, and spiritually to embrace her new life.

The Dream Process

To understand the dream process, we must first describe the basic sleep cycle. Most people dream at least four or five times each night. About ninety minutes after falling asleep, we typically enter that stage of sleep marked by rapid eye movement (or REM) activity. Although dreams can appear during other sleep stages, it is during REM that our dreams generally occur. Laboratory sleep research shows that most sleepers, when awakened from REM sleep, will usually recall a dream.

At the beginning of the night, our first REM period may last only five minutes; toward the end of the night, a REM period may last as long as thirty minutes. This stage of sleep is marked not only by rapid eye movements but also by a loss of muscle tone, sexual excitation, and brain waves resembling those that characterize wakefulness.

The reason for REM sleep is unclear, but it may facilitate memory storage, maintain brain equilibrium during bodily repose and, among infants, may accelerate the development of the brain and the coordination of the eyes. All of these potential goals of REM sleep indicate that its psychological activities are superimposed on more primary biological functions. While dreams may assist the dreamer to become aware of life issues, identify personal myths, and solve problems, these psychological activities are secondary to the biological purposes served by REM sleep.

According to one widely-held theory, during a REM period, a cascade of potent chemicals (including seratonin) is released. This stimulates the visual and motor centers of the brain, evoking the dreamer's memories. No matter how they are elicited, it is these memories that the dreaming brain uses as building blocks for the dream—recombining them in original, vivid, and often baffling ways to create a story. The dreaming mind may create the story by providing a script that has been waiting patiently for the material that would allow it to surface, or by producing an on-the-spot narrative that matches, as best it can, the images that have been kindled.[1] In either event, the dreaming brain appears to have remarkable self-organizing properties that create several more or less coherent stories each night.

Some dream stories reflect basic problems in daily life with which we have wrestled for years, stories that hold deep meaning for the dreamer. Other stories may be more trivial in nature, reflecting events of the past few days or hours that surface as "day residue." Still others may be little more than a jumble of disparate pictures and events, lacking any coherent theme. Regardless of the type of dream story presented, the story-making process can be likened to what transpires when we use language while awake. In fact, dreams are often called the language of the night.

We can define dreams as a series of images—reported in narrative form—that occur during sleep. Our mental and emotional processes during dream time are, in many ways, quite similar to those we experience during wakefulness. In one study people were asked to make up a dream while awake. Surprisingly, the judges could not discriminate these imaginary accounts from the written reports of nighttime dreams. Both contained similar imagery reported in a narrative form. [2]

Dreams and Myths

Some dreams bear an uncanny resemblance to those stories we refer to as myths. To scholars of literature, myths are not falsehoods, but rather symbolic and metaphorical narratives that address important human issues. Dolores's dream exposed her to her "personal myth," a story she told herself over and over again. The dream informed her that her old myth of keeping herself from facing her unknown "shadow" was no longer appropriate, and that she needed to open herself to a new myth that would stimulate her further development. Although few modern cultures have unified mythologies that everyone accepts, each of us has personal myths, family myths, and institutional myths that can exert enormous power over our actions.

These myths largely operate outside of our awareness. In Western culture, where the interpretation of dreams is considered superstitious, dreamers are rarely aware of their personal myth except when it emerges in dreams. Even then, the myth usually takes the form of metaphors and symbols. Metaphors are activities that stand for highly complex human issues; symbols are images and pictures that do the same. When metaphors and symbols are used in dreams, their meanings differ from dreamer to dreamer. For this reason, there is no single meaning for an image from a dream. In Dolores's dream, for example, she felt the man knocking at the door represented an opportunity for her to look more deeply inside herself. However, for another woman, the figure might have symbolized the "animus," the masculine aspect of a woman's psyche, or perhaps a fear of intruders. To a woman who had been abused, the shadowy figure might have been a traumatic residue from the past. There is no one "correct" interpretation for each image.

Dreams That Create Experience

Dreams can illuminate our personal myths in several ways. Some "problem-finding" dreams help us to identify our personal myths. Other "problem-solving" dreams put our personal myths to use in resolving a personal or professional life issue. However, some dreams appear to have little to do with our life issues and problems. Because biological functions of dreams are primary and psychological activities are secondary, many dreams are merely replays of daily activities, retrospective accounts of past activities, rehearsals of future activities, or combinations of the past, present, and future that make little sense. The brain's propensity to stimulate itself during REM sleep sometimes introduces new imagery into an ongoing dream narrative. As these new images are worked into the dream story, many dreams take on a bizarre, surrealistic quality that reflects the brain's unpredictable activity. This activity may be described as chaotic, but the dreaming brain creates order out of chaos, and the result is a scenario that can be profound, provocative, or even silly.

Most dreams reflect our experience, usually events that have taken place during the past few days. However, some dreams appear to create new experiences. They seem to help us prepare for the future, generate a new idea, or provide helpful insights to our waking life. They may provide the breakthrough that is needed in articulating a new personal myth, rather than reflecting myths that already exist. We have referred to these dreams as "extraordinary" because they are strange and unusual, yet precious and beautiful.

Some extraordinary dreams fall into the category of what Rhea White calls "potentially exceptional human experiences." These dreams call attention to themselves because of their unusual or anomalous quality, but they also seem meaningful in some way. If one or more of these dreams is accepted as "genuine," and if it impacts the dreamer's life, White would call it an "exceptional human experience." [3]

The following is an example of an extraordinary dream that helped the dreamer to gain athletic skills. This lucid dream had a significant impact on the dreamer's life.

Eva's Dream

Eva, one of our colleagues, loved ice-skating but had not skated for twenty years. At age forty she decided to take up this sport again. The first night on the ice, Eva was afraid of falling, so she moved very slowly with great hesitation. After being on the ice for a week she had the following dream:

> In the dream I find myself watching an ice-skating performance. I want to go out on the ice but I am afraid. Suddenly I realize that I am dreaming. With no hesitation I enter the ice rink. One of the ice-skating champions holds my hand and encourages me to be free with my movements. I am skating beautifully with no fear. While holding her hands, I make a few spins, which I have never done before. Suddenly she lets go of my hand so I skate on my own. I slide and spin, then I feel elevated from the ice into the air. The excitement is so great it wakes me up.

The next day when Eva went ice-skating, her fear was greatly subsided. She began skating with renewed self-confidence and, because she was not fearful, she was able to recall the skating skills she had had as a teenager. The improvement was so dramatic that the ice-skating coach was surprised and approached her with many compliments as well as questions. This experience helped Eva not only with her ice-skating skills, but also gave her courage to take risks in other areas.

This type of extraordinary dream has not been widely discussed in books about dreaming. However, extraordinary dreams may provide us with valuable and meaningful dream content and offer a unique opportunity to apply and learn important new skills.

Content Overview

This book features a variety of extraordinary dreams that are worth studying. These powerful dreams are filled with potential meaning and direction that can be as valuable as waking-life experience. Each chapter focuses on one type of extraordinary dream. It provides a definition, a historical perspective, dream examples, and a way in which dream practitioners can appreciate, understand,

and/or work with the material in the dream. Among the variety of dreams discussed in this book are:

- Creative dreams, which assist us in our attempts to solve problems and bring new endeavors or aspects of ourselves into being.
- Lucid dreams, in which we are actually aware of dreaming while the dream is occurring, enabling us, to witness, or to choose a new direction inside the dream for exploratory, spiritual, or therapeutic value.
- Out-of-body dreams, in which we have the sensation of leaving our body during, or even after, the dream experience.
- Pregnancy dreams, which may alert us to a variety of unconscious attitudes and feelings that may accompany the impending arrival of a new child.
- Healing dreams, which can signal oncoming health problems or point out needed preventive or remedial action.
- Dreams within dreams, in which we dream about having a dream or dream-like experience or a "false awakening" in which we think we are awake but we are actually dreaming.
- Collective dreams, in which two people report similar dreams on the very same night or dream of each other in a common space and time, independently remembering similar events about the dream.
- Telepathic dreams, in which we appear to identify the thoughts of another person physically distant from us at the time of the dream.
- Clairvoyant dreams, in which we seem to perceive distant events about which we have no ordinary way of knowing.
- Precognitive dreams, in which the dream seems to provide information about an event that has not yet occurred.
- Past life dreams, which appear to detail past events we could have known little about unless we had been there at the time.
- Initiation dreams, which introduce us to a new reality or vocational path.
- Spiritual dreams, in which we may experience some form of entry into a spiritual realm or be visited by ancestors, spirits, or deities.

Included at the end of each chapter are exercises to aid in working with dreams. These exercises are not a substitute for counseling or psychological therapy. Individuals in need of counseling or psychotherapy require the help of a trained therapist. Most readers, however, will find that working with their dreams can help them clarify and often resolve inner conflicts. As psychotherapist Anny Speier maintains, the interpretation of dreams, whether attempted by a mental health professional, a layperson, or the dreamer, must reflect the individual's unique personality characteristics as well as his or her present life situation.[4]

Extraordinary dreams are not uncommon. By recalling our dreams, we open a magic theater with an endless array of dream experiences. However, to open the doors to these new realms, we need to take the time to record our dreams as completely and accurately as possible. Dream reports are the only tools available for dream interpretation. When we work with dreams, we are always dealing with the memory of a dream, not with the actual dream itself as experienced during sleep. While we assume that the dream report is fairly accurate, we cannot be certain unless scientists someday develop ways to film, televise, or record a dream while it is happening. Until that distant time arrives, here are some techniques to help you more fully remember and record your dreams.

Remembering and Recording Dreams

Synesius of Cyrene, writing in the fourth century C.E., observed, "It is an excellent idea to write down one's dreams . . . to keep, so to speak, a dream diary." [5]

When we write down our dreams, or record them on tape, we are expressing an event that typically connects a series of action-oriented images, usually visual in nature. However, because dreams occur in an altered state of consciousness, one in which the biological and chemical brain ecology differs from that during wakefulness, many people have difficulty recalling these images or recording them coherently when they awaken.

It helps to have a pad of paper and a pencil at your bedside to jot down a dream if you awaken in the middle of the night. Some people use a tape recorder. Others use a penlight to see what they are writing. Whatever technique you decide on, preparing to make notes about your dreams will give your psyche a message that you will honor your nighttime creativity. This message may suffice for ensuring dream recall. Later, you can transfer your dream reports to a notebook or to a computer diskette, adding details. As an alternative, you may choose to record your dream by making a drawing of the images or dreamscape. Or, if the dream is especially lyrical, you may be inspired to write a poem.

Remembering one dream per week is sufficient to start working with your dreams. If you cannot meet this modest quota, you might try self-suggestion. Before going to sleep, simply tell yourself (silently or aloud), "I will remember a dream when I wake up. I will remember a dream when I wake up." Adapt the words to your own purposes, then repeat the message twenty or thirty times. After a few nights, this technique should begin to yield results.

Once you have recorded a few dreams in your notebook, you can start to work with them. One direct approach is to deal with them as stories. Give each dream a title, just as you would a poem or short story. Then identify the different parts of the dream. We have found that everything in a dream falls into one or more of eight categories, a list originally conceptualized by Calvin Hall and Robert Van de Castle.[6]

1. Activities: Any type of action or behavior.
2. Setting: The place where the activities in the dream occurred; sometimes the dream will also include the time when the activities took place.
3. Objects: Any object made by humans; objects not occurring in nature.
4. Nature: Any natural object; objects not made by humans.
5. Characters: Any entity with a distinct personality.
6. Emotions: Any subjective mood or feeling experienced by a character.
7. Sensations: Any non-verbal stimulation of the senses experienced by a character.
8. Modifiers: Any adjective used to describe something in the dream.

All of these eight elements can be found in Dolores's dream. The activities were walking, talking, knocking, and telephoning. The setting of the dream was her home in the middle of the night. Articles included Nisrock's clothing, doors to Dolores's home, her telephone, and her Spanish dresser. The full moon was a natural object. Dolores, Nisrock, and the telephone operator were the three characters in the dream. The emotions in the dream were fear and confusion. The "banging" sound was a sensation. "Shadowy" was a modifier that described the figure.

Identifying these elements helps when dreamers begin to record their dreams because they call attention to aspects of the dream that would otherwise be ignored. Once dreamers become adept at dream recall and are able to use more sophisticated dreamwork methods, they often discontinue these techniques. However, it is helpful to retain the practice of giving their dream reports titles as this helps identify the dream's central theme. This theme often serves as what chaos theorists refer to as an "attractor," something that organizes other material. In this way, your dreaming brain is a self-organizing system that provides you with a constant flow of stories, many of them ordinary

Chapter 2

Understanding Dreams and Dreaming

𝒯he interpretation of dreams goes back to prehistoric times. Tribal shamans took dreams seriously, working with their own dreams as well as those reported by members of their tribes. Various tribes interpreted dreams differently; for members of the Mohave tribe, dreams were sources of knowledge and messages from the Great Spirit, while the Iroquois Indians saw dreams as "wishes of the soul" (a position similar to that taken by Sigmund Freud when he posited "wish fulfillment" as the exploration of dreaming).

To the early Greeks and Romans, interpreting dreams was seen as a way of understanding messages from the gods. In Greek mythology Hypnoswas the god of sleep. Hypnos and Thanatos, the god of death, were twin brothers, the sons of Nyx, god of the night. Hypnos's son, Morpheus, brought dreams to human beings. His brother, Icelus, was thought by the Greeks to bring dreams to animals, while a third brother, Phantasus, brought dreams to inanimate objects.

The Roman god of sleep was Somnus, whose name was combined with the Latin term *ambular*, or "to walk," to produce the word "somnambulism," or sleepwalking. The term "somnambulist" is also used by some psychologists to refer to an individual capable of having especially profound hypnotic experiences. The word "hypnosis" itself was derived from the name Hypnos, because many early investigators incorrectly assumed that hypnosis was a form of sleep.

Clay tablets have been found, dating to about 2500 B.C.E., that contain interpretive material for Babylonian and Assyrian dreamers. Negative dream content was attributed to spirits of the dead and malevolent demons. Flying dreams were said to indicate forthcoming disasters. Imbibing wine forecast a short life but drinking water foretold a long one. This interpretive approach provided the same meanings for everyone, regardless of individual differences and the context of the dream.[1]

The Egyptian papyrus of Deral-Madineh was written about 1300 B.C.E. and gives instructions on how to obtain a dream message from a god. This is probably the oldest manual in existence that was prepared to help people understand their dreams. Much of the information is startling in its modernity; dream associations, allegorical material, and puns were used to interpret dreams, as was information regarding the dreamer's background, character, and physical appearance. In other words, individual differences were considered when interpreting dreams. The Egyptian god of dreams was Serapis; several dream temples or "Serapeums" were located throughout Egypt and later in Greece and Rome. Incubation, the deliberate effort to induce dreams through sleeping in these temples, was widely practiced. "Stand-in" dreamers were even sent to the serapims to have a dream on behalf of someone who could not make the journey personally.

The sacred Veda of India contains lists of favorable and unfavorable dreams. This literature, probably written sometime between 1500 and 1000 B.C.E., contains specific interpretations for dream symbols. However, dreams from different periods of the night were given different interpretations, and the dreamer's temperament was considered before an interpretation was made. Furthermore, the early philosophers of India conjectured that there were four states of the "soul": waking, dreaming, dreamless sleep, and mystical unity.

The earliest Chinese work on dreams is the *Meng Shu,* dating to about 640 C.E. The Chinese classified dreams according to whether their source was external or internal. They believed that dreams usually came from an internal source, the dreamer's "soul," but that external physical stimuli could also be important. Sleeping on a belt, for example, could induce a dream about snakes. Dreams were seen as an avenue to self-knowledge, but their proper interpretation depended on their context. The positions of the sun, moon, and stars, as well as the season of the year, were taken into account in working with the dream.

Cicero wrote about dreams, taking a naturalistic approach rather than attributing dream content to deities and spirits. But sometime later, translating the Bible, St. Jerome consistently mistranslated a Hebrew word. As a result, "seeking guidance through dreams" in the Western world became equated with "witchcraft"; it remained so for more than a thousand years, the only exceptions being the occasional dreams seen as messages from God. Even so, many authorities in the Roman Catholic Church prohibited dream interpretation.[2]

In *The Tempest*, William Shakespeare wrote about "such stuff as dreams are made on." Some of his contemporaries, most notably Cervantes, Calderon, Quevado, and Gongora, also took dramatic advantage of the similarities between dreams and theater. But these were exceptions in an age in which dreams were either ignored or suspect. Working with the "stuff of dreams" only became respectable as a result of two scientific undertakings: the psychoanalytic exploration of the unconscious and the naturalistic study of sleep.

Freud, Maury, and Hervey de Saint-Denys

The use of electrophysiological monitoring devices to study sleep was preceded by the work of two nineteenth-century scholars, Alfred Maury and the Marquis d'Hervey de Saint-Denys. They practiced self-awakening, and sometimes used accomplices who periodically awakened them. Maury made detailed records of his sleep awakenings and his mental content. In addition, he conducted experiments to determine how external stimuli were incorporated into dream content. Hervey de Saint-Denys filled twenty-two volumes with his dreams, self-observations, and hypotheses. They both broke with past traditions by taking dreams seriously, by studying their naturalistic origins, and by observing their creative and problem-solving capacities.

In 1895, Sigmund Freud's *Project for a Scientific Psychology* was published, followed a few years later by *The Interpretation of Dreams.* Freud's publisher published the book in 1899, but he advanced the date on the book's title page to 1900 to herald the new century. However, only 351 copies were sold in the first six years after its publication. The importance of Freud's work was not initially recognized.

It was clear to Freud that he, like Maury and Hervey de Saint-Denys, was making a distinct break from the prevailing opinion by assuming that dreams could be interpreted. Pointing out that philosophers and psychiatrists of his day considered dreams "fanciful," Freud stated, "I must affirm that dreams really have a meaning and that a scientific procedure for interpreting them is possible."[3] But Freud differed from Maury and Hervey de Saint-Denys by insisting that dreams were disguises for unwelcome drives, motives, and wishes. As a result, Freud reinstated the importance of dreams for Western culture.

For Freud, dreams served the function of "wish fulfillment." The raw materials used in dream construction included recent experiences, such as events from the day immediately preceding the dream. Freud termed these elements "day residues" that were "worked over," yielding the ultimate dream product, a complex and bizarre patterning of the original material. Although these day residues typically represented rather inconsequential daily occurrences, Freud felt that they could serve as screens, disguising socially unacceptable impulses and wishes that needed to be discharged in the dream. Hence, the dream helped maintain a psychological equilibrium by allowing an outlet for disturbing thoughts and feelings, especially when the dreamer was asleep and more vulnerable to incursions of unconscious material.

Freud differentiated between the "manifest" and "latent" levels of dream content, the former being the disguised content as the dreamer reports it and the latter referring to the actual meaning as it emerges during the psychoanalytic session. Freud's central notion was that censorship, usually of repressed wishes, was the central principle governing information processing during dreaming.[4]

Adler and Jung

At one time a follower of Freud, Alfred Adler took issue with his former mentor. Adler felt that day residues were important in and of themselves because they represented waking concerns. The function of the dream, therefore, was to work through unresolved problems from waking life rather than discharge unconscious and repressed problems. Whereas Freud saw the dream as the "royal road to the unconscious," Adler saw it as the royal road to consciousness. He felt that the dream's purpose was to reinforce the dreamer's emotional power, motivating the dreamer to use that power to obtain his or her goals in waking life.[5]

Both Adler and Freud thought that day residue served as the raw material for nighttime dreams. However, Adler proposed that the individual's concerns were openly revealed in the dream, whereas Freud held that these concerns were disguised. Adler also argued for a continuity between sleep and wakefulness; for him, the dream expressed one's lifestyle, serving as an integral part of the individual's mental functioning. The dream, being the creation of the dreamer, reflected his or her personality. Hence, Adler considered the dream to be purposive in nature, seeking to solve problems in a manner consistent with the dreamer's typical daily behavior.[6]

Both Adler and Freud erroneously concluded that people who function well in their daily lives rarely dream because they deal adequately with their problems while awake. However, electrophysiological research has demonstrated that virtually everybody dreams several times each night. Furthermore, neither Freud nor Adler proposed that the brain itself might be the source of dream information, a point of view that has gained popularity as the result of contemporary laboratory investigations.

For Adler, dream images were a type of language that represented the individual's current life situation. His emphasis on the symbol that expresses rather than on the symbol that disguises was consistent with his emphasis on the continuity between waking-style and dream-style. For Carl Jung, another of Freud's early associates who later broke with him, the dream symbol also revealed the inner life rather than concealed it. Jung, however, held that one's dream-style often contradicted one's waking-style; the dream may represent a suppressed or poorly developed function, or it may represent a pattern of behavior to be expressed in the future.[7]

In addition, Jung believed that dream images frequently represented emerging forces in a person's life rather than the repressed sexual wishes and troublesome past experiences stressed by Freudians. In contrast to Freud, Jung found it valuable to have his clients write down both their dreams and waking fantasies, and to take an active role in interpreting their dreams. He often used the technique of "amplification," in which both cultural myths and personal memories would be considered in order to understand the dream more fully. To Jung, a major function of dreams was compensatory, a mode by which the unconscious expresses in symbolic form a homeostatic reaction to the one-sided position of the conscious mind. The dream is seen as a self-representation of the psyche, emerging as part of the continual regulation of one's psychological processes.

Despite their differing positions on many critical issues, Freud, Adler, and Jung all saw the function of the dream as facilitating some type of resolution or equilibrium within the psyche. Whereas Freud was more likely to emphasize conflict and Adler and Jung to focus on balance, all three found dreams clinically useful. Later clinicians continued to acknowledge the unconscious determinants of the dream, but generally emphasized ways in which the dream directly mirrored the dreamer's conscious concerns and problems. Most contemporary dream practitioners differ with Freud, acknowledging the ability of dreamers to avoid undue self-deception and defensiveness when attempting to understand their dreams. The conception of the dream as an authentic presentation of personality dynamics rather than a disguised product of repression is common to most current dream interpretive schools. This notion would have been ridiculed by many early psychoanalysts who took the position that only the therapist could tell a client what his or her dream signified, an extreme position not taken by Freud himself.

Foulkes and Neisser

Sometimes the images in our dreams make little sense if we presume that they only refer to the people or objects they depict. In those instances, they are probably symbols referring to something other than themselves. Freud complicated the issue by asserting that the symbols occurring in dreams often express, in disguised form, wishes the dreamer has repressed. However, this assertion implies a discontinuity in nature. Most current dream practitioners believe that the symbol-making process in dreams exhibits more commonalties than differences with the symbol-making process in other fields of human endeavor, such as the arts.

This continuous, "cognitive" position is taken by David Foulkes, a psychologist who sees dreams as meaningful and symbolic, but not as predetermined, encoded messages that need to be "translated" (as a linguist would translate a foreign language). The human mind can be treated as an abstract formalized system, a kind of computer that transforms and rearranges symbolic material. Ulric Neisser, another cognitive psychologist, understands dreaming as a type of imagination, a cognitive activity that often anticipates waking information. He groups dreams with other imaginative products including after-images, hallucinations, and motion pictures in which the perceiver is being systematically misinformed by the "real environment." The dreamer's visual system simulates an object by providing some of the information that would be available if that object were actually present.[8]

According to Foulkes, the dream is "knowledge-based" and "bound to reflect some of the ways in which the dreamer mentally represents his or her world." Dreams are seen as vivid imagery, closely related to waking imagery. Indeed, Foulkes has found that almost all people awakened after a dream are able to identify some events as having rough parallels in their waking experience.[9] He argues that dreams are little more than waking consciousness stripped of most sensory input, and freed from the obligation of making coherent connections to the external world.[10] Yet some differences between waking cognition and dreaming cognition do exist. Dreams typically manifest cognitive limitations such as the inability for advanced planning and the inability to choose between two or more alternatives.

Charles Rycroft, a psychoanalyst, notes that if dreams are poetry, they are incomplete poems. It is the nature of dreams to cast their meaning in symbols that are both highly personal, yet, in addition, represent the shared legacy of the dreamer's culture. In most cases, however, dream imagery is too dependent on the dreamer's personal experiences to be convertible into works of art with wide appeal.[11]

There are exceptions, of course, most notably Henry James, Robert Louis Stevenson, Bram Stoker, and other authors who drew upon their dreams for inspiration. Nevertheless, the cognitive approach to dream interpretation sees these efforts, as well as less spectacular examples, as cognitive plans for dealing with memories that are more or less randomly activated during sleep. Some cognitive approaches to dreaming see the brain as a super-computer that has the capacity to generate dreams; however, this argument does not easily explain the highly creative dream that brings something new into the dreamer's world—and often into the world at large.

Hobson and McCarley

An even more basic type of random activation is central to the work of the neurophysiologists J. Allan Hobson and Robert W. McCarley, who have hypothesized that the elements in dreams derive from a synthesis of information produced by activation during sleep of the brain's motor pattern generators and sensory systems. This internal information is linked and compared with information about the organism's past experiences. They conclude that dreams are not a result of an attempt to disguise, but are a direct expression of this synthetic effort.[12] In other words, the brain is first internally activated, it then scans its memory for images that match the activation, and then synthesizes this information to form the dream narrative.

Hobson and McCarley have produced laboratory data indicating that during REM sleep, brain stem neurons activate higher brain centers and generate rapid eye movements as well as various sensory-motor and emotional processes. The brain uses its stored information to synthesize dream imagery and construct plots to fit this activated material. The role of emotion is critical in Hobson and McCarley's hypothesis; dream intensity is associated with the dreamer's respiratory rates, heart rate, and fluctuations of skin potential.

If dream content were a function of the distinctive pattern of neural events occurring in REM sleep, one would expect it to be rather bizarre in nature. The highly activated cortex must synthesize volleys of neuronal information from many sources in REM sleep; at other times during the night, the cortex is not highly activated and fewer neural stimuli impinge on it. Hobson tested this hypothesis by taking 146 pairs of sleep reports from 73 subjects; one report was obtained from REM sleep and one was not. A "Bizarreness Scale" that establishes discontinuity, incongruity, and uncertainty was applied to the dream plot, as well as to the characters, objects, action, dreamer's thoughts, and dreamer's feelings as reflected in the reports. About 70 percent of the REM sleep reports could be classified as bizarre, versus about 20 percent of the non-REM sleep reports, supporting Hobson and McCarley's theory.[13]

If Hobson and McCarley are correct, dreams result from attempts by higher brain centers to "make sense" of cortical stimulation by lower brain "dream generators." Dreams take the stimuli produced by these dream generators and use the images as story material. As a result, any number of psychological functions can be superimposed upon the basic biological process, such as, integrating daytime experiences with those memories already stored away; providing a "safety valve" so that the dreamer can deal with upsetting issues and events; and addressing one's unsolved problems and coming up with tentative solutions. A few writers would claim that dreams function only to purge unnecessary brain cell connections produced during wakefulness and that dream content is best forgotten.[14] But even if this neurological function occurs, the advice to forget one's dreams is not necessarily logical because divergent thought may contain creative ideas. In a further rebuttal of this position, Hobson states:

> Since dreaming is universal, it stands as testimony to the universality of the artistic experience. In our dreams, we all become writers, painters, and film makers, combining extraordinary sets of characters, actions, and occasions into strangely coherent experiences. . . . I thus strongly object to any implication that the artistic experiences of waking or dreaming are fundamentally pathological, defensive, or neurotic.[15]

Hobson and McCarley do not agree with Freud's notion that a repressed wish organizes the dream. Instead, the brain's creative processes produce a meaningful narrative from the randomly evoked images, activities, and memories that occur during REM sleep. As a result, dream practitioners (or "dreamworkers"), can discard the idea that dreams merely relive previous experiences; instead, dreams often are capable of fabricating new experiences. These emerging ideas, novel feelings, and unusual views of old problems can be amusing, innovative, and practical. It is this novelty that can be put to use by people who want to study their dreams and learn from them.

In confirmation of Maury's trail-blazing work, Hobson and McCarley observed that external stimuli can be incorporated into one's dream content. External fluctuations in light, heat, and sound can influence dreams, even though the laboratory attempts to measure this phenomenon have produced capricious results. Sometimes a dreamer will hear a doorbell ring but awaken to an alarm clock. An increase in room temperature may shift the setting of a dream to a hot, sandy desert. The fact that dreams can synthesize so many elements from internal stimuli, external stimuli, and one's memory bank demonstrates their remarkably creative potential.

Many orthodox psychoanalysts and other psychotherapists insist that there are psychodynamic determinants for every bit of dream content. However, this dogmatic position was never taken by Freud, who admitted that external sensory and internal somatic stimuli could initiate dreaming. Freud simply assigned a more critical role to psychodynamic factors, concluding that the objective sensory stimulus encroaching upon sleep plays only a modest role as a dream source and that other factors determine the choice of the memory image to be evoked. Hobson and McCarley also have given the key role to internal stimulation. One's memories, no matter how pressing at the time, may not appear in the dream at all if they do not match the internally generated patterns of light and other sensations. And if Hobson and McCarley are even partially correct, one should not expect all elements of the dream to make equal sense; some items may reflect internal or external stimuli that one's memory bank can not easily match. This is apparent when the content of extraordinary dreams is examined.

Antrobus and Solms

Objections to Hobson and McCarley's proposal about dream generation have come from several investigators. John Antrobus, for example, has described a "feed forward" system that is lawful rather than random. Eye movements are directly associated with this system because the dreamer is "looking at" the action in the dream, and periods of dense REM activity reflect a dream's vividness and clarity. According to Antrobus, higher brain centers and more complex cognitive processes are involved in dream production right from the beginning. This is a "top down" model in contrast with Hobson and McCarley's "bottom up" model.

Antrobus concedes that lower brain centers may trigger REM activity, but holds that their contribution is to determine the rate of REMs rather than specific features of dream imagery. Thus, there is more control by the cortex than Hobson and McCarley credit. Antrobus also disputes the uniqueness of REM dream reports; his data indicate that many differences between REM and non-REM dream reports disappear once the number of words in a report are taken into account. In other words, REM dream reports are more bizarre than non-REM reports, in part, because they are longer. As a result, some non-REM reports can be extraordinary in nature.[16]

Another dissenting position is taken by Mark Solms, whose research has convinced him that dreaming and REM sleep are controlled by different brain processes. The brainstem mechanisms associated with REM sleep can only generate the psychological phenomena of dreaming with the help of a second forebrain mechanism. This forebrain activity also is responsible for non-REM dreams. Both "REM on" and "non-REM on" mechanisms stand outside dream formation itself, which is mediated by an independent "dream on" mechanism located in the forebrain.[17]

Solms' data indicate that up to 10 percent of non-REM dream reports have all the characteristics of REM dream reports. He elicited similar reports from epileptics after their seizures, supporting his hypothesis that dream reports are similar to material obtained from states of consciousness other than REM sleep. His work with brain-injured patients produced further support for his hypothesis; some recalled no dreams in either REM or non-REM sleep, and some reported dreams even though the lower brain (site of the alleged "dream generator") was severely damaged. The former group of patients lacked some of the highest regulatory brain mechanisms, those to which Solms attributes dream production.[18]

Boss, Ullman, and Globus

Some dream theorists urge the dreamer to accept dream images and dream experiences in their own right and on their own terms. The existential psychiatrist Medard Boss denies that a hidden, symbolizing agent lies within the dreamer. He recommends working with dreams by having clients try to determine the emotional connections between themselves and the dream. The therapist might ask:

> Does it not strike you that you found yourself, in your dreaming state, standing high up on a shaky iron scaffolding, clinging in terror to its iron

shafts lest you fall down to your death? Do you perhaps have an inkling now, in your waking state, of an analogous position?[19]

At this point, the client may relate a feeling of anxiety consistent with the dream images. Some critics would claim that Boss is using symbolism, to some extent, in his approach. Nevertheless, Boss is a welcome counterbalance to those therapists whose extremely intellectual approach to symbolism in a dream ignores the feeling quality of the dream itself. Medard Boss insists that both dreaming and waking are unique forms of human existence, providing two ways of confronting the human condition. Dreaming contains the possibility of revealing an "unveiled world" if individuals reflect upon their dream experience and learn from it.[20]

Montague Ullman represents a humanistic approach to dreamworking, seeing dreams as having a potentially healing influence. The dreamer must feel safe as he or she moves into the intimate domains of the psyche. The dreamer also needs to be helped to understand the dream images that he or she is reluctant to face alone. For dreamwork to be effective, it has to meet both of these needs. Nonetheless, claims Ullman, anyone who is sufficiently motivated can learn the necessary skills.[21]

Ullman takes the position that there is a crucial difference between dreaming and the dream. Dreaming is a function of the sleeping organism and occurs in repetitive cycles during the night, irrespective of whether or not the dreamer recalls the process. The dream report is something quite different; it is a memory in the waking state of some aspect of the dreaming experience. Although clearly related to dreaming, it lacks the involuntary and spontaneous quality of the dreaming experience. In other words it is a report that may or may not be faithful to the dreaming process.

Dreaming consciousness differs from ordinary waking consciousness. Dreamers are involuntary witnesses to a symbolic and metaphorical display of some aspect of their lives, usually in the form of visual imagery, although other sensory modes may also occur. Some dreamers report considerable auditory imagery as well as touch, smell, taste, and feeling. The dreams of individuals who have been blind since birth are reported almost entirely in these other sensory modalities. Ullman points out that dream content, although borrowed from the world of the dreamer, is not a photographic representation of that world. Dream images and activities are often transformed into symbols and metaphors that portray facets of a current life predicament in a highly specific and selective way.

Ullman gives the example of a young man, still in the middle of a difficult divorce, who had become seriously involved with another woman. They had discussed marriage, even though his divorce was not yet final. In the young man's dream, he sees himself leaving one hotel and walking down the street toward another hotel. While in the street, he tries to put on his tie, but discovers that he is already wearing one. In this dream, the movement from one hotel to another is a metaphor for moving from one relationship to another. The young man's ties could be seen as symbols for marriage—one actual marriage and one contemplated marriage.

Ullman's approach is humanistic because it stresses individual differences, examines the social context of the dream, and sees dreams as partaking in a growth-oriented process that is intrinsically honest and authentic. It is also humanistic in the sense that dreamworking is seen as a skill readily available, not just to a specialized practitioner such as a psychoanalyst. Ullman disagrees with Freud's notions about the dream's proclivity to disguise and conceal. For Ullman, the three basic features of the dream are: its relevance to an active issue in the dreamer's life; the mobilization of material from the dreamer's past to better understand this issue; and the ability of the dream to puncture outworn personal myths and bring the dreamer closer to a realistic appraisal of the issue.

Over the millennia, the source of dreams has been seen as divine, demonic, the dreamer's "soul," the dreamer's environment, the dreamer's unconscious, the dreamer's imagination, and the dreamer's brain. For some, dream interpretation is a waste of time because dreams are meaningless; for some, dream interpretation must be done by an expert, while for others, dreamers can learn the skills needed to understand their own dreams. Gordon Globus, an existentially-oriented psychiatrist, believes that the dreamer temporarily lives in a special "life-world"; therefore, dreaming is worth considering on its own terms. The dream is a spontaneous production in which the dreaming "life-world" is created each night; it is a "firsthand" production, not a "secondhand" effort.[22]

Dreams and New Paradigm Thinking

New paradigm thinking takes into consideration advances in general systems theory, quantum mechanics, mathematics, and chaos and complexity theories. According to John Arden, "The changes . . . throughout the past century have significantly altered our perspective on how the universe operates. Instead of a deterministic and mechanistic universe in which complete objectivity is possible, we see a fluid, probabilistic and interconnected universe."[23]

This new paradigm has shaped emerging theories that seek to account for the complexity of the dreaming process: the organism is seen as an open system, in constant flux in multiple dimensions—physiological, psychological, and sociological. For human beings, the process of developing and maintaining a healthy sense of self takes place via autopoetic, or self-creating, processes. Dreams provide "self-referential themes that contribute to the organization of a cohesive self. In species that have more complex neuronal systems and sociocultural systems, a more complex cohesive self is critical."[24]

As we have seen, the activation-synthesis model of Hobson and McCarley provides a possible description of the mechanisms that trigger REM sleep, a kind of biological clock trigger involving interaction of neurotransmitters in specific brain cell groups. However, in their model, dream images precede symbolic meaning; little is said about what brings the dream together in the synthesis phase. Taking a non-linear perspective, Arden argues that while the brain is put in a chaos-like destabilized state during the REM cycle, "the self system acts as an attractor that pulls and organizes the neuronal activity and imagery. This personalized imagery may be seen as a . . . "self"-organizing process. The dream process organizes and integrates nocturnal neuronal stimuli, making them more relevant to the self system."[25]

The most constant image in dreams is the image of one's self. The dream presents situations by which we can observe how the self is "updating" itself by trying to make sense creatively of ongoing emotions, cognitive and existential changes that take place simultaneously within itself and in the world. It is a form of creative reorganization made possible by the on-going "self"-organizing production of the dream. So, according to the physicist Fred Alan Wolf, "we dream to develop a sense of self."[26]

This self-organization takes shape in the narrative or story form. George Baylor and Daniel Deslauriers have demonstrated how, in the dream story, there are many "choice" points (or "bifurcations") that could lead to different outcomes.[27] Their analysis shows how social scripts and personal scripts interact to stage a creative exploration of a self-defined problem. Each dream could be explored further in waking life to reveal the personal mythology or the set of significant beliefs that underlies them.[28]

In new paradigm thinking, dream analysis is viewed as a collaborative process between people. Daniel Deslauriers and John Cordts maintain that in a therapeutic encounter, the pursuit of dream meaning involves dream sharing.

> In the context of a shared reality, dream meaning is not something abstractly attributed by only one participant in the dream sharing dialogue, be it the dreamer, the therapist, the researcher or any dream worker. Rather, it is a process that can be described more realistically as a joint venture. . . . Depending on the context, meaning arises between the dreamer and the researcher, the therapist, and the dream worker.[29]

Therefore, the concept of an independent, objective reality gives way to a more fluid reality of a participative universe. In such a universe the way we question a dream will influence the meaning of the dream. Psychological theories of dreams that focus on one aspect over another are not necessarily seen as incorrect but rather as presenting complementary aspects of the complex, multifaceted phenomena of dreams and dreaming.

Researcher and author Harry Hunt proposes an elaborate, diamond-like model of this multiplicity that includes lucid, archetypal, somatic, problem-solving and telepathic dreams.[30] Furthermore, Hunt argues that "research on the multiplicity of dreams . . . offers some of the most convincing evidence for the potential unity amidst endless diversity that constitutes the human mind."[31]

Thoughts, memories, and emotions, as well as other components of our conscious experience, are themselves processes that ebb and flow moment by moment, hour to hour, and day to day, in a chaotic rhythm. Contrary to the notion that dreams are "psychotic," most dreams, from both REM and non-REM sleep, seem very much like waking experiences.[32] Nevertheless, dreams are often saturated with an emotional intensity lacking in waking hours, and the lack of critical thinking in dreams permits an acceptance of shifts in people, objects, and settings that make little sense in wakefulness.[33] Once experienced, the dream becomes a "text," and like other "texts," dream reports are available for multiple readings and varied interpretations.[34]

All these dream models and theories bring different perspectives to dream understanding. We will rely on these sources in the forthcoming chapters to assist you in arriving at a better understanding of your extraordinary dreams.

Creative Dreams

From ancient times, writers, artists, musicians, scientists, and a variety of individuals in other professions have used dreams as a source of creativity. Dreams have been included in such great creative works as *The Epic of Gilgamesh*, *The Iliad*, and *The Odyssey*. According to a report dating back to about 2500 B.C.E., King Gudea of Mesopotamia dreamed of a god-like man "as tall as the sky." This impressive creature ordered King Gudea to construct a temple in his honor, going so far as to design the architecture. King Gudea recalled the plan when he awakened and had the temple built.

The word "creativity" has several possible meanings. To most observers, it denotes the ability to bring something new into existence. For others it is the psychological process by which novel and valuable products are fashioned. But it can describe the product itself—the artwork, poem, statue, machine, or recipe that is the end result of the process. For still others, it describes a unique interaction between a person and an environment that affords an opportunity for creativity. Thus, there are at least four aspects of creativity: the creative process, the creative product, the creative person, and the creative situation.

The psychologist E. Paul Torrance provides a definition of creativity that is congruent with what seems to happen in dreams. For Torrance, creativity is a process of being sensitive to problems, deficiencies, gaps in knowledge, missing elements, and disharmonies. The process identifies problems, searches for solutions, makes guesses, and formulates hypotheses about these problems. It then tests and retests the hypotheses, possibly modifying and again testing them, and finally communicates the results.[1] Similar to creativity in Torrance's concept, dreams sometimes identify problems, search for solutions, and test hypotheses, then communicate the results to the dreamer.

R. W. Weisberg states that creative problem solving occurs when a person produces a novel response that solves the problem at hand.[2] Therefore, we might include in the category of creative dreams those in which the dream content helps to resolve one of the dreamer's problems. Indeed, Carl Jung once wrote that a dream is a theater in which the dreamer is the scene, the player, the prompter, the producer, the author, the public, and the critic.[3]

Creative Problem Solving in Dreams

Creative problem solving in dreams can take place either by considering dream activities and images as realistic representations or as metaphors or symbols. On one level or another, dreams reflect a process of creative synthesis at work. Dreams synthesize the activity of various parts of the brain and many sources of dream content. An example of a creative dream as a realistic representation is one recalled by William Blake, the poet and artist. The image of Blake's dead brother came to him in a dream and showed him a process of copper engraving. Blake immediately verified the technique and put it to use to engrave his illustrated songs.

An example of a creative dream that was metaphorical is that of Elias Howe, the inventor, who had been trying to construct a lock-stitch sewing machine. For several years, Howe had used needles with holes in the middle of the shank, but none proved to be useful. One night, he dreamed that a tribe of savages had captured him. Their king bellowed, "Elias Howe, I command you on pain of death to finish this machine at once!" Frustrated, Howe cried for mercy. This plea did not move the monarch, who commanded his warriors to execute Howe. Although overcome with terror, Howe noticed eye-shaped holes near the tips of the spears his executioners were carrying. He realized that what was needed to make his machine work was a needle with an eye-shaped hole near the point. Howe awakened and whittled a model of what he saw in his dream.[4] In this case, the image of the spears was a symbol for the needle required to bring the lock-stitch sewing machine into actuality.

Montague Ullman lists four reasons why we can say that every dream partakes in the creative process. First, all dreams are original; they join various elements to form new patterns. Second, dreams, like many other creative processes, are involuntary experiences; they occur naturally. Third, dreams contain metaphors and symbols; they employ creative imagery. Fourth, humankind's capacity to produce them spontaneously demonstrates their creative potential.[5] Taking a somewhat different view, psychiatrist Silvano Arieti calls dreams "original," but not "creative." Arieti claims that dreams can be of value once they are interpreted, but "then they are no longer dreams; they are translations of dreams."[6]

Nevertheless, some dreams are associated with extraordinary creativity. The mathematician Jerome Cardan had a recurring dream that ordered him to write *De Subtilitate Rerum,* his most celebrated book. Whenever Cardan was lax in his writing habits, the dream returned with great force. Giuseppe Tartini, the composer who invented the modern violin bow, had not been able to complete a sonata. One night he dreamed that he found a bottle on a beach; inside, a demon begged to be released. Tartini agreed, on condition that the demon assist him with his unfinished work. Once let out of the bottle, the demon seized a violin and, according to Tartini, played "with consummate skill a sonata of such exquisite beauty as surpassed the boldest flights of my imagination." Upon awakening, Tartini recalled and transcribed the music as best he could, creating what is often called "The Devil's Sonata." It became Tartini's most acclaimed composition, yet Tartini lamented, "The piece . . . was the best I ever wrote, but how far below the one I had heard in my dream."[7]

Research into Creative Dreams

An early attempt to study dreams and creative problem solving was initiated by M. E. Maillet, who obtained eighty replies from mathematicians to whom he had sent questionnaires. Four of them cited mathematical dreams in which they had found a solution to a problem. Eight mentioned that the beginnings of solutions had occurred in dreams. Fifteen mathematicians stated that they had awakened with complete or partial answers to mathematical questions, even though they did not recall dreams about them. Another twenty-two said they recognized the importance of mathematical intuition, even if they did not recall specific dreams about their problems.[8]

Robert Davé attempted to determine if dreams could facilitate creative problem solving by conducting a study of twenty-four people who were at an impasse in solving a problem. One group of eight subjects was hypnotized; a "hypnotic dream" was evoked, and the subjects were told that they would have nighttime dreams offering solutions to their problems. Another group was given instructions on how to solve their problems through activities emphasizing rational, cognitive thought exercises. Eight other participants served as a "control" group and were simply interviewed regarding their problems.

Davé judged the experiment a success for six of the eight members in the hypnotic dream group. For example, one group member was a writer who had completed extensive research for an article about an art store, but was unable to develop a format for the piece. His hypnotic dream image consisted of three piles of material, indicating to him that the article could be divided into three parts. In a subsequent nighttime dream, he found himself floating into an art store, observing the activities that constituted the subject matter of his proposed article. In the hour after he awoke, he composed a draft of the article, using a format that took the reader on a walking tour of the store. Another subject was blocked in her efforts to complete a poem. She had only been able to write one stanza prior to hypnosis. On the third night following her hypnotic session, she awoke from a vivid dream that motivated her immediately to compose three stanzas. In contrast, only one member of the rational-cognitive group reported a problem-solving breakthrough and no one in the control group reported success.[9]

Michael V. Barrios and Jerome L. Singer queried forty-eight volunteer subjects about their creative impasses, finding that most had been blocked for over three months. Their reported difficulties involved completing literary or artistic works, professional or vocational projects, or scientific or technical tasks. The subjects were administered a battery of psychological tests, then divided into four randomly assigned groups of twelve—waking imagery, hypnotic dream, rational discussion, and the control group.

The subjects in the waking imagery group engaged in ten directed imagination exercises and subsequently generated three waking fantasies that related to their creative projects. Those in the hypnotic dream group were exposed to a hypnotic induction procedure and subsequently produced three hypnotic dreams that related to their creative projects. Subjects in the rational discussion group were led through a highly focused and logical collaborative examination of their creative projects in which distractions and task-irrelevant thoughts were avoided. The control group was simply encouraged, in a non-directive fashion, to discuss their projects.

Results of the experiments indicated that waking imagery and hypnotic dreams were most effective in promoting the resolution of creative blocks. When the psychological test data were examined, it was found that subjects who had the ability to regulate their attention and showed a low level of negative daydreaming (involving guilty or hostile fantasies) were most likely to demonstrate positive changes. For example, a writer in the hypnotic dream group had published poetry and nonfiction but was having difficulty writing fictional material. With each successive hypnotic dream, however, the action and dialogue of her proposed short story became more elaborate. Elements of conflict between characters, which initially had been notably absent to that point, began to emerge and enliven the plot. Following the test, the writer reported a high level of satisfaction in relation to the story and also reported enhanced productivity in writing poetry.[10] In other words, the two techniques that involved imagery appeared to be the most successful. As the study demonstrated, it is the imagery in dreams that often leads to creative breakthroughs.

On the basis of these and other research studies, Christopher Evans concluded that during a period in which one is working on a problem, analyzing the key features in a dream may yield a solution. To benefit from such a dream, however, one needs to exert a certain amount of effort. As Evans explains, the solution "may leap at you in a sudden flash of insight, but more likely you may need to work at it to tease it out."[11] In other words, dreams are no panacea; they do not solve everyone's problems. Nonetheless, the track record of dreams is encouraging enough to warrant the attention of the dreamer. Creative dreams have assisted in solving problems for some celebrated people as well as ordinary people. Dreamwork will probably result in self-knowledge and growth in some areas of the psyche, even though the specific path, like so many of life's adventures, is difficult to predict.

Christy's Dream

Christy, one of our students, was a junior in high school when she first discovered that her dreams provided her with unique problem-solving opportunities. As she entered college, she continued to tap into her dreams for answers whenever she became challenged in her undergraduate courses, especially organic chemistry. In one dream:

> I am at my study desk and I open my calculus textbook. I am normally nervous when I try to do my homework problems, but this time I am confident. I know deep down inside that I am a mathematical genius and so I turn the page to problem #13. This problem is the most difficult in the set. Within seconds, I write down two pages of algebraic notations. I become ecstatic and awake with my answer in mind.

On waking, Christy immediately wrote down the calculations. Later, at school, she discovered that she was one of few students in the class to successfully solve problem thirteen. Inspired by her problem-solving dream, Christy shared the details of her experience with her study partner. The two decided to use their dreams to creatively solve mathematical problems when they could not arrive at solutions in waking. When a solution or clarification was needed, they would study the material shortly before taking a nap. Typically, they would dream about the study material and then wake up with a clearer understanding of the problem. Incubating dreams for problem-solving became an important process, which enabled them to pass their exams.

As Christy's experience shows, some problem-solving dreams come in a literal language, others come in a symbolic form. The following is an example of how metaphoric dreams can alert us to certain problems, and how we can creatively take action in waking.

Marilyn's Dream

Marilyn, a business executive, was considering a joint venture with a high-tech company involved in multimedia. This was a direction that she was very interested in pursuing for her company. The high-tech company had made strong overtures to finalize a deal that Marilyn thought would be advantageous for the future of her firm. A contract was ready to be signed in a meeting the next morning. However, there was something she could not identify about the prospective partnership that was bothering Marilyn. That night she incubated a dream, asking if this would be a positive direction for her company's future. In the dream:

> I am walking to my car when suddenly an intruder comes up behind me and puts a gun to the back of my head. He forces me into the car and tells me to drive. I begin driving while he continues pointing the gun at my head. In the next scene, I find myself locked in the trunk of my car while the intruder is driving my car away.

Marilyn woke up feeling alarmed and anxious. Upon reflection, it became clear the dream was telling her that if she chose to proceed with the contract, the other company would be in the driver's seat and that she would lose future control and direction of her company. Immediately she called an early meeting with her staff to review the contract provisions. As her group reviewed the contract more closely, they discovered clauses that would have effectively given control of all future work to the prospective partner. Later she confronted the president of the high-tech company and her worst fears were confirmed. She discontinued all further negotiations with the high-tech company.

Working with Creative Dreams

It is quite likely that we engage in creative problem solving in our dreams, whether or not we remember the dreams. To invoke this type of dream:

- Review the elements of a personal dilemma before going to sleep.
- Reflect on a task or a project on which progress has been blocked.
- Use as many sensory modalities as possible.
- Read any material that is pertinent to the task.
- Speak out loud when considering alternative solutions to the problem.
- Draw diagrams that illustrate the problem.
- Focus on any emotional elements of the dilemma.

In the morning, review all your dreams to determine whether any of them relate to the activity of the previous night. If you do not recall a dream, approach the task again. You might be surprised to find that a solution is now available to you that was not apparent before the pre-sleep exercise.

Stanley Krippner collected 1,666 dream reports from participants in his workshops in Argentina, Brazil, Japan, Russia, Ukraine, and the United States between 1990 and 1998. From this collection, 5 creative dreams were identified. In each case, an element of the dream was useful as a creative approach to an issue in everyday life. For example, a Ukrainian man reported:

> While awake, I had been trying to find a proper ending to a piece of fiction I had been writing, but none of my solutions worked out. During my dream, I was at my desk, writing. I seemed to be working on the same fictional piece that had been giving me trouble when awake. Then I saw a scene enacted before me involving two men and a woman, the main characters in my story. Instead of choosing one or the other, the woman rejected them both. I laughed in my dream, as the ending was very appropriate. When I woke up, I put this dream into writing and was quite satisfied with it.[12]

This problem-solving process is often called dream incubation, as it was in ancient Egypt and Greece when pilgrims went to temples to have dreams that would address their problems. One set of instructions from an Egyptian papyrus reads: "To obtain a vision from the god Besa, make a drawing of Besa on your left hand, envelop your hand in a strip of black cloth that has been consecrated to the goddess Isis, and lie down to sleep without speaking a word."[13]

A more recent form of dream incubation has been developed by the psychologist Gayle Delaney. Like the Egyptian and Greek practices, it contains several steps:

1. Choose the right night. Select a night when you are not overly tired, and one in which you can take between ten and twenty minutes to incubate your dream.

2. Review your thoughts and feelings of the day. If you have been keeping a diary or a journal, review your entry for the day. If not, write a few lines on paper that will summarize the day's events.

3. Write down the various aspects of your problem. What are its causes? What are the alternative solutions to the problem of which you are aware? How do you feel emotionally as you write about the problem? What benefits might you be gaining from perpetuating the problem? Does living with the problem feel safer than resolving it? How would your life be different if the problem were resolved?

4. Write a one-line request for a dream. Your incubation phrase might be like one of the following: Help me understand why I am afraid of flying and what I can do about it? What can I do to improve the relationship I have with my spouse? Please give me an idea for my next painting.

5. Concentrate on your request. Repeat it over and over as you go to sleep. Delaney believes that this is the most important part of the incubation procedure.

6. Fall asleep. Your creative potential is aware of your incubated concerns and is quite capable of responding to them.

7. Record your dream content as soon as you awaken whether you awaken in the middle of the night or in the morning. Write down as much as you remember about the dream. Include any feelings, thoughts, or fantasies that may come to mind. Write down any associations and draw any unusual dream images. In the morning, close your eyes and try to re-experience the dream; you might recall some elements that you missed earlier.

8. Attempt to understand the message of your dream. If you did not recall a dream, simply try again the following night. If the dream does not seem to be related to your problem, it may be that your random brain activity has not stimulated the images relevant to your question. Again, repeat the procedure the following night. But do not discard the dream you recalled. It may address other issues in your life. And at some future time you may discover answers in the dream that were not apparent earlier.[14]

Dream incubation is a valuable technique that can be used to evoke all of the extraordinary dreams we discuss in this book. But it is especially helpful in addressing creative or problem-oriented questions because of the opportunity it gives to tap into the creative capacities of the dreaming process.

André's Dream

André Percia de Carvalho, one of the authors of this book, frequently uses his dreams for creative problem solving. He incubates dreams before going to sleep and reviews the information that he has about his project by placing such objects as photographs, drawings, and books near his bed. Then he repeats the incubation phrase. For example, he needed to produce a book proposal for a Brazilian publisher, but did not know what parts of the book to highlight. In his dream, the entire outline of the book appeared on a chart like a movie screen. He remembered this outline when he woke up, copied it, and sent it to the publisher. The publisher accepted the proposal and the book was published!

A number of studies suggest that people with high scores on creativity tests tend to recall more dreams.[15] In her book *The Art of Dreaming*, Veronica Tonay focuses on creative people and their dreams. In this self-help book, readers are invited to keep a journal and look through their dreams to find and develop creative dreams.[16] In addition, the book *Dreamworking* is entirely dedicated to creative problem solving in dreams with examples and extensive references on the topic. Each chapter ends with exercises that can be used for incubating dreams and working with dreams in a variety of techniques.[17] More recently in her book *The Committee of Sleep*, psychologist Deirdre Barret also connects dreams and creative problem solving by citing anecdotes from writers, filmmakers, musicians, scientists, and artists.[18]

Exploring the connection between creativity and dreaming represents an important inquiry into the realm of consciousness. This exploration can offer great possibilities and insights into the nature of the human psyche.

Chapter 4

Lucid Dreams

*I*n 1913, the psychiatrist F. W. Van Eeden published a lecture on lucid dreaming that he had delivered to the Society for Psychical Research in London. Here he coined the term "lucid dreaming," and described some of his own experiences.[1] However, there are descriptions of similar types of dreaming in ancient Tibetan Buddhist texts where lucid dreaming is called "dream yoga." In the Hindu traditions the practice of lucid dreaming is referred to as "dream witnessing." Both of these traditions circumvented dream manipulation in favor of "merging with the light," "being fully present," and practicing other forms of meditation while dreaming.

Aristotle also mentioned lucid dreams in his treatise *On Dreams*. The illustrious Greek philosopher observed that sometimes "when one is asleep there is something in consciousness which declares that what often presents itself is but a dream."[2] Hervey de Saint-Denys, the innovative French professor and dream investigator, used his own lucid dreams to explore the process of dream formation. One day he designed a thought experiment and was able to carry it out into a dream. He experienced the following lucid dream:

> I wish to see an absent friend and immediately see him lying asleep on a sofa. I change a porcelain vase into a rock-crystal fountain, from which I desire a cooling drink—and this immediately flows out through a golden tap. Some years ago I lost a particular ring whose loss I felt deeply. The memory of it comes into my mind, and I should like to find it. I utter this wish, fixing my attention of a piece of coal that I pick up from the fireplace—and immediately the ring is in my fingers.[3]

But Saint-Denys' contemporary, Alfred Maury, doubted the existence of lucid dreams, perhaps because he himself had never had one.

In 1909, the second edition of Sigmund Freud's *The Interpretation of Dreams* was published. Freud had added an observation that some people, while they are asleep and dreaming, are able to direct their own dreams. While discussing what is now felt to be one of his own dreams, Freud described a dreamer who found himself in a sexually exciting situation. Even though he had attained dream lucidity, the dreamer declined to take advantage of the woman in the dream, fearing he would have a nocturnal emission and exhaust himself.[4]

The psychologist Patricia Garfield recorded dozens of her own lucid dreams, reporting that two thirds of them were associated with "the flow of sexual energy." In nearly one half of these dreams, the activity led to sexual orgasm, usually with Garfield's husband, but sometimes with other men, "a male angelic creature," a woman, a half-man–half-woman, or Garfield herself.[5]

On the basis of the data provided by these investigators, both past and present, we can describe lucid dreams as those that are characterized by impressions that the dreamer is aware that he or she is dreaming during the ongoing dream. Sometimes a dreamer is able to modify or change the action or the outcome in the dream; at other times, the dreamer knows that a dream is occurring, but is unable to refashion the flow of the dream.

Awareness While Dreaming

Born in 1877 in the United States, Edgar Cayce was a "psychic sensitive" who advocated the study of dreams. Cayce's statements about dreams were remarkably astute for his time: he asserted that dreams may reflect past experiences, health conditions, or spiritual connections. Cayce advised dreamers to make a firm decision about the topic on which they needed guidance before going to sleep. Cayce taught that this form of dream incubation directed the dreamer's awareness to the responding dream.[6]

One of Edgar Cayce's students, Elsie Sechrist, relates that her husband William Sechrist, was unsure about where he should start a car rental business. In a dream, an inner presence recommended Houston, Texas, as a location to start his business. Sechrist became lucid during the dream and asked why Houston would be suitable. Three images appeared in his dream: a star, a running water faucet, and a family on a houseboat. Once he awakened, Sechrist understood that the dream indicated that Houston would be the "star" of the South with ample water and incremental growth as a vacation center. Sechrist moved to Houston and opened his business. It quickly became a successful venture.[7]

In 1974, Patricia Garfield's book *Creative Dreaming* was published. In this volume, Garfield gave her readers examples of lucid dreams as well as exercises to heighten their own capacity to dream lucidly.[8] Other instructions have appeared in books by Stephen LaBerge, Jayne Gackenbach and Jane Bosveld, and Malcolm Godwin.[9]

The following example illustrates how powerful lucid dreams can be as a source of both inspiration and information.

Eric's Dream

Eric Snyder, an artist, attended a baby shower for one of his friends, Suzanne, who was about to have her first child. During the gathering, people were speculating whether the child would be a boy or a girl. Eric thought about this on the way home and before he fell asleep. That night he had a long lucid dream and towards the end of the dream he experienced the following:

> The next thing I become consciously aware of was standing in front of a door covered with a heavy drape. All at once the drape is pulled back and I see Suzanne with her newborn baby. I am now completely lucid and am amazed at the reality of what I see. She holds the baby in her arms and I see that it is a boy with reddish skin. I see the shape of the face and the color of the eyes. I look at him exactly as I would if I were going to try and remember each detail for a painting.

The next day, Eric recorded his dream. As he reflected upon his experience, "I felt a sudden wave of inspiration, as if light was pouring down into me." He was inspired to write a poem:

> A wellspring of the earth
> orange and red
> whose feeling is so great
> one loves your company
> strong one in midst of
> tumultuous times
> orange and purple

Eric had a "felt sense" that his lucid dream might also be a precognitive dream giving him a glimpse of what might occur in the future. He decided to type his dream, date it, and seal it in an envelope. A few weeks later, Suzanne gave birth to a baby boy and Eric visited her, recalling:

> The experience was like a déjà vu. I walked into a darkened room, just as I had in the dream. Suzanne was sitting in the same position holding the boy and he was exactly the same person I had seen in the dream, even the shape of his head and color of skin [was the same]. Suzanne read what I had written and agreed that it described her baby.

Lucidity and Dream Control

The advisability of dream control is a controversial issue. Some dream practitioners believe that dreams should not be manipulated; individuals who overuse lucidity may find that the spontaneity and creativity of their dreams suffer as a result. Other practitioners suggest that dream lucidity can be used for therapeutic purposes, making connection with deceased relatives, eliciting creative insights, and even treating chronic nightmares. Psychologist Franklin Galvin and psychiatrist Ernest Hartmann have attempted to teach individuals afflicted by frequent nightmares to attain lucidity during terrifying dreams. Most patients report that once they attain lucidity, the nightmare's uncontrollable quality decreases, threatening images can be changed or dismissed, the story line can be transformed into a pleasant narrative, and the dreamer can gain an understanding that the imagination has created the dream, just as it may have created needless anxiety in the waking state.[10]

Psychophysiologist Stephen LaBerge, founder of the Lucidity Institute in California, has persuasively stated the argument in favor of lucid dreaming. LaBerge observes,

> If fully lucid, you would realize that the entire dream world was your own creation, and with this awareness might come an exhilarating feeling of freedom. Nothing external, no laws of society or physics would constrain your experience; you could do anything your mind could conceive. Thus inspired, you might fly to the heavens. You might dare to face someone or something that you have been fearfully avoiding; you might choose an erotic encounter with the most desirable partner you can imagine; you might visit a dead loved one to whom you have been wanting to speak; you might seek self-knowledge and wisdom. By cultivating awareness in your dreams, and learning to use them, you can add more consciousness, more life, to your life. In the process, you will increase your enjoyment of your nightly dream journeys and deepen your understanding of yourself. By waking in your dreams, you can awaken to life.[11]

Research in Lucid Dreaming

In 1978, Keith Hearne (a British investigator)[12] and Stephen LaBerge independently discovered that lucid dreamers could communicate with the outside world by moving their eyes, clenching their fist muscles, or flexing their arm muscles in a predetermined pattern during a lucid dream. During REM sleep, there are the "phasic" period when the muscles, especially those around the eyes, are more active, and the "tonic" period, which is more placid. Most lucid dreams appear to take place in the phasic portion. Some lucid dreams occur in non-REM sleep. Furthermore, the events experienced in lucid dreams produce effects in the brain and the body that are remarkably similar to those that would be produced if the events were experienced while awake.

An exception is sexual orgasm. Lucid dreamers frequently report erotic encounters to the point of orgasm. But the male lucid dreamer rarely has a nocturnal emission, probably because of the complex nature of the reflexes involved in sexual orgasm. The female lucid dreamer shows increased vaginal activity but only a slight increase in heart rate during sexual orgasm in the dream. Perhaps this is why dreams seem so real. To the brain, and to a lesser extent, to the rest of the body, dreaming of a certain action can be similar to the same action in waking life.[13] These results are based on very few subjects, indicating a wide open field of future research.

Although lucid dreams are fairly common phenomena, research studies indicate that people who are frequent dream recallers have more lucid dreams. Meditators tend to have more lucid dreams than non-meditators, as do individuals who have somewhat androgynous gender role identities.[14] People who have a better sense of balance tend to have more lucid dreams. Frequent lucid dreamers also tend to be "field independent" on personality tests, that is, they do not need to rely on context to move about in physical or psychological space. Field independence can be of great assistance in lucid dreaming, since a person who can stand back from the events of the dream has a better chance of being able to realize the actual nature of the events than one who is fully embroiled in the plot.[15]

When lucid dreams and ordinary dreams are compared, lucid dreams tend to occur more frequently in the early morning. In addition, lucid dreams contain more auditory and kinesthetic imagery. Most dreams are basically visual in nature and involve considerable movement, probably because the visual-motor cortex of the brain is stimulated during REM sleep. In lucid dreams, there is more conversation, but fewer dream characters. In one study, ordinary dreams had happier and more successful endings than lucid dreams. However, in most comparisons, lucid and ordinary dreams were similar despite individual differences.[16]

Pierre Weil, a French-Brazilian psychologist, has written a fascinating account of his study of "dream yoga" with a Tibetan lama. By practicing various types of meditation, visualization, and breathing during wakefulness, Weil was able to attain lucidity in his dreams. Weil kept a dream diary in which he recalled his dreams each morning. Not only did he have more lucid dreams during the three years he studied with the lama, but also he recalled more dreams in general. However, once his studies stopped, so did his dream recall and his dream lucidity. For example, in 1983, Weil recorded nineteen lucid dreams; he recorded thirty-seven in 1984 and thirty-one in 1985. During the two years following the end of his work with the lama, his dream lucidity dropped to zero. He was still able to recall dreams, but at a lower frequency than before. Nevertheless, Weil felt that the work was worthwhile, and that he had been able to incorporate the elements of lucidity into his daily life.[17]

Many lucid dreamers report spiritual experiences in lucid dreaming. Scott Sparrow, author of *Lucid Dreaming: Dawning of the Clear Light*, reported a lucid dream that changed the direction of his life. After becoming lucid in a dream, he wrote: "I stand outside a small building that has large black double-doors on its eastern side. I approach them to enter. As soon as I open them, a brilliant white light hits me in the face. Immediately I am filled with intense feelings of love."[18]

Fariba Bogzaran's study, "Experiencing the Divine in Lucid Dreaming State," showed that the mere intention of wanting to have a spiritual experience in lucid dreaming can actually lead to such experiences. Incubation and intention prior to sleep are the two most important elements in cultivating spiritual experiences in lucid dreaming. Transpersonal experiences in lucid dreaming vary with each individual; however, there are common reports of visiting one's spiritual teacher or contacting spiritual figures who appear in a personalized form. Also, there are reports of spiritual encounters with white light or dark light, geometric shapes, non-representational forms, unrecognizable images and events, and multidimensional spaces during the lucid dream.[19]

George Gillespie, author and a lucid dream explorer, has experimented and reported several transpersonal experiences in his own lucid dreams. He describes in detail powerful imagery and mystical experiences that occur while he is lucid in his dreams. Sometimes he sees "light patterns, with color and movement." At other times, he has encountered "disks of light," which often appear in the shape of a moon or planet, either stationary or moving. If he can lose the sensation of his dreaming body, he may enter a state that he calls "total elimination of objects of consciousness."[20]

Gillespie also describes his encounters with "the Light," which he claims appears only in his lucid dreams. Often the Light appears while he is in darkness or engaged in some religious activity. The experience of the Light, according to Gillespie, is a moment of bliss and joy, or "union with the spiritual world."

For their book, *Control Your Dreams,* Jayne Gackenbach and Jane Bosveld interviewed a professor of physics and long-time practitioner of transcendental meditation. In the interview the professor, who preferred to remain anonymous, explained five stages from lucidity to witnessing. These five stages, similar to those in a categorization Gillespie set up, start with awareness of dreams and images as something outside the self, then proceed to recognizing that the images are inside the dreamer. The last stage is the entrance into the transcendental state, which is referred to as "pure consciousness."

In this state, the professor claims that he encounters forms not seen in a non-lucid dream. "They will be much more abstract and have no sensory aspects to them, no mental images, no emotional feelings, no sense of body or space. There is a quality of unboundedness to them. One experiences oneself to be a part of a tremendous composite of relationships."[21]

Another of Bogzaran's studies, "Images of the Lucid Mind," suggests that when one moves from ordinary lucid dreaming to a multidimensional dream, images slowly transform into more abstract patterns such as light lines or energy lines, spheres, dots, and circles. In this state of consciousness that she calls "hyperspace lucidity" lucid dreamers often experience the transformation of their dream bodies into particles of light, or the dream body slowly or suddenly disappears but awareness continues. [22]

Keelin's Dream

After two weeks of attempting to incubate a spiritual dream, Keelin experienced the following dream during which she became lucid:

> I become aware of being in a vast limitless darkness that is at the same time brilliant with countless stars and very much alive. Something emerges from darkness. It looks like some kind of living, molecular model/mathematical equation—extremely complex, three-dimensional, fluorescent, neon-orange in color—very thin lines, very clear and sharp visually. It seems to unfold itself, multiplying, constantly changing, form-

ing more complex structures and interrelationships. It is filling up the Universe. This growing movement is not erratic, but consistent and purposeful—rapid but at the same time determined. . . . This is the best way I can describe the space. It is rapid, yet there is a feeling that the knowledge or reality of it already exists, or that it is being born, exists in its entirety and visually manifest all in the same one moment.[23]

When Keelin awoke from this dream, she experienced a tingling sensation throughout her body. She described the sensation as the opening of the energy centers in her body. She referred to this experience as a powerful and transformative experience of her life.[24]

Working with Lucid Dreams

There are many ways to enhance dream lucidity, but one of the simplest methods is to pay attention to every dream. The more dreams that are recalled, the more likely one is to remember an occasional lucid dream. Self-suggestion will often enhance lucidity in dreams. Before going to sleep at night, simply repeat this suggestion: "Tonight I will become aware that I am dreaming and will remember that dream when I wake up." Repeat this suggestion twenty or thirty times; do not be discouraged if it is not effective immediately, as this technique rarely works during its first few applications.[25]

Carlos Castaneda wrote that his purported mentor, the Yaqui sorcerer don Juan Matus, had instructed him in lucid dreaming. Before sleep, Castaneda was told to place his hands in front of his gaze. Eventually, he reported that he had found his hands in a dream and had lifted them to the level of his eyes. At this point he realized that he was dreaming. Castaneda used this technique of looking for his hands in his dreams to become lucid on a regular basis. From this vantage point he claimed to be able to perform wondrous feats.[26]

Several years earlier, Kilton Stewart claimed that the Senoi tribal people in the Malay peninsula had developed dream lucidity; when they encountered a terrifying creature or situation in their dream, they would become lucid, would face their fear directly, and either conquer it, make friends with it, or surrender to it.[27] The consensus of contemporary anthropologists is that neither Castaneda nor Stewart accurately presented the practices of the native groups they claimed to have studied. Nevertheless, the techniques they describe actually seem to be effective for some people.

Charles Tart used Kilton Stewart's procedure whenever he had a nightmare, and he taught the technique to his young son. In both cases, the occurrence and severity of their nightmares abated,[28] although Tart stated that "Stewart dreamwork" is probably a more accurate title for the procedure than "Senoi dreamwork." Castaneda's approach has also been effective with some dreamers although it probably has little to do with Yaqui Indian practices.[29] Stanley Krippner practiced the Castaneda technique, placing his hands at eye level before falling asleep. After a few nights, he became aware of his hands in a dream and immediately obtained lucidity. Once lucid, he was able to make choices in his dream. He talked with plants and animals, and instructed other people in his dream to become lucid as well.

Practicing lucidity during waking fantasy has increased lucidity in dreams for some individuals.[30] The basic procedure is to "re-dream" a dream while awake, pretending to be asleep. During this period of re-entry, one can attempt to work with the problems presented in dreams by facing the problems and working through them to gain more insights. Eventually, this procedure may evoke lucidity during nighttime dreams.

The "critical question" technique, utilized by a variety of dreamworkers, differs from the "intention" technique of self-suggestion and from the "re-dreaming" technique involving daytime fantasy. The "critical question" involves asking, am I dreaming? One can ask this question at regular intervals during the day (for example, every thirty minutes) or whenever observing an item that frequently appears in dreams, for example, food, water, a timepiece. In the latter instance, one would ask the question, am I dreaming? whenever looking at a clock or a watch during the day. Then one would make a "reality check" to test waking consciousness. A "reality check" involves looking away from the timepiece then looking back at it again and noting whether the timepiece has changed. If changes are noted in the timepiece, this indicates that one is indeed in a dream.

Using this exercise, one slowly builds a conditioned response in waking that allows the mind to remember to ask the "critical question" in the dream. For example, when the timepiece appears in a dream, the dreamer is likely to automatically ask, am I dreaming? and then make the reality check. If there is still any doubt, the dreamer can look around the environment to see if it is familiar. The dreamer then can observe the people in the dream to determine whether or not their behavior is bizarre. If so, the answer is, yes, I am dreaming, the dream becomes lucid.

The process of becoming lucid in the dream often involves some of the following experiences:

- Waking up due to excitement caused by becoming aware in a dream.
- Being actively involved in the dream while fully lucid.
- Witnessing the dream event without being involved in the dream activity.
- Deliberately changing objects in the dream.
- Leaving the dream scene by intending to be in another space or time.
- Confronting nightmarish characters and working therapeutically with the fear.
- Visiting deceased relatives and friends.
- Having transpersonal experiences; contacting a higher being, God, or spiritual entity.
- Entering a multidimensional space, "hyperspace," either spontaneously or by incubation.[31]

One simple technique to foster lucid dreaming is to fall asleep on the right side. On the average, lucid dreams were three times more likely while sleeping on the right side of the body than on the left, in a study reported by Lynne Levitan. There were no gender differences, and those people sleeping on their backs also reported more lucid dreams than individuals sleeping on their left sides.[32] This research finding corroborated the advice given to yogic adepts for many centuries by Tibetan Buddhist instructors.[33]

As is the case with other dreams, we can gain insights from the power of the lucid dream experience and the resulting symbols and metaphors. The following dream is an example of how a lucid dream can assist in self-awareness and insights.

Steve's Dream

Steve, one of our students, went camping by himself on Mount Shasta in California to meditate and enjoy the wilderness. He incubated a dream every night to guide him toward the next step in his life. On the fifth night, he had the following lucid dream:

> I am in a cave with a group of old men. They are drinking water from an old bowl that is being passed around. As the bowl comes closer towards me I realize that this must be a dream. An old man with dark skin and dark hair sitting next to me hands me the bowl. I take it and drink the water. As I am drinking the water the sensation feels more real than waking reality. I suddenly hear a humming sound and as I look up the men have disappeared and a beautiful white deer is walking in the light in the far distance. I awake feeling ecstatic.

Steve considers his lucid dream to be initiatory in nature. He later shared his dream with his dream group and discovered even more insights into his dream. Steve realized that his dream was not only about male initiation, but healing his past wounds. He grew up with three sisters and an absent father. He was influenced by the women in his family to express the feminine aspect of his psyche in life's situations and he never had a male role model.

One of the members of his dream group believed that the bowl and water represented the emotional containment that reflects his feminine aspects. She suggested that these dream images were asking him to integrate the feminine and masculine principles of his personality. Another member of his group experienced the dream as if it were her dream. She believed that the disappearance of the men and the appearance of the white deer were a sign of transformation from receiving old wisdom to receiving new vision.

For Steve, the ending of the dream was an indication that it is through the dark that the light originates. This dream had a great significance in his life, because it brought greater awareness to the masculine and feminine aspects of his psyche. The fact that he became lucid was a sign of becoming aware of the unconscious process that was waiting to emerge.

Krippner, in his cross-cultural study of 1,666 dreams, found lucid dreams to be the most common "extraordinary" dream. Of the 29 dreams in this collection, dreamers from Argentina and the United States reported more lucid dreams than did dreamers from other countries. Sometimes lucid dreams were also scored as creative dreams, or as dreams within dreams.[34]

The value of lucid dreams can be determined after a few lucid dream experiences. Some people may decide that ordinary dreams bring so much enjoyment and understanding that lucid dreams add little if anything to their wisdom and appreciation. In his book, *The Sun and the Shadow*, psychotherapist Kenneth Kelzer reports numerous accounts of his own spiritual experiences in lucid dreams and concludes that "The lucid dream is, above all else, a pathway toward a direct and personal experience of The Light."[35] Others may find that lucid dreaming is an altered state of consciousness that brings excitement, delight, and knowledge that can be obtained in no other way. Some dreamers claim to have held conversations with God in their lucid dreams, while others report that their lucid dreams are more constricted and less creative than their ordinary dreams. Lucid dreaming represents a continuity of content as well as cognition, so there will be many individual differences among lucid dreamers.[36] Each person must decide for him or herself whether lucid dreaming is worth the effort. Some may stop after one or two lucid dreams, but others may find them so exhilarating that they make lucid dreaming part of their regular spiritual practice.

Out-Of-Body Dreams

*T*he significance of dreaming is discussed in the *Mandukya Upanishad*, one of the ancient Hindu scriptures. Out-of-body experiences were also recognized in Hindu philosophy. It was held that the "subtle body," referred to as the *sukshma sharira*, was able to separate from the physical body under certain conditions.

The ancient Egyptians were convinced that during dreaming the *ba*, or soul, detached itself from the body and blended into the cosmos. During these moments, dreamers were permitted to enter into communication with the deities, the dead, and even with demons, thus gaining information about their own destiny. Thutmose IV, in about 1450 B.C.E., dreamed that, while out-of-body, he had spoken with a god who promised him a great kingdom. The god also told Thutmose that if this gift were granted, he would need to clear away the sand that had accumulated in front of the Sphinx at Giza. Thutmose became the most powerful monarch of his time, sanctified the area around the Sphinx, and erected a stela on which this compelling dream was engraved.[1]

Some out-of-body experiences appear to be stimulated by vivid dreams, particularly when waking consciousness is aroused by some irregularity in the logic of a dream. For example, a dreamer may recognize the familiar environment of his or her own room but notice that the wallpaper is the wrong design and color. This irregularity may trigger the realization that this must be a dream, and can result in one finding oneself moving independently of the physical body.

"Soul Travel" during Sleep

It is common for tribal cultures to conceptualize dreams as journeys of the soul during sleep. Barbara Tedlock has collected several examples in her edited

book *Dreaming*;[2] the information that follows is drawn from this book, especially from the chapter by E. B. Basso. Among the Sambia tribe, in Papua,
New Guinea, dreams are called *wunju*, and are viewed as occasions when the
soul leaves the body and roams in different places, "sliding on the wind." The
soul takes one's thoughts with it, leaving the dreamer's body empty. Dream
reports are not viewed as memories of dreams, they are viewed as the recall of
actual events. The dream world, a world filled with supernatural entities, is
held to parallel the ordinary world. If a member of the Sambia tribe dreams
about a friend, the image is conceived of as the friend's "spirit." The most
feared dream characters are the *boongu*, evil nature spirits who try to engulf the
dreamer's soul.

For the Zuñi in the southwestern United States, the *pinanne* or "breath
soul," can leave the body at will. During sleep, the *pinanne* can travel to other
places, as well as to the past and the future. Dreams are classified as positive or
negative, depending on the dreamer's emotional feeling upon awakening. The
worst dreams are those in which the dreamer appears to be in a type of sleep
paralysis and can perform no voluntary movements.

Among the Quichè Maya in Central America, the *nawal* or "free soul"
wanders during sleep, while the *uxlab* or "life soul" remains in the body.
Dreaming may involve visits with the deceased, but is rarely seen as threatening because it only involves one of the dreamer's souls. The Quichè are eager to
put the dream into words because the ability to speak articulately is seen as the
defining feature of human beings.

The Aguaruna tribe of Peru places great importance on the *iwanch*, or
"shadow soul." Some members of the tribe have told anthropologists that it is
the *iwanch* that travels during sleep, but others claim that it would be dangerous for the "shadow soul" to leave the body under any circumstances. This dis-
crepancy might reflect the influence of Christian concepts of "soul" on the
belief system of tribal members.

The Raràmuri Indians of northern Mexico attribute dreams to the activities of a person's "principal soul" during sleep. Dreams are considered to be real
events, and anthropologists often do not know if an experience being related by
a tribal member occurred in waking life or in dream life. The word *rimúma*
means "to dream" in the Raràmuri language; there is no word for "a dream"
because what occurs in a dream is considered a human activity, just like any
other.

Among the Kalapalo Indians of central Brazil, dreaming is said to occur
when a person's *akua* (that part of the self that interacts with the environment)
rises out of the body and wanders until it has an experience. These activities are

triggered by visitations from powerful dream spirits who are attracted to the *akua* when it detaches from the physical body and begins to roam. A member of the Kalapalo tribe told an anthropologist, "Two friends went traveling. At night, while they were both lying down . . . one of them saw his friend get up from himself. 'What's the matter with my friend?' This other person got up and walked away, but his friend's body was still lying down. But when in the morning the man woke up, he was all right."[3]

Research on Out-of-Body Dreams

When individuals have out-of-body experiences during wakefulness, they often notice a rush of energy and bodily vibrations, and hear strange sounds; sometimes a sensation of bodily paralysis precedes the out-of-body experience. To the sleep researcher, these strange symptoms are remarkably similar to sleep paralysis, which typically takes place when a person is waking from or falling into REM sleep. During REM sleep, the muscles of the body are immobilized, with the exception of the eye muscles and those responsible for circulation and respiration. This immobility prevents dreamers from acting out their dreams. Occasionally, this paralysis remains active after the individual is fully awake, and might give the sensation of being out-of-body.

This possibility is supported by an investigation conducted by the British psychologist Susan Blackmore. Over 85 percent of her respondents said that they had experienced out-of-body experiences while resting, sleeping, or dreaming, rather than while being fully awake.[4] A survey by another British researcher, Celia Green, revealed that most out-of-body experiences take place while people are in bed, ill, or resting, with a smaller percentage taking place while people are drugged or medicated.[5]

Although people who have had out-of-body experiences are more likely to have had lucid dreams as well, the two experiences are generally quite different.[6] During an out-of-body experience, the individual is typically convinced that the event is actually taking place in the physical world, and not in a dream. In a lucid dream, dreamers are certain that their experiences are taking place within a dream. The exception would be a lucid dreamer who has an out-of-body experience during a lucid dream.

In 1991, Stephen LaBerge reported on a study of 107 lucid dreams; of those, 9 percent included an out-of-body experience. This type of lucid dream often involved feelings of bodily distortions, an awareness of being in bed, or the sensation of floating or flying. LaBerge also discovered that out-of-body experiences during lucid dreams occurred more often when a person re-entered

REM sleep shortly after awakening, or just after having become aware of being in bed. A questionnaire study of 572 individuals resulted in similar findings; of the 452 respondents who claimed to have had at least one lucid dream, 39 percent also reported having had at least one out-of-body experience. Only 15 percent of the respondents who never recalled a lucid dream claimed to have had an out-of-body experience.[7] It is important to point out that out-of-body experiences are not an indicator of mental illness. Several surveys have been conducted, finding no link between out-of-body experiences and psychosis.[8]

Dreamers from all of the six countries included in Krippner's collection of 1,666 dreams reported out-of-body dreams. An Argentine woman recalled, "I felt as if I were dying, but it was not as traumatic as I had imagined. It was a profound sensation. There was an appearance of vivid white light. I felt as though I was leaving my body and that I was dying. I looked down on my body; it had turned into a golden brown. I was wearing clothes but my skin was golden brown."[9]

There is a continual debate about whether out-of-body experiences take place "in" the body or "out" of the body. Blackmore has given a provocative philosophical answer to this question based on the teachings of Buddhism.[10] She reminds us that the Buddha considered the ego to be an illusion. Humans assume all too easily that they are some kind of persistent, stable entity inhabiting a material body. According to Buddha's teachings this "reality" is only a construction of our information-processing system, modulated by our social milieu. Our sense of identity, or ego, is also a social construction.

Are out-of-body experiences "in" or "out" of the body? Blackmore answers "neither," because the ego and other socially constructed experiences have no location. Out-of-body experiences, near-death experiences, and mystical experiences can dispel the illusion that humans are solid selves within a body, which may be why many people find these experiences so enlightening and liberating. As the following example illustrates, out-of-body experiences can have transformative power.

Rochan's Dream

Rochan is a successful financial broker in New York. At age sixteen, she had an out-of-body dream experience that left a strong impression within her psyche about the realness of the dream world. She remembers falling asleep one afternoon while reading a magazine. She then dreamt the following:

I suddenly see my dream body next to my bed, but I can also see my "real" body in my bed. I realize that I must be dreaming. I look around the room and everything looks just the way my room looks in waking life, but the colors and textures are more intense. Suddenly, I feel myself being lifted up to the ceiling. I look out through my bedroom window from high above my bed and I see a white car parked outside with a crunched brown bag lying in front of it. I look down and I can see my real body still in bed. I suddenly become scared and begin screaming, but my voice will not come out. I think that maybe I can go back to my real body, so I slowly calm down and enter my real body again. I actually feel my dream body face entering my real body's face.

When Rochan awoke from this dream, she initially felt disoriented because she did not know what had happened to her. Her curiosity about her dream experience led her to walk outside her home to see if she would actually see what she had seen while experiencing her out-of-body dream. She found a white car parked by her house with a crunched brown bag lying in front of it.

At age sixteen, Rochan was too frightened to share this experience with her parents, but now, at age forty, she claims that her initial out-of-body experience led her to numerous other extraordinary dreams, such as precognitive and telepathic dreams. These dream experiences have assisted her as she made significant life changes.

Rochan's dream is only one type of out-of-body dream. In another common type, the dreamer is flying, then looks down to see his or her body on the bed, on the street, or on the ground. Still another variety involves experiences in which one's "soul" is taken from the body by an angel for a flight into heavenly realms. Out-of-body dreams may also contain narratives concerning abductions by aliens from UFOs, journeys to other worlds with native shamans, or magical powers that enable dreamers to engage in distant travel while their bodies remain in familiar surroundings.

Sleep Paralysis and Out-of-Body Dreams

One of the most common experiences people have at the beginning or end of out-of-body dreams is an awareness of sleep paralysis, a common phenomenon that occurs when the "mind" awakens from a dream, but the "body" is not yet fully awake. People report wanting to scream or move but being unable to make a sound or move a muscle. This state is often frightening, since one has the impression of being fully awake. As the dreamer becomes more fearful, the fear can evoke nightmarish images, but it is a state that can easily move the dreamer into an out-of-body experience.

Fariba Bogzaran found that she could transform the frightening experience of sleep paralysis into an out-of-body dream, and then a lucid dream. One night she experienced two episodes of sleep paralysis. During the first, she became completely frightened. As her fear increased, she imagined monsters with no heads and legs, which approached her and eventually sat on her body, pressing down her chest. The mythical image of an "incubus," a medieval demon, often is reported to visit the dreamer in this state. Bogzaran tried to scream or move her body, but was unable to do so. Finally, she was able to jerk herself out of this frightening state. When she realized that she had produced the nightmare out of her own fear and that her body and mind needed time to coordinate and come into balance, she decided to go back to sleep by using this suggestion: "If I have a sleep paralysis, I will breathe and relax into the experience." One hour later, she found herself in a second paralysis. Although frightened at first, she soon remembered her suggestion to breathe.

> I slowly let go of the fear by breathing and relaxing. I started to feel lighter and lighter in my body. Soon I felt I was sitting in bed, but I could also see my body lying in bed. I knew this was a dream. I stood up and looked out the window. A geyser of colored light particles came through it. I stood there with a sense of awe. I reached out with my hands, wanting to touch the particles. As I moved my hands, the particles became colorless, weightless, and I felt the beauty of their energy all through my body. I awoke with an ecstatic feeling of joy.[11]

Based on this experience, Bogzaran developed a method of working with sleep paralysis to induce out-of-body experiences or lucid dreams. This technique has been usually implemented in her classes and students are able to transform sleep paralysis into a new and positive dream experience. Bogzaran proposes a 5-step procedure in working with sleep paralysis:

1. Upon experiencing sleep paralysis, identify the state by telling yourself "I realize I am in a sleep paralysis." With this confirmation, much of the fear subsides.

2. Instead of struggling to move or make sound, relax and let go of any negative thoughts.

3. Concentrate on your breathing while relaxing your body.

4. Stay aware without thinking or moving; at the same time, continue relaxing into the experience.

5. You can practice dream re-entry or observe the creation of the new dream. You might even decide to fully awaken.

Working with Out-of-Body Dreams

LaBerge believes that out-of-body dreams are most often associated with the onset of sleep, when dreamers lose input from their sense organs while retaining consciousness. If so, these dreams may be expected to occur in hypnagogic states or when the dreamer passes from wakefulness directly into REM sleep—an event that is rare, but possible. In both instances, a mental model is created independent of sensory input. Usually, the dreamer is aware of his or her physical body, and obtains constant feedback from the sense organs in the muscles, tendons, joints, and viscera. In REM sleep, however, the information from the dreamer's senses in the physical body is blocked. As a result, it is easy to dream about dancing, flying, being dismembered, or actually leaving the body. LaBerge speculates that as the sensation of gravity shuts down, the dreamer may feel lighter and begin to float upward in his or her dream.[12]

If LaBerge is correct, hypnagogic imagery is one event that might trigger an out-of-body dream. Another stimulus is to develop lucidity in dreams to such an extent that an out-of-body experience can be evoked during a lucid dream. Such a program might include the following steps, adapted from these suggested by Patricia Garfield.[13]

1. Regard dreams as playing an important and meaningful role in your life. Keep a dream notebook, join a dreamworking group, discuss your dreams with other people, read books and articles about dreams, and apply what you have learned from your dreams to your daily life.

2. Realize that you can be awake and aware in your dreams. Every time you have a lucid dream, review this dream intensely. Determine at what point in the dream you became lucid. This will give you the confidence you need to become lucid in your dreams more frequently.

3. Use self-suggestion before going to sleep. Read an article about out-of-body dreams or about out-of-body experiences in general. Tell yourself that you will have a lucid dream, and that you will travel out of your body during the dream.

4. Learn from your previous out-of-body dreams. Were they preceded by some other activity, such as flying? Were they accompanied by an emotional feeling, such as peacefulness, excitement, or anticipation? When your dream

becomes lucid, try to recreate that activity and feeling. This may propel you into an out-of-body experience in your dream.

5. Have a clear-cut reason for having an out-of-body dream. Is curiosity your main motive? Is it metaphysical? Is your goal to obtain a better understanding of the mind? of the spirit? of death? Be honest with yourself so that you will not be ambivalent about the experience.[13]

Some dreamworkers have negative feelings about out-of-body dreams, claiming that the "dream body" is a critically important aspect of the dream. They maintain that if a dreamer can recall body feelings, body activities, and the appearance of the dream body, these memories can be used to great advantage in understanding one's dreams. Why would anyone want to leave the body in a dream if the dream body is able to provide the dreamer with so much information?

Arnold Mindell, who organized the Research Society for Process-Oriented Psychotherapy in Zurich, Switzerland, feels that couples can learn a great deal about each other and about their relationship by focusing on these dreams, and, in particular, on the dream body in each other's dreams.[14]

All intimate relationships involve awareness, courage, and humility. An intimate relationship between two (or more) people is not easily attained. Whether the relationship is romantic, sexual, or professional, or whether it occurs in a family, a friendship, or a business, the interaction of separate human beings requires skills that need to be learned and nurtured. Dream sharing often can assist in this process.

One person in a relationship might have dreams, for example, in which the dream body is very clear and expressive; the other person in the relationship might have dreams in which his or her dream body is unclear and ephemeral. Some people cannot recall ever seeing their body in a dream. If such dramatic differences occur in dream content, it is possible that similar differences exist in the routines of the relationship. One member of the relationship might be very physical in nature, while the other person might live in the imagination. Once the partners are aware of their dissimilarities, these differences could lead to an exciting, complementary relationship, rather than a difficult, conflicting one.

Mindell suggests that dreamers in a relationship examine several aspects of the dream body. What are the boundaries of their dream body? Where do the boundaries of one person stop and the boundaries of another person begin? How does the dream body communicate with other dream characters? Is the communication achieved through speech, touch, or gesture? What is the dream body wearing? Are the clothes clean or dirty, modest or flamboyant?

Mindell tells of a client who surprised him by wearing an alluring dress to his office one day. This was out of character for her, but the reason became apparent when she discussed her dream. On the previous night, the woman had dreamed about a nightclub singer. The singer flirted with the men in the nightclub, and the dreamer was both fascinated and repelled by this dream character. Mindell realized that the nightclub singer was the "shadow" of his client—a side of her personality that she hid, even from herself. But the identification was apparent because of the daring dress the woman had selected to wear that day.

In addition, Mindell describes how a psychotherapist can observe body signals both in clients' dreams and in their body language in the office. Sometimes the client's body signals are different in dream life and waking life; they might be very expressive in the dream, but quite inhibited in his office. This dissonance will often assist the psychotherapist as he or she decides what direction to take in the therapeutic process.

Another psychotherapist, Eugene Gendlin, has proposed a 16-step procedure in which dreamworkers can utilize body image and bodily feelings to help their clients. These questions can be summarized as follows:[15]

1. What comes to mind as you think about the dream? Notice your immediate associations to the dream.

2. What was your feeling in the dream? Choose the most vivid part of the dream and let a felt sense of it come to your body.

3. What did you do, and what did you think about and feel, the day before you had the dream? Determine if any of these activities, thoughts, and feelings are related to the dream.

4. Where and when did the dream take place? Sense what the dream setting felt like to you.

5. What was the basic story contained in the dream? Ask yourself if there is anything going on in your life that resembles that story. Again, let your felt sense guide you to any comparison that may emerge.

6. Who were the other characters in your dream? Ask yourself what physical feeling each of the characters would give you if you encountered them while you were awake.

7. Do any of the characters remind you of yourself? As you experience the physical feeling of each character, one or more may feel very much like a part of yourself. Or a character may act the way you would act under certain circumstances.

8. Can you imagine yourself as each of the dream characters? Let the physical feeling of each character come into your body. How would the character walk, sit, or speak? Does that character's movement remind you of anyone?

9. Go back to the most vivid part of the dream. Feel it as fully as possible and wait for something further to happen. If the dream continues, what is your feeling about what happened next? Does this give you a clue as to the meaning of the dream?

10. Were there symbols or metaphors in the dream? A bridge in the dream might represent a crossing point in your life. Imagine your feelings as you cross the bridge. A policeman in the dream might represent an enforcer of the law. Imagine your feelings as you encounter the policeman, or as you become the policeman. What laws are being broken, or what laws are being enforced?

11. Could any of the dream images be symbols of your body or of your bodily functions? The top floor of a building might represent your head, your thinking process, or being removed from your feelings. The ground level of the building might represent your feelings, your sense of being "grounded," or being able to combine thoughts with actions. The basement of a building might represent the unconscious, something unknown, or feelings that you do not want to acknowledge.

12. Was there anything in the dream that differed from the situation in waking life? If the dream story seemed to go out of its way to change the actual situation, why would it have made those changes? Perhaps it wanted to "correct" your waking attitude, or draw attention to something that you have ignored.

13. What childhood memories come to you in relation to the dream? Sense your bodily feeling if you recall something from childhood. This may resemble a feeling about something going on in your waking life at the present time.

14. Could part of the dream refer to your personal growth? Sometimes a dream will illuminate ways in which the dreamer is unconsciously developing some aspect of his or her character or personality. If so, what does this change feel like to you? For example, do you feel pleased with the growth, or fearful of it?

15. Could part of the dream represent a sexual feeling or activity in waking life? Examine the dream story to see if it contains sexual symbols or metaphors. Something long and pointed might represent the male sexual organ; something hollow and deep might represent the female sexual organ. In

the dream, such bodily feelings as pulsing, throbbing, entering, and leaving might represent sexual intercourse.

16. Could part of the dream represent your creative or spiritual development? Sometimes there are dimensions in the dream that bring the dreamer's attention to activities you may ignore in your waking life. A death in the dream might represent the need for a part of you to change so that something better can be reborn. A bright light in the dream might express the need for spiritual illumination on a crucial life issue.[15]

Gendlin also suggests that dreamers use their bodies to correct any unconscious bias that might occur while they are interpreting their dreams. Sometimes dreamers distort the meaning of the dream so that it fits some preconceived belief or desire. But if this interpretation is taken back to the body, one's "felt sense" will often indicate that something about the assessment is incorrect. Gendlin recommends staying with the body feeling for a few minutes, and considering its reaction to important dream interpretations before the dreamer takes the action suggested by the dream.

Can dreamers learn more from going out of the body or by staying with the dream body? Or can both avenues of exploration be helpful? These are questions that each person must answer. Like most other extraordinary dreams, the out-of-body dream is not for everyone. But many of those dreamers who have experienced it are convinced that it has provided them with unique and valuable insights about their dreams, themselves, and the nature of reality.[16]

Chapter 6

Pregnancy Dreams

*D*reams during pregnancy have been given special attention by many cultures throughout the world. For example, members of the Tlingit tribe in North America believe in reincarnation, that deceased individuals are reborn into a new body. A French anthropologist in the 1800s noted, "It happens often that if a pregnant woman sees in a dream some relative long deceased, she will declare that this same relative has returned in her body and that she will put this person back into the world."[1]

Maya, mother of the Buddha, reportedly dreamed that a six-tusked white elephant ran, trumpeting loudly, into the palace. It circled her bed three times, then plunged into her womb through the right side of her rib cage. Upon awakening, she claimed that the dream was an omen that her child would bring a special gift to the world.

The birth of Alexander the Great was said to have been presaged by dreams from both parents. His father, King Philip of Macedonia, dreamed of seeing an imperial seal with the figure of a lion on his wife's abdomen. Queen Olympias dreamed she was sleeping with Ammon, the horned god of Libya. Later, she used this dream as proof that her son was a demi-god, and that Philip was not Alexander's actual father.

When pregnant with Augustus Caesar, Atia dreamed that her intestines were being carried up to the stars and stretched over all lands and seas. This was supposedly an indication that her child would rule a great empire. In Christian scripture, the New Testament reports that Mary's husband, Joseph, dreamed that an angel told him that his wife would "bring forth a son [who] will save his people from their sins."

Why Pregnancy Dreams Are Different Than Other Dreams

The unusual nature of pregnancy dreams could be related to the unusual nature of pregnancy: Hormonal changes; possible life style changes; irregular sleep patterns.

Patricia Maybruck's research has convinced her that all three of these factors work together at various times during pregnancy. Hormonal upsurges during pregnancy contribute to a greater variety and intensity of emotions while the pregnant woman is awake. Pregnant women may experience episodes of depression and euphoria, mood swings, and outbursts of crying, especially during the first trimester of pregnancy. This high degree of emotionality could be mirrored in the pregnant woman's dreams, and may account for many of their vivid images and colorful narratives. In addition, pregnant women rarely have a night of uninterrupted sleep, especially during the last trimester when the pressure of the enlarged uterus on the bladder necessitates frequent trips to the bathroom. Furthermore, dream research has repeatedly demonstrated that most dreams tend to reflect the dreamer's concerns and experiences during waking life. Pregnancy is a time of change and transition, hence differences in dream content would be expected.[2]

These changes may also affect expectant fathers. Their dreams often reflect such concerns as: Will I be displaced in my wife's affections? Will my wife and baby be physically healthy? Can I support my child financially? Can I nurture my child emotionally? By recognizing and discussing the possible implications of their own personal dream themes, expectant mothers and fathers can enrich the transitions they are both experiencing.

Many psychotherapists and obstetricians are beginning to encourage expectant parents to discuss their dreams. Their concerns about health, delivery, and childrearing can be acknowledged and confronted. Once dreamers face these fears directly, they report fewer nightmares and a greater sense of well-being. A discussion of dreams can accompany classes in natural childbirth as well as programs in prenatal care. Such discussions can reduce or eliminate the need for drugs to reduce tension and anxiety during pregnancy and enable the expectant mother and father to await the birth of their child with greater joy and with less apprehension. Pregnancy dreams are one area in which dream reports can be put to practical use.

Research on Pregnancy Dreams

At the turn of the nineteenth century, Sigmund Freud discussed a pregnancy dream told him by a Viennese woman:

A subterranean channel led directly into the water from a place in the floor of her room (genital canal-amniotic fluid). She raised a trap-door in the floor and a creature dressed in brown fur, very much resembling a seal, promptly appeared.[3]

Freud noted that the seal-like creature resembled the dreamer's younger brother, to whom she had always been like a mother. He also conjectured that the subterranean channel and the water symbolized the birth canal and the amniotic fluid.

The first reported study of pregnancy dreams has records of dreams that are strikingly similar to the dream recorded by Freud. Robert L. Van de Castle and Peggy Kinder collected the dreams of fourteen pregnant women in the United States, finding that small animals were frequently mentioned in the dream reports.[4] Kittens, puppies, bunnies, and other small creatures were also considered typical symbols of the fetus in other dream studies conducted in the United States.[5] Another common dream image in these studies was water, which might symbolize the waters of the amniotic sac in which the fetus is suspended.

A number of studies indicate that dream content changes remarkably both during menstruation and during pregnancy. Van de Castle once obtained dated dream reports from fifty nursing students, along with a calendar of their menstrual cycles. He found that menstrual dreams contained more references to rooms (perhaps symbolizing the uterus) and to anatomy, as well as more infants, children, and mothers.[6] Krippner and his associates also studied pregnancy dreams, finding that pregnant women's dreams tended to contain more references to architecture, shopping centers, the human body, small animals, and babies of various shapes and sizes.[7]

Patricia Maybruck collected over one thousand dreams from sixty-seven pregnant women, finding that expectant women reported more dreams than most non-expectant women. Again, pregnant women are probably able to recall their dreams more easily due to the irregular sleep patterns and frequent awakenings that characterize pregnancy. The data Maybruck collected were consistent with earlier studies of pregnant women in the United States and Canada. Also consistent with earlier studies, Maybruck found many dreams were concerned with water, again probably a symbol for the amniotic fluid. Again the pregnancy dreams also contained architectural references, perhaps symbolizing the dreamer's body, especially the uterus. There were many threatening dreams (such as, robbers, intruders, fires, earthquakes)—possibly a representation of the dreamer's fears of pregnancy complications, or references to the past (many of them metaphors for unresolved conflicts of childhood or adolescence).[8]

Maybruck observed that 40 percent of the pregnancy dreams she collected were nightmares; another 30 percent contained anxiety-provoking elements such as funerals and catastrophes. However, there is some evidence that frequent nightmares may help pregnant women resolve the issues that contribute to stress and tension during wakefulness. In one study, the pregnant women who had had more nightmares had shorter labor with fewer complications.[9] Maybruck replicated this study, and discovered that the more assertive the dreamer was in her nightmare, the shorter her labor was during childbirth. Maybruck also provided evidence that dream content changes from the first to the third trimester of pregnancy; anxiety and fear were more likely to be present in the last trimester, especially for women expecting their first child.

Steven-Lauria Albon found that dreams during pregnancy could increase the possibility of conflicts in analysis. A case study of a thirty-six-year-old analysand during different stages of her pregnancy cited regression to early childhood and abandonment issues. Albon concluded that the intensity of the dreams in pregnancy creates immediate access to personal conflict.[10]

Susan Sered collected dreams from fifty-five postpartum women on the maternity ward in a hospital in Israel. Her research and data showed that women with complicated obstetrical histories reported more dreams during pregnancy.[11]

Alan Siegel studied the dreams of expectant fathers. He found that these men often dreamed about rejection and exclusion, probably because they feared the baby would take their place in their wives' affection. Siegel observed that both men and women had frequent animal dreams during the pregnancy period, and that the animals related directly to the expectant parents' fantasies and concerns about the baby and the birth process. One of his clients had the following dream:

> I am fishing at the beach with Will, my younger brother. Out of a bubble comes a "boo" sound that startles me. Then, as I pull in my line, I feel no resistance. There is a white, fluffy, ripply thing attached to the end. Then I get it up on the beach, and I see it's a very old dog. It is alive. I have a feeling that it lived in the ocean to be protected so no one knew that it was alive.[12]

Although there is no specific mention of children or birth, this dream is filled with symbols and metaphors of pregnancy and birthing. It portrays the mysterious arrival of an animal, barely alive, which was hidden under water for protection. Emerging from a placenta-like bubble, with a shout, the dream dog could be a symbol of the baby's arrival.

Luis Zayas studied the dreams of ten first-time expectant fathers during three two-week periods in their wives' pregnancies. When compared to the dreams of ten non-expectant married men, the dreams of expectant fathers contained a considerable number of symbolic references to the womb, and feelings of loneliness and exclusion during the first stage of pregnancy. During the middle and late stages, the feelings of loneliness and exclusion decreased as did references to the dreamer's work environment and threats to oneself. In other words, dreams revealed the expectant father's initial fear of exclusion, which gradually gave way to greater confidence and the turning of one's attention to the home.[13] Zayas also conducted a pilot study in which the dreams of two expectant fathers were examined during the final months of pregnancy. These men had several dreams about their own fathers, as if they were trying to reconcile their relationship to their father in preparation to establishing their own paternal identity.[14]

Cross-Cultural Research on Pregnancy Dreams

Postpartum depression strikes a number of women in industrialized countries, and is thought to be caused by a combination of stress, hormonal changes, and unresolved personal conflicts. Sara Harkness studied new mothers in rural Kenya, using interviews and dreams to understand the emotional status of these women. Harkness found no evidence of postpartum depression among the women she interviewed. The role of dreams in the study was important, because without exploring this inner dimension of the participants' lives, critics could have alleged that rigid cultural role expectations simply repressed the women's depression.[15]

Fred Jeremy Seligson has collected over two thousand pregnancy dreams in the Republic of Korea, and has found that they are interpreted according to local folklore. Some folk beliefs were corroborated in predicting the gender of the child; cherries, strawberries, and watches predicted girl infants, while grapes, dates, and bears predicted boy babies. Other images were also fairly accurate. Flowers and apples, for example, represented girls, while dragons and tigers represented boys. However, in some cases the number of dreams in the sample was small, and there were other images that did not match the correct gender. Also, each species of animal, as well as most plants, has two possible genders in Korean language, further complicating the issue.

Seligson also found that the yin or yang qualities of a dream were held to predict gender. The sun is brilliant, or yang, while a cave is shadowy, or yin. A sour or hot (yang) fruit supposedly predicts a boy's birth, while a cool or sweet (yin) fruit predicts a girl's birth. According to Korean folklore, the personality characteristics of the child are also predictable from dreams: A black-skinned vegetable or animal indicates a sensual, pliable personality, whereas the color red indicates passion and the color blue indicates virtue.

The amount of activity a dream image engages is also salient in Korean folklore. A wild, fast, aggressive beast indicates a boy, especially if it bites the father. A tame, slow, shy animal suggests a girl baby, especially if it moves closely toward the father or if it is seen walking with its mother in the dream. An animal that bites the mother is indicative of a girl baby as well.[16]

Changes in Dream Imagery during Pregnancy

Each trimester of pregnancy is accompanied by different physical changes, both in the fetus and in the mother's body; these changes can be reflected in dream reports if the pregnant woman or expectant father keeps a dream note-book. Dreams can help the expectant parent understand and appreciate the pregnancy process, and his or her own reaction to it.

During the first trimester, dreams about obstetricians and the dreamer's body image are common for some expectant parents, especially during the first pregnancy. One woman had a Japanese obstetrician; she dreamed that when he arrived to deliver the baby, he was dressed in a traditional Japanese robe. Once in a while, these dreams may contain romantic fantasies on the part of the woman and references to jealousy on the part of her husband or partner. This is not unusual, because the obstetrician examines the most intimate parts of a woman's body. One woman dreamed that her obstetrician told her that he loved her. An expectant father dreamed that he caught the obstetrician and his wife in bed together. But at other times, the dreamer will reveal her changing body image; one woman dreamed she was carrying a spare tire around her waist.[17]

Dreams during the first pregnancy may contain fertility symbols. These dream images may be flowering gardens containing fruits and vegetables. One woman dreamed of a bowl filled with papaya and mangoes. Cuddly animals, birds, and fish might begin to appear in pregnancy dreams at this point. One woman dreamed, "I am holding a white rabbit under my arm, and I am stroking it." Another woman dreamed, "I have two little swans, and I know they will swim into the sunlight and become human babies." Architecture may appear, especially rooms, tunnels, and other features symbolizing the uterus and the birth canal.

If a pregnant woman decides to have an abortion, she might dream about that process at this point. Abortion dreams often contain hospital scenes and medical instruments. If a woman or her partner is considering abortion, their dreams may contain metaphors for feeling trapped, being overburdened, or looking frantically for a solution to a problem.

Some expectant fathers experience the symptoms of pregnancy during their dreams. In fact, from 10 to 30 percent of expectant fathers experience the "couvade syndrome" in which they have morning sickness and dizzy spells during the day, unusual food preferences, and even labor pains. This sympathetic response to their wife's or partner's pregnancy may appear in their dreams as well. The expectant father's personal myths about pregnancy and child-rearing often appear in his dreams and can help him separate those beliefs that are helpful from those that are dysfunctional.

During the second semester, personal myths about one's adequacy as a future parent may appear in one's dreams. Sometimes, these take the form of unresolved issues with the dreamer's own mother. In addition, babies appear more often, replacing small animals for many pregnant dreamers. Around the sixth month, when expectant mothers feel the movement of the fetus, dreams about infants may increase dramatically. Symbols for the pregnant woman's body may be more pronounced than during the first trimester, and appear in the form of houses, boats, cars, and trucks. There also may be dreams about fertility—gardens, flowers, and fruits.

In the third trimester, dreams often try to decipher whether the baby will be a boy or a girl. Maybruck's study revealed that expectant parents' dreams were correct half the time and incorrect half the time, exactly what one would expect by chance. During this final trimester, the personal myths concerning the changes in the couple's relationship can also be detected in dreams of both expectant mothers and expectant fathers. The content of these dreams may reflect on how the relationship will change once the baby is born.

One expectant father dreamed, "There is a party and I am having a wonderful time. There are many women, but I am not interested in them. I think to myself, 'This must be what it is like to be married.' Then I realize that I actually am married already." When the dreamer awakened, he thought that the dream indicated that he was thinking of infidelity. But when he brought the dream to a dreamworking class, he discovered the opposite was true. The dream appeared to be more a reaffirmation of his commitment to his wife and expected baby than a desire to be unfaithful with one of the ladies at the party.

Dreams about journeys, large animals or buildings, physicians, and hospitals may increase during the third trimester, and dreams about the labor experience are common. However, many of them are unusually brief; the baby simply "pops out," or is already there in the crib. In some cases, the baby is perceived as a teenager or young adult, probably symbolizing the dreamer's wish that the baby would arrive in the world well past the dangers inherent in childbirth and infancy.

Some dreams about the unborn baby may foretell future events, as in the case of one of our students, Jill. Jill was about six weeks pregnant. One night she had a fever of 104 degrees and had the following dream:

> There is a little boy in a black suit standing on the garden side of a glass sliding door. He was looking into the bedroom with tears streaming down his face. I am sitting in bed and around me are women, family, and friends. They are all wearing black.

This dream caused Jill great concern. Soon after, she visited her doctor, who told her that the fetus had stopped growing and that the pregnancy had been terminated. The black in this dream represented mourning. The boy was standing outside the glass door on the "other side," looking in. To Jill this indicated her fetus had passed through the threshold of life.

With her second pregnancy, Jill had another high fever. She was understandably worried about the safety of her baby, and she had the following dream:

> I am sitting in bed and in front of me there are rows and rows of children, or angels with wreaths on their heads, and they are all singing.

Jill woke up with the felt sense that her child would be fine. To Jill, the rows of children signified the abundance of creativity, and their singing was a positive feeling that gave her assurance that the baby would be healthy. Jill did not experience any difficulties with her second pregnancy.

Some dreams may show the new baby as a grotesque monster instead of a healthy child. These dreams are neither unusual nor unhealthy. They simply reflect an expectant dreamer's concern about the health and appearance of the infant. When partners share and discuss dreams of this type, they often find that it adds a new dimension to their relationship. They are better able to communicate their mutual fears and concerns about pregnancy and childrearing. In other words, dreams and dream sharing can enhance the relationship and expand the partners' range of experiences.[18]

Working with Pregnancy Dreams

Researchers at Johns Hopkins University interviewed 104 pregnant women who had chosen not to know their babies' gender through prenatal testing. Of the women who based a prediction of the baby's gender on a "feeling" or a "dream," 71 percent were correct and *all* the women who cited a dream were correct. Those results differ from those of Maybruck and the researchers concluded that maternal-fetal connections need to be more thoroughly explored.[19] There is one pregnancy dream recorded in Krippner's collection of 1,666 dreams from six countries. In that dream, a Brazilian woman correctly stated that she would give birth to a girl.[20]

Paul Trad has recorded case studies with pregnant women in psychotherapy. In these case studies, mothers who expressed emotions and disclosed their dreams and fantasies during pregnancy were better able to cope with the transitions and challenges of motherhood after the infant was born.[21]

The following dream by Elizabeth (one of our students) shows just how helpful dreamwork can be in gaining insights about pregnancy-related issues. Elizabeth was three weeks into her pregnancy but did not know that she was pregnant until the following dream:

> I feel an injection into my uterus by some strange entity; it is a little blue ball. I watch it inside of myself and see that it moves slowly. I am fascinated that I can see inside my own body. This little blue ball soon expands and I see a baby boy growing. I am initially excited, but suddenly I become scared. I wonder, "How do I take this baby out of me?"

Elizabeth realized she was pregnant one week following this dream, and a few months later learned that the baby was a boy. This was her first child and she had a petite frame.

As Elizabeth worked with the dream, a number of important insights came to her. The dream showed that she was concerned about how to "bring this baby out." In actuality, the fetus *was* growing so large that she was not certain if she could physically give birth to the child. It occurred to her that she had been a Cesarean baby and that the dream might be revealing the possibility that her baby might also be a Cesarean baby.

Metaphorically, Elizabeth also may have seen the baby boy in the dream as the masculine aspect of herself that she was beginning to discover. The birth and growth of the baby also may have represented for Elizabeth a "birth" of her creativity. Elizabeth's masculine energy had been repressed by her mother, who expected her to behave like a "proper little girl." During her childhood and adolescence, Elizabeth had difficulty staying in school and holding down jobs. She thought that her "job" as a woman was to be a wife and raise children. This dream gave Elizabeth a new perspective. During her pregnancy, she started studying so that she could finish her education. She decided that she wanted the responsibility of a job in her life. Once again, this case study demonstrates that extraordinary dreams can enhance daily life, enrich one's self-understanding, and improve one's creativity.

Chapter 7

Healing Dreams

*D*iagnostic and healing dreams assumed great importance among ancient peoples. Many indigenous people believed that dreams represented a domain as important as the ordinary world and that what occurred in the dream world was as real as what happened in the waking world. Many tribes contended that the deities had "dreamed" the ordinary world into existence; in a similar fashion, a human being could "dream" an event into something substantive. Therefore, dreams of sickness and health were carefully scrutinized for their impact upon the well-being of the dreamer. The Ojibway Indians of the Lake Superior region in North America made "dreamcatcher" nets that hung over the beds of their children to catch unfavorable dreams; only favorable dreams would pass through, and it was assumed that they would facilitate the childrens' health and well-being.

The Egyptian physician and architect Imhotep, who supposedly lived about 2900 B.C.E., became the patron of the ill. Individuals incubated their dreams at Serapeums or healing temples and reported their dreams to the *katochoi*, or dream scribe. If the *katochoi* did not deem the dream to be satisfactory, the patient remained in the sanctuary until an appropriate dream was reported. Patients often reported that Imhotep himself appeared with a diagnosis or a prescription. There is a historical link between the temples of Imhotep in Egypt and the healing temples of the Greek god Asclepius, which were especially popular in the fourth century B.C.E.. In the Greek temples, patients allegedly received diagnosis and treatment in their dreams during a visit from Asclepius or from one of his sacred animals.

Diagnostic dreams were studied by Hippocrates and later by Aristotle, both of whom explained dreams naturalistically rather than supernaturally.

They were of the opinion that diagnostic dreams reflected bodily processes too subtle to be registered during wakefulness. Hippocrates saw dreams that reproduced recent experience without distortion as a mark of health. Hippocrates "was concerned with dreams in which the soul, awake while the body slept, indicated somatic changes and hence the proper prophylactic treatment. Prayer was particularly indicated in dreams that involved the heavenly bodies or the earth."[1] Especially bizarre dreams reflected some inner struggle in somatic functioning; disturbances in specific internal organs often were portrayed in the dream as streaming water, windstorms, or heat from the sun.

Aristotle observed, "It is evident that the beginning of disease and other bodily afflictions will be small, and these necessarily will show themselves more in dreams than in the waking state." The concept that dreams could create as well as reflect waking life events was first articulated by Aristotle in an essay on prophetic dreams. He wrote, "The movements in sleep are often the starting points for the activities of the day, because the thought for the latter is already started on its way in our nocturnal fancies."[2] In the second century C.E., the Greek physician Galen stated that it was necessary to consider patients' dreams to form an accurate diagnosis and prognosis of their ailments.

Native American shamans made considerable use of dreams in their work. A contemporary shaman, Leslie Gray, has described her experiences with a healer from the Pomo Indian tribe. This healer told Gray that all of his healing ability and knowledge emanated from his dreams. For example, in his dreams he was instructed to move his hands in a vibrating manner to transfer the "healing energy" that is transmitted through him to his clients. Gray worked with the Pomo healer as well as with a Cherokee shaman when a severe neck injury did not respond to conventional medical treatment. Her work with the two Native American practitioners was successful and eventually led her to go beyond her university training in clinical psychology to obtain additional instruction from North American Indian shamans.[3]

Throughout the Middle Ages, the primary concern of European theologians was whether a dream was divinely inspired, or whether it was sent by demons. However, in the thirteenth century, a number of individuals speculated about dreams and illness. Michael Scot, an astrologer in the court of Frederick II, believed that dreams could be used to diagnose imbalances of blood, cholera, "melancholy" conditions, and unusual dryness, coldness, or heat in the body. Brother Bartholomew of England, a Franciscan monk, believed that natural bodily conditions were among the causes of dreams. Saint Thomas Aquinas wrote that dreams were the result of natural causes, among them bodily conditions. Albertus Magnus, a teacher of Saint Thomas, used dreams in his medical diagnosis.

From the Renaissance to the eighteenth century, there was little interest in dreams on the part of most Western philosophers. The major exception was Thomas Hobbes who speculated on the organic causes of dreams. Hobbes suggested that the erratic behavior of the body's internal organs during sleep contributed to the disordered sequences of thoughts in dreams.[4]

Health Diagnosis in Dreams

In 1967, the Russian psychiatrist Vasily Kasatkin reported on a twenty-eight-year study of over eight thousand dreams, concluding that dreams could warn of the onset of a serious illness several months in advance.[5] Kasatkin often observed changes in dream content shortly before an illness appeared; sometimes he was able to save a patient's life through early diagnosis and treatment.

In general, dreams announcing the onset of a disease were often found to contain frightening images, including scenes of war, fire, battles, and damage to the body. Unpleasant thoughts and feelings were also more often present, as were such emotions as terror, loneliness, and panic. Physical pain was not characteristic of many of these dreams, probably because the brain stores pain memories in an area far removed from the visual-motor cortex, the main area activated during REM sleep.

As the symptoms of the indisposition worsened, so did the dream content. But as the illness ran its course, the dream images reflected the recovery. Kasatkin reported that recurrent dreams of bodily wounds revealed the most serious conditions. For example, patients with repeated dreams of chest wounds often suffered serious heart attacks. Patients reported other dream images that proved to be symbolic of their ailments as well. One of Kasatkin's patients, for instance, had recurring dreams about a blocked chimney just before being diagnosed as having respiratory problems. Kasatkin's work with dream symbols and health has brought humankind full circle. Just as many native people believed that dream images could impact ordinary reality, many physicians and psychotherapists now believe that dream images can assist not only in identifying health problems but also in restoring one's health and well-being.

Carl Jung once accurately diagnosed a cerebrospinal condition in a man he had never met, solely on a description of one of the man's dreams. The neurologist Oliver Sacks tells of a woman who had a series of disturbing dreams. In one of them, she was imprisoned in an inaccessible castle that had the shape of her own body; in another she had become a living statue made of stone; and in another she had fallen into a sleep so deep that no one could awaken her. In this case, the dreams were ignored. One morning the woman's family had difficulty waking her; she had become catatonic and had succumbed to Parkinson's disease.[6]

In Krippner's cross-cultural collection of dream reports, there were three dreams in which information in the dream had practical health consequences. A Russian woman reported this dream:

> Suddenly, a small black snake appears and bites me in the right side of my neck. I squeeze it with three fingers and it opens its mouth. I squeeze the poison out of it, and try to find a place to put the snake. I find a glass box and open it with great difficulty. I put the snake in. When I wake up, I am still squeezing my hands. But that action decreases my recurring headaches. I still use that squeeze when I have headaches, but they have almost disappeared.[7]

Another dramatic example was provided by William Dement, a pioneer investigator of REM sleep. He recalled the following dream:

> Some years ago I was a heavy cigarette smoker—up to two packs a day. Then one night, I had an exceptionally vivid and realistic dream in which I had an inoperable cancer of the lung. I remember as though it were yesterday looking at the ominous shadow in my chest X-ray and realizing that the entire right lung was infiltrated. The subsequent examination in which my colleague detected widespread metastases in my . . . lymph nodes was equally vivid. Finally, I experienced the incredible anguish of knowing my life was at an end, that I would never see my children grow up, and that none of this would have happened if I had quit cigarettes when first I learned of their carcinogenic potential. I will never forget the surprise, joy, and exquisite relief of waking up. I felt I was reborn. Needless to say, the experience was sufficient to induce an immediate cessation of my cigarette habit. The dream had anticipated the problem, and solved it in a way that may be a dream's unique privilege.[8]

As Dement experienced, healing dreams become crucially important when one discovers a correspondence between dream life and waking life. Rosalind Cartwright, a psychologist, selected a number of psychotherapy clients who seemed as if they might end their therapy before significant progress had been made. The clients were asked if they would like to enroll in a two-week sleep and dream program. Forty-eight accepted her invitation. Of this group, sixteen were regularly awakened during REM sleep, sixteen during non-REM sleep, and sixteen went directly into psychotherapy. Each morning, the sleep laboratory subjects were asked to recall and talk about the dream reports they had made to the experimenter during the night. Compared with the subjects who went directly into psychotherapy and those awakened during non-REM sleep, the subjects awakened during REM sleep were more likely to remain in psychotherapy for at least ten weeks. Furthermore, of the participants in the three groups, those subjects made the most changes in their lives.[9]

Award-winning author Marc Ian Barasch was able to detect his thyroid cancer through a series of nightmares that pointed literally and metaphorically to a problem in his neck. He writes: "after one terrifying dream—torturers had hung an iron pot filled with red-hot coals beneath my chin, and I woke up screaming, the odor of searing flesh in my nostrils—I couldn't ignore them any longer."[10]

Barasch sought the advice of physicians and the only symptoms he had were his nightmares! With the initial tests, doctors were unable to detect any problems but his dreams continued warning him. Barasch insisted on being thoroughly examined. Finally the doctors were able to detect a hard lump—a thyroid nodule. The lump turned out to be cancerous. Were it not for his haunting dreams, his cancer would not have been detected early. It is possible that his nightmares saved his life.

Carl Simonton and his associates worked with a young male patient who reported a dream of an "unorthodox doctor" who told him that he had come to help him. This dream doctor told the patient how to remedy his weight loss, improve his muscle tone, overcome his fear of women, and express his sexuality more fully. The patient began to gain weight, developed an exercise program, and improved his social relationships. Simonton and his colleagues suggested that the dream doctor symbolized their patient's "inner healer," and that his advice was closely attuned to what the young man needed for his development.[11]

Research with Healing Dreams

Robert C. Smith has conducted a number of studies on the "early warning" properties of dreams. In one study, he collected recent dreams from a group of individuals hospitalized for various medical problems. In follow-up visits, he discovered that men in the study who had dreams about death had a worse prognosis than men who did not have these dreams. Women who had dreams about separation had a worse prognosis than women who did not have this type of dream. The men and women who had the negative dreams were more likely to die, or to experience complications of their illness or re-hospitalizations than the other subjects studied, although all groups had been in equally serious condition during their original stay in the hospital.[12]

One terminally ill man in the study had the following dream about death one week before his first admission to the hospital:

> My brother and I visited our old house . . . , and mother was there in her casket. It was all black except for a weird glowing red stripe. . . . She tried to get out, but then fell back and seemed to disappear; she was a goner for sure now. We took her to the cemetery and almost got killed ourselves in a flood on the way. There weren't many people there. Dad was dead for years.

A woman who was admitted to the hospital because of breast cancer had the following dream about separation. She died six months later, after several re-admissions:

> I can't find my husband. He's never gone this long. I keep searching. I miss him. Then a strange dog comes in. I worry about Betsy, our cat, but can't find her. I'm more lonely and call my daughter, but she's not there.[13]

This study provided some of the first evidence that traumatic dreams might be warnings of underlying medical problems. However, Smith's method was retrospective; he began with the prognosis and then looked backward in time to see what the patients' early dream content had been. In a later, more rigorous study, Smith started with the death and separation dreams, made a prediction about the outcome, and then determined whether the prediction was correct. Using a group of patients being examined for possible heart disease, he predicted that the more traumatic the patients' dreams, the more serious their diagnosis would be. His prediction was confirmed; the greater the number of death dreams (i.e., for men) or separation dreams (i.e., for women), the more severe the heart disease was found to be.[14]

Frederic J. Boersma conducted an intensive investigation of the dreams of a woman diagnosed with ovarian cancer. Boersma worked with the woman's dreams in psychotherapy, as well as hypnosis, active imagination, and poetry. Her recovery was remarkable and was mirrored in her dream content. Boersma identified six themes in her dreams: unfinished business, conflict, blockage, psychological defenses, death, and spiritual healing. He based his psychotherapeutic intervention on these themes, assisting the woman to release past heartache and resentment, deal with psychological and physical pain, and express her deep feelings honestly and directly. The woman's dreams included many images of body armor and shielding. Boersma saw these as symbols of her psychological defenses against acknowledging her feelings. In active imagination exercises, he invited her to let down these defenses and use the newly acquired energy for healing purposes.[15]

Harry A. Wilmer studied the dreams of 103 Vietnam War veterans receiving Jungian-oriented psychotherapy for posttraumatic stress disorder. Although they had been back in the United States for at least seven years, 53 percent of their 359 reported dreams depicted actual combat events. A second cluster of dreams depicted combat events in metaphorical form. A third group of dreams portrayed fantastic events that appeared to be metaphors for healing and recovery. Wilmer observed that the veterans who recovered from the posttraumatic stress gradually moved through the three types of dreams. Originally, they would dream about being under attack, or about killing enemy soldiers. As their therapy progressed, the dreams would become metaphors for the battles and for associated life issues. Finally, the dreams would reflect resolutions of the issues raised and a coming to terms with the war events.[16]

Psychologist E. W. Kellogg has reported a number of case studies in which he used lucid dreaming to heal an injury. In one case, Kellogg himself reported that he had punctured his tonsil with a wooden skewer while he was eating Japanese food. His tonsil became swollen and infected. He attempted an out-of-body experience to heal his tonsil, but instead had the following lucid dream:

> I became lucid and tried to heal my throat. I looked in a mirror and my throat looked healthy, but the tonsils looked more like the middle section [i.e., uvula] than like tonsils. So, in my dream body my throat looks healthy, but different. I use affirmation for healing to occur and my throat does feel much better.

Upon waking from this dream, Kellogg did not feel any pain and the next day the right tonsil looked almost normal. He reported that 95 percent of his infection disappeared within twelve hours of his lucid dream.[17]

Citing many case examples, Robert Moss shows how dreams can facilitate healing from a shamanic perspective.[18] His case studies demonstrate that shamanic traditions retain powerful techniques that can assist contemporary dream practitioners. For example, he took one man with cancer on a guided imagery journey in which he encountered a figure covered with blue tattoos. This strange figure seemed to emanate energy that was directed to the cancer cells. Moss' client felt the tattoos represented a new "blueprint" for his life and began work with the images that the strange figure had pointed out to him; soon, his cancer was in remission.[19]

Bogzaran has been using dreams as a diagnostic tool and working with dreams for healing. The following is her personal account of a dream related to illness, and how she took charge as the dreamer and worked with the dream.

In the turning of the season, when many people suffer from the flu, Bogzaran felt herself on the verge of an illness. She took a nap and had the following dream:

> I am walking in a street and suddenly I am attacked by a ferocious group of bugs. I am trying to defend myself but they are too aggressive. I become more and more anxious.

Bogzaran woke up with a headache and a sore throat. Reflecting on the dream, she saw the attack of the "bugs" as a possible attack of the flu virus. The "bugs" were weakening her immune system and the sore throat was her body's defense against the virus. Using a dream re-entry technique, she visualized herself once again walking in the street. As the bugs came towards her she put out her hands, imagining a liquid stream coming out of her fingers to repel the bugs. As the imaginary liquid jet came out of her fingers, her body began to feel lighter. She managed to repel most of the insects. Instead of being the passive victim, she took an active role to defend her body. When she ended the dream re-entry experience, Bogzaran felt much better. Her headache was completely gone and her sore throat slowly disappeared within couple of hours. She did not catch the flu.

Working with Healing Dreams

Patricia Garfield has devoted a considerable amount of time to working with healing dreams. Based on her extensive interviews and her collection of case studies, Garfield recommends a 6-point program for working with dreams to explore their diagnostic or therapeutic properties.

1. Describe the dream in the present tense. By writing or telling the dream as if it were an ongoing story, you can recall the emotions in it more fully and begin to discharge any anxiety associated with the emotions. Retelling the dream in the present tense allows you to appreciate the concerns expressed and use the dreamworking process therapeutically.

2. Recall your emotional feelings in the dream. Did your emotions change over the course of the dream? When were they the strongest? What were the most pleasant and unpleasant parts of the dream for you? By identify-

ing your feelings during the dream, you will clarify potential areas of concern as well as support.

3. Identify events and emotions in your waking life that might be related to the dream. Ask yourself what has happened recently in your life, and what your reactions have been. Could the dream be a reflection of these events and attitudes? Remember that dreams often exaggerate feelings and serve as metaphors for waking events.

4. Associate to the key images and activities in the dream. First, consider the main activity. What was it about? Can you make any associations to your waking life? Then turn to the most puzzling image of the dream. It may be a person, an animal, a building or an activity. Ask yourself what is special about that image. How would you describe it? You might imagine you are describing that image to a child in very simple terms. Does this description fit you or any-one around you? Does it fit anything in your waking life? Imagine yourself inside of that dream activity or image. What does it feel like? If that dream ele-ment could speak, what would it say? Identify the setting of the dream. What does it feel like to be in that location? Does this remind you of any situation or locale in your waking life?

5. Substitute your own personal associations for the actions in the dream. Put your associations to work by telling the dream in those words. For exam-ple, suppose the theme of your dream was "President John F. Kennedy is dead." Examine your associations to Kennedy. You might have considered him an idealistic politician, or a dangerous social reformer, or a charming and mag-netic personality. Your associations to "dead" might reflect "inactive and non-functional," or "the end of life," or "the final stage of growth." Now put them together. Perhaps the idealistic part of you is inactive. Perhaps a dangerous part of you can bring about the end of your life. Perhaps your personal charm has taken you as far as it can go, and you must now develop some other aspect of your personality.

6. Decide what you plan to do about this situation in your daily life. You can state this intention in the form of a personal myth. Using the examples in the Kennedy dream, these myths might reflect the determination that, "my ideals need to be revived," or "I will be more cautious and will curb my danger-ous behavior," or "compassion, empathy, and loyalty are more enduring per-sonality traits than superficial charm."[20]

Garfield pays special attention to the metaphors in healing dreams, noting that the word comes from the Greek terms *meta*, meaning "over" and *pherin* meaning "to carry." Therefore, a metaphor "carries over" a meaning from one item to another. Aristotle recognized this property of dreams when he wrote,

"The most skillful interpreter of dreams is the person who has the faculty of observing resemblances." Garfield has found many metaphors in healing dreams: a dreamer walking down a rickety staircase might have a spinal problem; a dreamer putting too much fuel into a furnace might be overeating in waking life; a dreamer who can not stop a car because of faulty brakes might need to slow down his or her activity level.

A house is a common symbol for a dreamer's body. The electrical wiring may represent the nervous system, the back door may represent the anus, and the front door might represent the mouth or the vagina. Another common symbol for the dreamer's body is the automobile. The steering wheel often represents the brain, the horn may stand for the dreamer's voice, and the fuel may denote the dreamer's energy level. As healthy body functions go awry, the disturbances often are mirrored in dreams. Garfield likens work with dreams to the procedures carried out in Egyptian and Greek dream temples. But instead of depending on a deity or supernatural entity to guide one's dreams, the dreamer can use his or her own "inner guide" to benefit from healing dreams.

Robert Moss underscores the importance of attending to repetitive dreams, focusing on the intention of a dream before going to sleep, protecting oneself during sleep by "self-defense" rituals, and remembering that the planet as well as the individual is in need of healing. "Visionaries," asserts Moss, "had a direct line to high knowledge. They acted on their dreams, not to hurt but to heal, as we must today."[22]

In Argentina, Roberto Rocca has used the concept of personal mythology in his treatment of psychoneuroses. He has obtained clues from his clients' healing dreams concerning the best direction in which psychotherapy should proceed. He and his clients have worked together to restructure those personal myths that are dysfunctional, using active imagination and waking fantasy.[23]

As this research has shown, healing dreams can be used by dreamers themselves, or by dreamers in conjunction with their physicians and psychotherapists to identify and resolve physical, psychological, or spiritual ailments, problems, and disorders. As Montague Ullman has pointed out, there is great potential in healing dreams. That potential can be turned into actuality through the wise use of dreamworking.[24]

Chapter 8

Dreams within Dreams

*D*reams within dreams are multilevel dream experiences in which the already-dreaming dreamer enters either an old dream or a new dream. Sometimes dreamers think that they have awakened but soon realize that they have simply awakened to another dream. This "false awakening" can be repeated several times from one dream to the next. One of our friends, Richard, illustrates the experience of a dream within a dream. Richard had recently lost his mother to cancer. A month after her passing he had the following dream:

> I find myself in the basement of my grandmother's house rummaging through old books and papers. I find an old notebook that belonged to my mother. I begin to read the words and slowly they begin to disappear off the page. This experience seems very strange to me and I say to myself, "I must be dreaming." I become emotional and wake up. [At this point Richard enters into a false awakening.]
>
> I wake up and begin writing my dream experience on a piece of paper. As I am writing it down I hear a strange noise outside. I open the door and see a few of my college friends outside of my house. I say to myself, "How can they be here?" The excitement of seeing them wakes me up immediately.

After this "second" dream, Richard actually awakened and realized that he had had a dream within a dream.

While contemplating this dream, Richard realized that this dream had taken him to the time in his life when he felt emotionally secure and close to his mother. The death of his mother was a shock to him. Although he was in the basement of his grandmother's house in his dream, he saw his dream as a direct message from his mother. The basement to him represented a passageway into the "underworld" where he could discover messages from the "book of his ancestors."

When Richard shared this dream with a close friend, he gained several insights. He learned that in recent years he had become overly analytical, and as a result he had not allowed himself to grieve the loss of his mother. Although he did not see his mother in the dream, the multilevel nature of his dream stirred memories and emotions about his mother and her death. For example, his college friends were the same friends who had visited him when he lived with his mother. To Richard, those friends represented a sense of community and support that he lacked in his present life. This dream brought him closer to his emotions and he was able to grieve the loss of his mother. In addition, he became much more open, sharing his experiences and feelings with close friends and family members.

One of the common examples of dream within a dream or false awakening is the "bathroom dream." In these dreams the desire of emptying one's bladder incorporates into the dream scene and creates a challenging situation for the dreamer. The following is a dream of a colleague, Sandra, who experienced this phenomenon:

> I find myself in a shopping center; I am looking for a toilet. I have to stand in a long line, and when my turn finally arrives the toilet gets smaller and smaller while changing shapes. I realize that I am in a dream, so I wake up having my bladder full. I run to the bathroom, but I realize that the bathroom has been moved to another building. I begin walking in different hallways to get to the bathroom. I get frustrated and wake up. This time, I really wake up and find the bathroom.

In Sandra's dream within a dream, we can see her mind and body at cross-purposes. Sandra's mind continues dreaming, as best it can, even though her body is directing her to empty her bladder. It could be conjectured that part of Sandra's psyche wants to remain asleep, while another part wants to wake up. A compromise is reached in which she seems to awaken. But this compromise is an unworkable solution because her physical needs are now more acute than ever. The confusion in the dream may reflect the cross-purposes that exist in her body as it wrestles between wanting to sleep and wanting to urinate.

Sandra's dream dramatically demonstrates how a full bladder or colon, or an empty stomach cramping with hunger pains, can lead to dream images that accurately reflect these conditions. It is interesting to observe how ordinary bodily processes create sensations that are converted into dream images, just as symptoms of illness can sometimes create images that prove to be useful in the diagnosis and treatment of ailments. When dreamers' bodies are disturbed, their dreams can provide the first sign of this discomfort or disequilibrium.

Another common experience of a dream within a dream occurs in the second dream when Sandra frantically tries to resolve her dilemma.

REM sleep is associated with the activation of sexual responses in both men and women.[1] Sexual arousal in males and females is a natural part of the activation that some bodily systems experience during REM sleep.[2] Adolescent males frequently have erotic dreams accompanied by an ejaculation of semen. Did the dream provoke the erection and ejaculation? Or did an accumulation of seminal fluid in the testes create swelling pressure that stimulated the dream? Both possibilities appear to exist; penile erections are firmer and stronger during sexual dreams than during non-sexual dreams accompanied by erections. And when the dreamer is sexually deprived or excessively stimulated, the typical arousal of the sex organs during REM sleep is intensified and often results in dreams with a carnal content.[3] These natural bodily processes can lead to dreams within dreams. One of our students Kescia, a computer programer, reported the following example:

> I see myself resting in my bed and feel a wave of passion engulf my being. I am alone and I begin to have a sexual fantasy. I see sensual bodies around me and feel the energy within me intensify. I begin to masturbate and shortly following my climax I suddenly awaken. I feel very light and relaxed. Within moments, I find myself floating high in the air above my bed with a beautiful woman next to me. Still floating, we begin to caress one another and together we experience one of the most intense sexual encounters of my life. We climax and I awake in my bed, alone with my inner thighs warm and wet.

Kescia's dreams stimulated her multiple orgasms, demonstrating that her bodily processes were at work during her dream state. Kescia realized upon her actual awakening that she had suppressed sexual energy that needed to be released. Having an intense sexual drive with an active imagination, Kescia's body often climaxes when she has erotic dreams. She believes that her erotic dreams allow her to express her sensuality and sexuality even when she is not in a sexual relationship.

Research on Dreams within Dreams

Dreams within dreams are frequently referred to in the psychoanalytic literature. Freud took the position that dreams within dreams are the client's attempt to resist or obscure what was dreamed. Leon Berman presented a case history confirming this hypothesis. His client had repressed a disturbing memory from childhood in which she watched her parents making love; to obscure the memory, the scene took place in the dream within a dream, attended by feelings of guilt and anxiety.[4] Austin Silber reported another example of a childhood sexual memory occurring in the first dream; the second dream—from which the dreamer awoke—was reportedly an attempt to encapsulate the disturbing memory of the actual event.[5]

Fred Lipschitz, another psychoanalyst, takes a different view. He contends that the phenomenon is an attempt at problem solving and self-discovery, and is often a substitute for unsatisfactory interpersonal transactions. As such, these dreams can be very useful for the psychoanalyst, as they suggest issues that the client would like to discuss.[6]

Brazilian psychiatrist Moises Tractenberg has dealt at length with Freud's notion of wish fulfillment in dreams and Freud's insistence that dreams almost invariably represent repressed wishes and the fulfillment of these desires—at least in one's dreams. But Tractenberg tells how Garman, a fellow psychiatrist, has proposed something quite different: that dreams are "mini-nightmares," masked re-enactments of traumatic situations. The fulfillment of wishes in dreams would act only to defuse the traumatic thought before it converts to a harmless hallucinatory fantasy. Another psychiatrist, Kemper, attempts a synthesis of these views, agreeing with Freud that dreams represent attempts at wish fulfillment, but adding that they contain creative aspects that prepare the dreamer for waking activity, searching and offering solutions for present conflicts. Some dreams can even have a premonitory aspect, announcing future events or containing predictions that actually occur.[7] If Kemper is correct, one dream might represent an attempt to fulfill a desire, which then gives way to another dream in which a more realistic solution to the conflict is given. The dream within a dream would then allow the dreamer to compare and contrast various alternatives.

In Krippner's cross-cultural collection of 1,666 dreams, there were 10 dreams within dreams; all six countries were represented. A Brazilian woman reported:

> I dream that I see an Indian man who is running. He has a knife in his hand, and is being chased by a leopard. I watch him fight with the leopard and I am frightened. But then I stop being a witness and become the Indian in the exact moment that the leopard jumps on him. I think I wake up and recall the dream, but actually I am still in the dream. But this time I am the leopard, and I attack the Indian![8]

Some dreams within dreams appear to point out internal conflicts or obstacles that the dreamer needs to resolve in order to move forward in life. In the following dream within a dream from a university professor, Lisa (one of our colleagues), the first dream presents an issue that she needs to address in her life; the second dream provides further clarification of the subtleties involved.

> I am looking through my closet for a dress to wear to an upcoming wedding. I am frustrated because I can't find a suitable dress. I search through different dresses and finally pull out a blue and white dress. As I look at the dress, I suddenly remember another dream.
>
> In this other dream, I wear the same blue and white dress to my own wedding, but I am not wearing any shoes. It is an extremely embarrassing situation for me. I tell myself, "Well, I know what will happen if I choose this dress for this wedding!" I think about my statement and decide to still look for the shoes that match the blue and white dress. I begin looking through boxes of shoes, but all the boxes are full of papers. I start to panic and open all the shoe boxes, but I can't find the right pair of shoes. I finally find the right pair of shoes, but when I put one on it is too small for my foot.

Lisa woke up initially feeling frustrated, but as she began working with her dream she soon realized that it represented a behavioral script in her personal life. She realized that throughout her life she had been experiencing a fear of commitment in her intimate relationships. For example, she was dating a man who had been asking her to marry him, but she felt "unprepared" for a committed relationship. In her dream within a dream, she was almost "prepared" to wear the wedding dress, but in both dreams there were obstacles that caused her to feel either embarrassed or frustrated.

Working with Dreams within Dreams

Daniel Deslauriers and George Baylor believe that "script analysis" allows the dreamer to find patterns, both in dreams and in waking life. Once the dreamer recognizes a pattern, she or he can work with the dream, transforming this pattern into a new script or story. To conduct a script analysis, the dreamer will want to use the following steps:

1. Look at the overall story of the dream.
2. Choose the important scene in the dream.

3. Identify the characters and their roles (e.g., Who is in charge? Who initiates the action? Who is the victim?).

4. If the dream story is not satisfactory, decide what choices would lead to a different outcome.

5. Undertake a "metaphor mapping" of the dream that identifies a pattern within the dream that may apply to a waking life situation.

6. Pay close attention to the emotions of the dream because they typically act as the bridge between the dream image and the waking situation.[9]

When working with a dream within a dream, this procedure can be followed with each individual dream, then with the total dream. The transition points are especially important. What feelings occur when the dreamer appears to be awake? Are there any immediate reactions to the dream during the false awakening? Is there a sharp contrast between the dreams, or are they similar? Is the second dream a continuation of the first dream, a commentary on the first dream, or a contrast to the first dream?

Sometimes, especially in the morning, a dream occurring during REM sleep will blend into a hypnopompic image. (Hypnopompic states of consciousness occur immediately preceding awakening.) While this type of dream experience appears to be a dream within a dream, it has some different properties. Hypnopompic imagery may be visual, auditory, or kinesthetic in nature, and may even involve tastes and smells. However, there is little narrative in hypnopompic imagery.

A similar type of imagery occurs immediately preceding sleep. This is the hypnagogic state. Once again, there is little narrative quality to these images; plots and stories are very rare during the hypnagogic state. The etymology of the word is in Hypnos, the Greek god of sleep, and *agein* or "leading to." Hence "hypnagogic" means "leading to sleep." *Pompe* is a Greek word meaning "procession"; "hypnopompic" means "proceeding from sleep into wakefulness."

Some dream practitioners use a simulated false awakening technique as a tool for working with dreams. They ask their clients to imagine the final scene of their dream, and then to imagine that they "awakened" to a continuation of the dream.[10] This technique, if done from an emotional rather than an intellectual perspective, sometimes allows the client to expand on the lessons or insights offered by the dream. Further, it is one of many dreamworking techniques that dreamers can learn to undertake themselves.

ᥱᠪᠥ ───────────────────────── Chapter 9

Collective Dreams

*C*ollective dreams have been recorded since before the time of Christ. The Assyrian King Assurbanipal, living in the seventh century B.C.E., was keenly interested in dreams and even kept a dream diary. One night, it is said, he and his priests had a collective dream in which the goddess Ishtar appeared to them, promising to lead them into battle. Encouraged by this dream, the Assyrian army fought valiantly and won the conflict.[1]

In William Shakespeare's play *Richard III*, several ghosts of people who were murdered by Richard during his illegal seizure of the throne visit him in a dream on the eve of his climatic battle with Richmond (the leader of the opposing army). Richmond dreams about the same ghosts that same night. For Richmond, this dream is a favorable omen, but for Richard it presages defeat on the following day.

Collective dreams of this type are referred to as "mutual dreams"—when two or more people have similar dreams on the same night. A second type of collective dream is the "shared dream," in which two or more people dream of each other in a common space and time, and independently remember similar surroundings, conversations, and interactions within the dream. Linda Lane Magallón, author of the book *Mutual Dreaming*, reports that "shared dreaming" often occurs when dreamers decide to go to sleep with the intention of meeting in their dreams. If they intend to have the same dream, dream about the same theme, and dream up the same symbols, deliberate shared dreaming may take place.[2]

A unique example of mutual dreams was reported by two Japanese women who contributed to Krippner's cross-cultural study—the only such dreams in the survey. The first woman dreamed: "I am in the lobby of a big hotel. There is a large pillar made of marble. My friend Aiko is there and I stab her with a knife. I don't know why I stab her. Nobody seems to notice what I have done." The second woman reported: "I am in a hotel lobby. There is a big pillar there and I am standing by it. My younger sister comes in. She walks right up to me and stabs me with a knife. My younger sister's name is Tomoko. I die from the stabbing." The fact that both dreamers reported being in the lobby of a big hotel with a marble pillar and experienced the same event makes this a remarkable example of a mutual dream. If the assailant had been the same person in both dreams, and each woman had appeared in the other's dream, it would have been a shared dream.[3]

Many factors can influence whether either type of dream will occur, for example, pre-sleep activities, common group interests, and coincidence. Telepathy may also be a contributing factor. The cultivation of mutual and shared dreams does not attempt to exclude sensory cues or any other stimuli that might provide a conventional explanation for the phenomenon. However, to dreamworkers interested in these topics, it is the dreams themselves, as much as the factors that contribute to them, that is of interest.

Dreaming Someone Else's Dream

Hornell Hart was a pioneer in the study of both shared and mutual dreams, and he reported numerous examples of shared dreams that he and his wife seemed to experience.[4] The British psychologist Ann Faraday has cited examples of mutual dreams in her well-known book, *The Dream Game.*[5]

Some groups of indigenous people have used shared dreams to make decisions for the benefit of all members of their community. This process of dream sharing usually takes place in public, and the tribal shaman assists in determining the common dream themes that will determine the action to be taken. Sometimes an individual member of the tribe may step forth with an important dream to share. This was a common practice among the Iroquois Indians in North America, where the community traditionally paid special attention to dream visions, songs, and dances. The Iroquois were also attentive to similarities in dreams reported by several members of their community.

Two psychologists, Robert Van de Castle and Henry Reed, have developed a modern-day version of the Iroquois dream-sharing practice, which they call the "dream helper ceremony." This ceremony focuses on evoking mutual dreams to assist one or more members of a group. When the group meets, the group leader asks, "Who among you is feeling particularly troubled or is dealing with a life crisis?" Typically, the specific problem of the volunteer (or volunteers) is not discussed openly until it is revealed the following morning. If the group is large enough, it can be divided, with sub-groups focusing on each volunteer, but usually one person is the focus of the entire group.

The volunteer enters the circle and the group leader asks the group to "open up" to that person's needs. The focus person loans personal items (keys, jewelry, clothing) to each member of the group to form a closer connection. A meditation session encourages the process as well. Before retiring for the night, the group leader reminds members that they will "donate" their dreams to the volunteer:

> Take the object that the focus person has given you and sleep near it or on it. Remember that tonight your dreams are not your own. You are donating them to assist the focus person. You have a responsibility to remember as many of your dreams as you can, so be prepared with a pad of paper and pen by your bed. Since the dreams belong to the focus person, do not censor your dreams. Even trivial details might be important. Parts of your dream that might be embarrassing need to be reported; those embarrassing details may very well be an important key to helping the focus person with the problem, whatever it is.[6]

Henry Reed has reported a striking example of this ceremony. One night a nine-person dream helper group was focusing on a young woman named Mary. Of the nine people in the group, only three did not recall their dreams. The dreams of the remaining six members contained a number of similar themes. One dreamer reported a dream of going to a supermarket. Another person dreamed of going to a drugstore to buy a shower kit that could fit in a pocket, but had difficulty finding the money to pay for it. The same dreamer also dreamed of going to a library. Another dreamed of a "Jewish mother" who never was convinced that her child was healthy. Still another person dreamed of holding hands with Mary, of going to a piano recital, and of a boy diving very deeply into a pool of water. Another dreamed of being underwater and emerging to fly over the building where the dreamers were sleeping. He saw Mary and heard a physician's voice report, "Her diet is too tight; water is very important." This dreamer also dreamed of being at a fashionable poolside park.

Reed also had several dreams that night. First, he dreamed that he was lying on the deck of a sinking ship. The water level was rising slowly, but was beginning to enter Reed's mouth. He began to choke and awakened suddenly with the impression that Mary had been ill and almost died. His second dream was quite different:

I dreamed I was in my childhood home and I heard Mom playing on the piano. I also saw her in the bathroom taking a shower. Then, I saw her standing in the kitchen, dripping from the shower, talking on the telephone to someone about how her piano playing was always interrupted. I also saw Dad lounging in the living room in his pajamas. Then I went outside to return a book to the library. Outside on the lawn was my personal library, and it was being soaked by a lawn sprinkler. Mom and Dad did not look like my parents at all.[7]

In the morning, the members of the dream helper group reported their dreams. Certain dream images had been repeated: water, shopping, the library, mother, and piano. Putting the dreams together, the group speculated that Mary's problem concerned her health, and that water might be a critical factor. At this point, Mary was asked to make a statement. She was deeply affected by the dreams, and explained that her problem was a recently canceled wedding. Although none of the dreams directly reflected a marriage theme, several dreams touched on matters that had been involved in the breakup.

Mary recognized the dream of the poolside party as the type of social situation she frequently had to attend with her ex-fiancé and his family. They came from different social backgrounds, and this difference caused problems for them. She said that the dream of the Jewish mother also reminded her of her ex-fiancé, for he had once been very ill and his mother continued to treat him like a sick little boy.

As to the water images, Mary responded with a story not previously shared with anyone. She had a chronic, epileptic-like condition with seizures brought on by tension. She said the themes of being under water reminded her of how she would feel "flooded" prior to a seizure, an image she had been concerned with recently. She said that Reed's drowning dream was an appropriate image of what had happened to her during a recent stay in a hospital. As an unexpected side effect to some medication she had received, she had developed a temporary partial paralysis in her sleep. As a result, while sleeping on her back she had been unable to swallow her saliva. It had filled her throat, choking her, and she had almost died from suffocation.

The phrase "diet too tight" reminded Mary of a related component of her medical condition—fluid retention—and she speculated that changes in her diet might assist her recovery. The library images reminded her of her ambivalence about going back to school. Concerning the piano, Mary recalled that she was the only non-musical member of her family. As she reflected on the images brought forth by the group, Mary felt exhilarated by the dream helper ceremony. The dreamers themselves were also pleased and surprised by the connections between their dream images and Mary's life issues.

Research with Collective Dreams

Psychologist Mark Thurston attempted to conduct a research study based on Van de Castle and Reed's dream helper ceremony. His experimental subjects were 465 members of the Association for Research and Enlightenment, a group founded to study the work of Edgar Cayce, the American "psychic sensitive." The subjects were randomly divided into two groups, each of which worked with a target person suffering from a chronic physical problem. One target person suffered from severe skin eczema; the other had a chronic kidney infection. The subjects whose dreams were most useful to the target persons were found to have had psychic experiences in the past, and to have scores similar to the target person on personality tests. The dreams of female subjects tended to be more congruent with the needs of the target person than those of the male subjects.[8]

In a dream course taught by Bogzaran, students were asked to attempt mutual or shared dreaming. The class was divided into four groups of five. Each group chose a specific night and a designated site in which members could meet each other in their dreams. Meditators John and Marcia, two members of the class, were assigned to the same group. The night of the mutual dream study, Marcia was absent from the class and was not aware of the class intention to have a mutual dream. John's group decided to meet each other in their dreams at Muir Beach near the Green Gulch Zen Center in Marin County, California.

John's First Dream

I am walking down the gravel path from Green Gulch to the beach, I see a sign on the path and I remember that I need to go to the beach to meet the group. I go to the beach and find Stephanie, one of the members in my group.

Three days after John's dream and two days before he told his dream to the class, John went to Green Gulch Zen Center for a meditation retreat. In one of the walking mediation sessions he began walking towards the beach on the same path he had walked in his dream. On the path he saw Marcia, walking back from the beach. As this was a silent retreat, they acknowledged each other by nodding as they passed.

John saw this event as more than just mere coincidence. Marcia felt as though she had participated in a waking-related dream experience. Magallón terms this type of synchronistic event a "dream-to-waking experience phenomenon."[9]

A week later John and Marilyn, other students in the class, decided to try a shared dreaming experiment at the same location—attempting to meet by the water at Muir Beach on Friday the 13th, 1996. They had the following shared dreams.

John's Second Dream

Marilyn and I were on Muir Beach, facing the water on the north end of the beach. Then we end up at the Pelican Inn, in the restaurant, sitting at a table near the fireplace, talking. Marilyn is wearing a burgundy sweater and black jeans.

Marilyn's Dream

I am walking along the path that leads from Green Gulch to the beach. I walk through the gate and I am noticing the rocky, gravel path. I arrive on the beach and walk towards the water. John is standing to my left close to the water. I see the back of his head and know that it is him.

When John and Marilyn were sharing their dreams, John noticed that Marilyn was wearing the exact clothes she had been wearing in his dream: a burgundy sweater and black jeans.

Besides the synchronous elements involved in these waking and dreaming events, Bogzaran asked the dreamers what shared dreaming meant to them. What emerged from the dialogue was that shared dreaming is another way of extending one's relationships with others. For John, the dreams were important events in his life, as he has been isolating himself due to his various spiritual practices. Shared dreaming had brought him into a closer relationship with others in the class. For Marilyn it was the expansion of her awareness beyond the apparent limitations of waking consciousness that helped her see life in a new way.

In this process, shared dreaming becomes a way of sharing and exchanging one's dream and waking activities with others. As members of the dream class reported, people felt they had connected with one another at much deeper levels. As a result of these dream experiences, John, Marcia, and Marilyn became very close friends. Although they have all graduated, they still keep in contact and are deepening their friendship.

Working with Collective Dreams

Robin Shohet, a British psychologist, has developed a systematic approach to dream sharing. He points out several advantages of working in a group: (1) the ability of other dreamers to identify dream meanings that have escaped the dreamer; (2) the usefulness of the group's combined knowledge in interpreting puzzling dream symbols and metaphors; and (3) the safety and support a group can offer to each individual member.[10] The very act of working with a group of dreamers will offer an opportunity for the emergence of both shared dreams and mutual dreams.

As we saw in Bogzaran's class example, dreamers can make deliberate attempts to foster shared dreams. The technique involves a group of people who agree to meet in the same dream at the same time, and to recall the details when they awaken. An underlying assumption is that shared dreaming is a learned skill, one that requires a great deal of patience as well as a joyous sense of play and adventure. Dreamers who are successful in sharing dreams soon realize that they have been launched into a mutual exploration of boundaries, both personal and social. Some individuals become anxious when they come to this realization and stop the process. Others become exhilarated and use shared dreams to develop intimate relations, to resolve conflicts, or even to create new projects.[11] Magallón and Barbara Shor, two pioneering dreamworkers in this field, have provided a number of suggestions for organizing and participating in shared dreaming experiences:

1. Group members must agree to meet in a jointly chosen "dreamscape" or dream setting for a minimum of six sessions.

2. One person should act as the "commentator." The commentator will collect the dream reports and will search them for group themes, group correspondences, and similarity to the dream setting.

3. Members need to make a social connection with other people in the group before they start the project. Whether the group consists of two or ten, all members should know each other's names, tone of voice, and personal appearance to be able to recognize them in a dream. Making eye contact, hug-

ging, or holding hands helps everyone connect at an emotional level. Having photographs of each person in the group is also helpful.

4. The group should select a dream setting that everyone will enjoy. Members should not plan to meet at the Iguassú Waterfalls if some people in the group do not know the location or do not like bodies of water. Some dream sharing groups have met at the Eiffel Tower in Paris, the Great Pyramid in Egypt, or in the parlor of a friend's home. The group should have pictures of the "dreamspace" so that everyone can concentrate on the setting before going to sleep.

5. The group may decide to set goals for the shared dream, such as to have a party, create a ritual or ceremony, or solve a community problem. Some groups select a setting for the dream, but do not determine the activity in which they will engage during the dream.

6. Before bedtime, each person in the group should relax and clear their attention of everything except their intention to have a shared dream. Members can then concentrate on trying to meet their fellow dreamers in the appointed setting by looking at the picture of the setting and at the photographs of the other dreamers, imagining the group together in that dreamspace.

7. Upon awakening, each member needs to write down his or her dream and date it. It is important for each member to do this before hearing from the other dreamers. A discussion of dream content before it is recorded might distort the recall, and similarities may be recorded that were not present. Each person's dreams should be sent to the person chosen as the commentator.

8. The commentator mails copies of the dreams to everyone in the group as well as his or her comments on group themes and correspondences. This material will provide feedback, and will give each dreamer some direction as to how to proceed during the next night of attempted dream sharing.[12]

In shared dreaming projects, dream partners may have the sense of participating in a communal event even though they don't necessarily identify one another in their respective dreams. During Magallón's carefully orchestrated Nexus project in February, 1989, the dreams of Melody and Tracy provided two views on a harmonious group meeting near a dreamland waterway.

Melody's Dream

All through the mansion and grounds are channels of water on which small boats are traveling. The owner of the mansion announces that we will be hearing a seminar. But if the audience loses interest in the seminar, one of the seminarians will sing to us.

Tracy's Dream

In the background are brightly colored boats and sails about 30 feet away. Melody asks me about our mutual dreaming group and I tell her a bit about it. She then asks if there are any "monks," which I take to mean people extraordinarily devoted to dreams. I say, "No, not exactly, but some people are more interested in it than others."[13]

Mutual Lucid Dreams

One of the rare types of mutual dreams is "mutual lucid dreaming." The controversial anthropologist Carlos Castaneda claims that Mexican sorcerers taught him this skill as part of his apprenticeship.[14] However, there are instances of mutual lucid dreaming that are better documented. In her exploration in lucid dreaming, Bogzaran constantly incubated lucid dreams of being in her home country and visiting an old friend whom she had not seen for eighteen years. One night, she had the following lucid dream:

> I am walking in my old neighborhood where I grew up. Suddenly I ask myself "how did I get here?" I do not remember taking a plane. At that point I become lucid. I continue walking and have a strong intention to see Yalda my old childhood friend [she has moved and I have never been in her new house]. I find the street where she lives and walk towards her house. The color of the door is pale blue. I ring the bell and she opens the door. I am overjoyed to see her. We cry and hug each other with overwhelming emotion. Embracing her feels absolutely real. The intensity of the experience wakes me up.

Bogzaran recorded the dream and in the morning she wrote her friend a letter enclosing the dream. In her letter, she detailed what she saw in her dream and described the location of her friend's new house. A week later she received a letter from her friend. In this letter, dated the day after the dream (indicating that she had mailed her letter around the same time as Bogzaran had mailed hers), her friend described the same dream. In Yalda's dream, Bogzaran came back home for a visit. Her friend described the same scene that Bogzaran had experienced, where Bogzaran knocked at the door and Yalda opened the door.

Surprised to see each other, they embraced with great excitement. At that moment Yalda also became lucid in her dream.

This mutual lucid dream helped them to have an experience that they had been anticipating for years. The experience was so intense and vivid that they had a strong felt sense that they had actually seen and visited each other. This mutual lucid dream was a profound experience, a gift for both friends. Five years later, after twenty-three years of separation, the two friends were able to meet in waking life. The moment they saw each other, they embraced with an emotional intensity similar to that in the dream they had shared. Their dreams were precognative, mutual, and lucid.

Both mutual and shared dreams can awaken a dreamer's awareness of the subtle connections that exist among all people around the world. These dream experiences can provide self-confidence and self-esteem, as the dreamers' conventional boundaries of themselves and their abilities are transcended.

The writer George du Maurier referred to shared dreams as "dreaming true," and he used them as the basis for his celebrated novel, *Peter Ibbetson*.[15] Another gifted writer, Doris Lessing, may have had shared and mutual dreams in mind when discussing global awareness. She asked her readers, "Do you imagine you dream for yourself alone?"[16] Most Western dreamers, whose world views insist that their psyches terminate where their skins end, would answer, of course. Indigenous people, however, would be more likely to reply, of course not when considering Lessing's question.

Chapter 10

Telepathic Dreams

*F*or as long as human beings have kept records of their experiences, they have described extraordinary occurrences: reveries in which they appeared to receive the thoughts of another person, dreams in which they seemed to become aware of faraway events, rituals in which future happenings were supposedly predicted, and mental processes that were said to produce direct action on distant physical objects. These purported occurrences may have been instances of phenomena that contemporary parapsychologists call telepathy, clairvoyance, precognition, and psychokinesis. Collectively, they are referred to as "psi"—reported interactions between organisms and their environment (including other organisms) in which information exchange or influence has occurred that cannot be explained through mainstream science's understanding of sensory-motor channels. They are regarded as anomalous because they appear to occur beyond the constraints of time, space, and energy. The noted Roman orator Marcus Tullius Cicero wrote a skeptical treatise on anomalous dreams entitled, "On Divination." In his treatise, he pointed out that,

> Those very persons who experience these dreams cannot by any means understand them, and those persons who pretend to interpret them, do so by conjecture, not by demonstration. And in the infinite series of ages, chance has produced many more extraordinary results in every kind of thing than it has in dreams; nor can anything be more uncertain than that conjectured interpretation of diviners, which admits not only of several, but often of absolutely contrary senses.[1]

Contemporary psychology is the scientific study of behavior and experience; parapsychology studies events that appear inexplicable by currently known mechanisms that account for organism-environment and organism-organism information and influence flow. Over the past century, considerable research has been conducted in an attempt to understand these reports and to determine whether they are worthy of continued attention and investigation.

Parapsychology began in the late 1800s with the collection and analysis of psi experiences recorded by participants and witnesses. However, many ancient and classical traditions incorporated psi into their world views, their mythologies, and their daily practices. The first reported parapsychological experiment was allegedly designed by King Croesus of Lydia about 50 B.C.E. Attempting to determine which of several oracles was the most trustworthy, Croesus had his messengers ask them what he was doing on a certain date. Only the oracle at Delphi answered correctly, telling the messenger that his king was boiling a tortoise and a lamb in a cauldron. Croesus then confidently submitted a critical question: What would occur if he invaded Persia? The oracle is said to have replied that, following the invasion, a great empire would be destroyed. Croesus launched the attack; however, Persia was victorious and the doomed empire was Lydia. The ambiguity of the Delphic oracle's second response continues to characterize purported oracles and "psychic sensitives." Even though their statements may satisfy their gullible clients, the enigmatic responses frustrate sincere researchers. However, the specificity of the ancient Delphic oracle's first response is the hallmark of those experiments that produce clear-cut results and reinforce serious interest in the field.

The Society for Psychical Research, founded in Great Britain in 1882, was the first major organization to attempt to assess psi scientifically, beginning with surveys that would later evolve into controlled experiments. The "Report on the Census of Hallucinations," organized by members of the society, analyzed and categorized some seventeen thousand responses to the question, "Have you ever had a vivid impression of seeing, or being touched . . . or of hearing a voice, which impression, so far as you could discover, was not due to any external cause?" Affirmative answers were obtained from about one in ten of the respondents, with more visual hallucinations reported than auditory or tactile hallucinations.[2] Psychologists Donald Marks and Peter McKellar refer to this collection as a veritable gold mine of data, noting that the investigators attempted a pioneering effort to categorize the reports into sensory hallucinations, ordinary sense perceptions, dreams, and what today would be considered eidetic imagery.[3]

This early survey did not claim to be a random sample of subjects, nor did it claim that the reports were necessarily accurate or anomalous. However, there were a number of provocative findings. For example, when analyzing hallucinations involving death, one in forty-three of these hallucinations occurred within twelve hours of (either preceding or following) the death of the person who was seen in the hallucination. On the basis of the death rate in England and Wales at the time, only about one in nineteen thousand individuals died in a given twenty-four-hour period. Therefore, it would be expected, on the basis of chance—if no other factors were involved—that only about one in nineteen thousand hallucinations would be within twelve hours of the person's death. Because reports of this nature can be consciously or unconsciously distorted, they are not necessarily trustworthy; nevertheless, they often provide leads that can be subjected to more rigorous inquiry.

A more recent questionnaire survey involving 375 college students focused upon auditory hallucinations. Overall, 71 percent of the sample reported some experience with vocal hallucinations in wakeful situations. Thirty percent also reported hypnagogic hallucinations (which took place as people were dropping off to sleep) and 14 percent reported hypnopompic hallucinations (which took place as people were waking up). Nearly 40 percent reported hearing their name being called when outdoors; 36 percent reported a similar experience indoors. Eleven percent claimed to have heard their own voice come from the back seat of their car, while a similar proportion stated that they had heard God speak "as a real voice."[4]

Some surveys have been conducted through the mail. One of them, published in 1979, obtained 354 completed questionnaires from residents of the Charlottesville, Virginia, area and 268 completed questionnaires from University of Virginia students. One question read, "Have you ever had, while awake, a vivid impression of seeing, hearing, or being touched by another being, which impression, as far as you could discover, was not due to any external physical or 'natural' cause?" This was essentially the same question asked by the British society a century earlier. It was answered affirmatively by 17 percent of the residential as well as the student respondents—about the same as the 13 percent giving positive responses in the earlier survey. However, the majority of hallucinations in the British group were visual, while the American groups' reports were predominantly auditory or tactile.[5]

A question from the same survey read, "Have you ever seen light . . . around or about a person's head, shoulders, hands, or body, which, as far as you could tell, was not due to 'normal' or 'natural' causes. . . . ?" Five percent of the townspeople and 6 percent of the students answered this question affirmatively. Another question asked, "Have you ever had, while awake, a strong feeling, impression, or 'vision' that a previously unexpected event had happened, was happening, or was going to happen, and [learned] later that you were right?" At least one such experience was reported by 38 percent of the towns-people and 39 percent of the student sample. In the majority of the cases, the event was said to have occurred within twenty-four hours of (before or after) the experience, and in over a quarter of the cases the respondents claimed that they had told someone of their experience before learning of the event. Therefore, a number of claims of this type are open to some type of verification.

One question was phrased, "Have you ever had a rather clear and specific dream that matched in detail an event during or after your dream, and that you did not know about or did not expect at the time of the dream?" At least one dream of this type was reported by 36 percent of the town sample and 38 per-cent of the students. About two out of three of these dreams were reported to be "more vivid" than respondents' ordinary dreams. In about one-third of the cases, the verifying event was said to have taken place within a twenty-four-hour span. In about 20 percent of the cases, the dreamer claimed to have told someone about the dream before learning of the verifying event.[6]

It is likely that most telepathic, clairvoyant, or precognitive dream reports can be explained on the basis of coincidence, faulty memory, or information that was actually available to the dreamer before the dream took place. For this reason, controlled experiments are necessary to determine if any of these reports could be truly anomalous, in other words, if they could be an exception to science's current understanding of time, space, and energy.

Dreaming about Someone Else's Thoughts

Biblical accounts are filled with stories of anomalous dreams. One of them is the well-known account of Nebuchadnezzar, the ancient Babylonian king, who awoke one morning from a powerful dream only to have it disappear sec-onds later. All he was left with was the strong impression that the dream must have been divinely inspired. He sent word to wizards, astrologers, and diviners that they must tell him what his dream had been and then interpret it. If they failed, he threatened to execute them all. When Daniel (the future prophet) heard of the situation, he prayed that God would reveal to him what the king had dreamed. It is said that the answer came that night, and Daniel brought the dream, as well as its interpretation, to Nebuchadnezzar the next morning. The king was satisfied, and the other dream interpreters no longer feared for their lives.

Sandor Ferenczi frequently corresponded with Sigmund Freud about var-ious anomalous phenomena. Before the First World War, a self-styled "psychic sensitive" requested that Ferenczi conduct some experiments to test his abilities. Ferenczi finally agreed and told the man that at a given time, immediately after lunch, he would concentrate on something and the psychic sensitive should try to identify his thoughts. At the given moment, Ferenczi picked up the statue of an elephant in his waiting room and reclined on his couch for about fifteen minutes, holding the elephant in his hands. A few minutes later, the telephone rang. It was Ferenczi's friend, Robert Bereny, who told about having a terrifying dream in which he saw Ferenczi in a jungle fighting with wild animals, among them an elephant. A few days later, the letter from the so-called sensitive arrived, but his statements were completely unrelated to elephants or other animals. The correspondence between Bereny's dream and Ferenczi's elephant could have been coincidental, or it could have demonstrated how impervious to rational control telepathic phenomena may be.[7]

The word "telepathy" was coined by Frederic W. H. Myers in 1882. With two other members of the British Society for Psychical Research, Myers collected thirteen hundred pages of case histories describing anomalous phenomena, many of them associated with dreams. Over half of the 149 cases of dream telepathy described in the book dwelled on the theme of death. However, the authors noted:

> Millions of people are dreaming every night; and in dreams, if anywhere, the range of possibilities seems infinite. Can any possible conclusion be drawn from such chaos of meaningless and fragmentary impressions? . . . Are any valid means at hand for distinguishing between a transferred impression and a lucky coincidence? . . . And what proportion of striking correspondences are we to demand before we consider that the hypothesis of chance is strained in accounting for them?"[8]

For this reason, it was necessary to develop research strategies that would address the questions of coincidence and chance.

Research on Telepathic Dreams

The most systematic research project on telepathic dreams was conducted by Montague Ullman and Stanley Krippner at Maimonides Medical Center in Brooklyn, New York, during the 1960s and 1970s. Researchers at the Maimonides Dream Laboratory undertook a series of studies that investigated anomalous communication during dream time, such as telepathy. The basic research procedure was to fasten electrodes to the head of a subject and take him or her to a soundproof room. Another psychologist would then randomly select a sealed, opaque envelope containing a colorful art print, and would carry the envelope to a distant room, open it, and study the art print. In the meantime, the research participant (in bed and asleep) would attempt to incorporate material from the art print into his or her dreams without ever having seen it.[9]

Upon completion of an experimental study, outside judges compared the typed dream reports with the total collection of art prints and attempted to identify the print used on the night of each experiment. About two out of three times, the laboratory team obtained statistically significant results, with odds against chance so great that coincidence was unlikely. In other words, there was no obvious, logical way to explain the correspondences between the dream reports and the art prints themselves. For example, one research participant dreamed about going to Madison Square Garden to buy tickets to a boxing match. On that same night, the psychologist in a distant room was focusing his attention on a painting of a boxing match.

To illustrate the variety of correspondences observed in the Maimonides studies, the eight-category system based on Calvin Hall and Robert Van de Castle's scoring system can be utilized. Categories include activities (any type of action or behavior); objects (any human-made object), characters (any entity with a discernible personality); emotions (any subjective mood or feeling experienced by a character); modifiers (any adjective used to describe an element of the dream report); nature (any object not human-made), sensations (any nonverbal sensory experience); and setting (the time and/or place where the dream was said to have occurred). The following list cites some of the examples from the Maimonides studies, and how the dream reports correspond to the art prints. All examples given are from files in the Maimonides archives.

1. Activities. The research participant was a male psychoanalyst, and the target picture was Edgar Degas' painting *School of the Dance*, which depicts a dance class in progress.

First dream report: "Being in a class. Now, at different times, different people would get up for some sort of recitation or some sort of contribution."

Second dream report: "I was in a class, a class made up of maybe half a dozen people. . . . Now, at different times, different people would get up for some sort of recitation. . . . It felt like a school."

Fourth dream report: "I was finishing getting ready for bed and we started having company. . . . There was one little girl that was trying to dance with me."

2. Objects. The target was a painting by Paul Cézanne, *Trees and Houses*; the research participant was a male clinical psychologist. No people are shown

in the painting, only a desolate house on a hill that is covered by stark, barren trees.

First dream report: "All I could remember is it was something about a house."

Fourth dream report: "There was a house. . . . There were no people involved and nothing going on. . . . It was just this isolated house that seemed very small in size . . ."

Sixth dream report: "There was no color, no movement. . . . It's been a very poor yield. It may be a great yield if there's a target picture in there that's a lonely shack sitting on a hillside . . . "

Post-sleep associations:

> Some concern with houses. . . . I have never had any evening that I can recall with only such brief momentary fragments without any type of continuity. . . . There wasn't one single kind of personal interaction of any consequence. . . . It would have to be without people. . . . Maybe some of those kinds of building-landscapes.

3. Characters. The research participant was a male college student. The target picture was *The Fiddler*, a painting by Marc Chagall; it portrays a bearded man playing a fiddle.

Second dream report:

> I was out walking . . . and it was weird, this guy who came up to me . . . was really soused, and he ended up by having an accordion. . . . It seems to me that the man had a mustache. . . . It's like an accordion except it's a seaman's accordion, . . . concertina, I guess is the name. Maybe that's not right either. But anyway, this guy knew some wild songs, and he went running . . . jumping to the sides and kicking his heels in the air and all the while singing these wild songs, and playing this thing at the top of its volume, just as loud as he could. . . . The drunk that was playing the concertina . . . had on a dark colored solid color shirt that was sort of gypsy style.

Post-sleep associations: "He . . . started to run and dance and was playing the concertina . . . and singing these really . . . obscene songs . . . It does bring to mind the association with the song book we have at home with the picture of the sailor playing the concertina and sort of clicking his heels in the air."

4. Emotions. The research participant was a male college student and the target picture was James Ensor's *Masks Confronting Death*. The painting shows a number of people dressed in masks portraying skulls and other aspects of death.

First dream report: "This guy in a room. Some kind of big bang. A big crash."

Second dream report: "A disturbance. . . . Bob had two electrodes near his mouth. . . . Unusual electrodes. They were black."

Post-sleep associations: "It was a violent scene. Death. Burglary. . . .It was strange to see Bob with the black electrodes near his mouth . . . Two of my dreams had crashing in them. Disturbance. Strange scenes. Violent. Moving around. Things going the way they shouldn't. Emotional."

5. Modifiers. The target picture was *The Moon and the Earth* by Paul Gauguin. This painting portrays a bronze-skinned native girl standing nude by a waterfall. The research participant was a female receptionist.

Fifth dream report: "We're in church . . . and somebody introduces a girl who is a dancing girl. She starts to dance in church and everybody is clapping for her . . . and she comes over and says, 'Oh, I want to get a tan . . .' And I'm yelling at her to stay in the sun instead of running in and out all the time."

Post-sleep associations: "I think the dancing girl was one of my girl friends who I'm close with. She's fair and doesn't tan very easily. . . . She was doing . . . a folk dance and . . . somebody came over and was kissing her shoulder. I said to her. 'Look, your shoulders are tan. If you take your time you can get the rest of you tan.'"

6. Nature. *Mystic Night*, a painting by Millard Sheets, was the target. It portrays a nighttime ritual in a wooded area surrounded by mountains. The research participant was a female clinical psychologist.

First dream report: "Being with a group of people . . . participating in something."

Second dream report: "Driving in the country . . . looking at . . . a lot of mountains and trees."

Fourth dream report: "Students out in this kind of grassy . . . parking place; trees. What strikes me most about the whole thing was the trees, again, and the greenery and the country."

Post-sleep associations: "There's some sort of primitive aspect. . . . I can almost see it as some sort of tribal ritual in a jungle."

7. Sensations. The target picture was a photograph of *The Perseus*, a statue by Benvenuto Cellini In it the Greek hero Perseus is holding the severed head of the sorceress Medusa. The research participant was a female actress.

First dream report: "Just a sense of being involved physically. My head. It's not a headache. It's dizziness. . . . My head is very heavy. . . . It's not thoroughly pleasant."

Second dream report: "An image came to mind. Something bloody. There's something disturbing and I don't know what it is. I don't know, but it's physical."

Third dream report: "It was like Central Park. . . . There was also a man . . . and his arms were out."

Post-sleep associations:

> Heavy-headed. . . . I remember being a little bit scared. . . . Something that was not of this century. Not of my life as I know it. . . . I was physically working. It felt as if I was sleeping right on top of my head. I was standing on my head. There was that much pressure. Not the front like where you get a headache, but the back. The whole skull. Then I had a picture of somebody with a bandage around their skull. . . . In the dream . . . there was . . . something bloody and there was vomit around it. . . . Something painful, very painful. It's something very disturbing about it. . . . It's kind of like a killing or something.

8. Settings. The research participant was a female journalist. The target picture was a painting by Giorgio de Chirico, *Departure of a Friend*. The painting portrays a shadowy twilight scene with two men standing in the background. Behind the men and extending into the foreground is a wall made up of arches and columns.

First dream report: "A group scene. The 'Shadow Song' is running through my head. . . . Walking outside a building. It was a large, municipal-type building."

Second dream report: "I was walking along a corridor with one other person. The colors were dark—browns, blacks, and grays. . . . I was giving flowers to my grandmother."

Post-sleep associations: "There were several personal dreams about me and my family. . . . The dark colors were unusual. So was the theme of walking around and coming back."

In these examples, the ways in which target materials seem to be incorporated into dreams are similar to the ways that day residue, psychodynamic processes, and subliminally perceived stimuli find their way into dream content. Sometimes the material corresponding to targets is intrusive (e.g., "There was one little girl who was trying to dance with me"), and sometimes it blends easily with the narrative (e.g., "This guy knew some wild songs"). At times, it is the central focus of the dream (e.g., ". . . some sort of tribal ritual in a jungle"); at others, it is peripheral (e.g., "Oh, I want to get a tan"). It can be either direct (e.g., ". . . just this isolated house") or symbolic (e.g., ". . . the black electrodes near his mouth"). Although these dreams and their correspondence with distant art prints had anomalous characteristics, their construction and description did not appear to differ in significant ways from other dreams collected in laboratory studies.[10]

Such prominent dream researchers as David Foulkes, Gordon Globus, Calvin Hall, Robert Van de Castle, and Keith Hearne attempted to repeat these findings.[11] Because the replication rate from other laboratories was inconsistent, the Maimonides team did not claim to have conclusively demonstrated that communication in dreams can sometimes transcend space and time. Nevertheless, they did open a promising line of investigation.[12]

Michael Persinger, a Canadian neuroscientist, reviewed the entire body of research data. He selectied the first night that each research participant in a telepathy experiment had visited the Maimonides laboratory as well as conducting a second study focusing on the research participant who spent more nights at the laboratory than anyone else. He matched the results of these nights with data collected at weather stations. He discovered that the subjects' telepathy was higher during calm nights with little sunspot activity than during nights marked by electrical storms and high sunspot activity.[13] If these results stand up, they indicate a potentially predictable pattern in such events, and an association with the environment that may lead to a natural explanation of anomalous events. Subsequent analyses with the research participant who participated most frequently in the Maimonides studies yielded similar results; his telepathic skills appeared to function best on calm nights with low geomagnetic activity.[14]

One example of a possible telepathic dream is from a high dream recaller who claims to have experienced frequent telepathic dreams. Parvin, a dream practitioner, was living in Canada at the time of this dream, and her mother lived four thousand miles away in another country. Her mother was seventy-eight years old and was suffering from diabetes.

Parvin's Dream

I am back home visiting my mother. She looks as if she is in pain. I take her to give her a bath. Everything looks very real. While I am washing her, my father, who has been dead for five years, appears with a loaf of bread in his hand. He offers the bread to my mother. I try to stop my father, but he keeps insisting that the bread is good for my mother. My mother finally accepts the bread.

Next, my mother is gone and I go back to the bath area. I see a small doll resting on the floor. I begin crying loudly and hold the doll in my arms. I wake up sobbing.

Parvin had this dream around 5:00 A.M. She woke up disturbed by her dream and a few hours later she called home to speak to her mother. To her great despair, she found out that her mother had passed away a few hours before she called. Although Parvin knew her mother was ill, this news came as a complete shock to her.

Parvin realized that the time of her dream and the time of her mother's death coincided exactly. Perhaps her mother had "sent" Parvin a telepathic message in the dream. Later, when Parvin worked with this dream, she also discovered many symbolic meanings. The bathing could have been a metaphor for her mother's purification before passing from one world to another. Her deceased father's offering of the bread was like a communion, an invitation to join the community of deceased. Although in the dream Parvin did not want her father to offer the bread, after later reflection, she felt relieved to know that her mother had joined her father. The bread also symbolized her mother's bodily transition to spirit, joining the community of the deceased. The wooden doll was a beautiful but lifeless object. When Parvin looked back at her dream she realized that the doll could mean many things to her. Her mother was beautiful like a doll. The doll became an object of comfort in the dream, and helped her deal with the passing of her mother. The doll also reminded Parvin of her childhood needs, of wanting the security of being with her mother.

This telepathic dream, although disturbing, prepared Parvin to go through the transitions involved in such a loss. The dream gave her a certain comfort; she believed that her mother would no longer be alone and that her father was there to welcome her into the next life.

Working with Telepathic Dreams

Telepathy is one of three phenomena often grouped together under the term "extrasensory perception" (or ESP), the others being clairvoyance and precognition. In Krippner's collection of 1,666 dream reports from six countries, there were 2 telepathic dreams, 5 clairvoyant dreams, and 17 precognitive dreams, with Japanese and Russian reports containing the most alleged ESP.[15]

Parapsychologist Loyd Auerbach believes that people usually sense that they have had a psychic dream, one that contains "extra information" and is somewhat different from an ordinary dream. It may contain more emotion, it may focus on the life of a close friend or family member, and it may incorporate vivid colors and images. Auerbach suggests that those people who want to work with telepathic dreams, as well as with other anomalous dreams, keep a dream workbook, make dream recall a part of their daily routine, and review the dream workbook on a regular basis. When a dream appears to be telepathic, they might try to identify the special qualities of that dream so that they will recognize those qualities if they recur in future dreams.

Auerbach then suggests that deamers purposefully try to repeat the pattern surrounding a telepathic dream. For example, following Auerbach's advice, if a dreamer's workbook indicates that telepathic dreams occur more often away from home, the dreamer should be sure to take his or her workbook along on every trip and record each dream remembered. Also, dreamers should examine the type of telepathic information in the dreams. Is it good news or bad news? Does it involve friends or relatives? Does it focus on a specific topic, such as illness, romance, or finances? For every potential telepathic dream, the dreamer needs to check it out with the person involved. Dreamers might also try incubating telepathic dreams by telling themselves before going to sleep, "Tonight I will have a telepathic dream and I will remember it when I wake up."

Auerbach has additional suggestions for people interested in conducting home telepathy experiments:

1. Have a friend select a number of pictures or illustrations from magazines. They should be as different as possible. Do not have your friend show these pictures to you. They are potential "telepathy targets." Have the friend make color xerox copies of each picture.

2. Have your friend place each of these pictures in an opaque envelope and seal them. Select another friend who will be the "telepathic sender." On the night of the experiment, he or she will shuffle through the envelopes and will select one at random. The telepathic sender will take the envelope home and open it just before going to bed.

3. The telepathic sender will spend several minutes trying to "send" you the images on the picture. You are the "telepathic receiver" and will record all the images that you recall having while dreaming as well as before and after sleep.

4. The following morning, your friend will share the color copies with you. You will choose the picture that comes closest to your dreams, as well as one or two "runners up." However, your friend should not be with you when you do the judging as he or she may give subtle clues that will influence your choice.

5. The telepathic sender will join you at this time, bringing the target picture. You will look at the target picture and will see if it was one of those that you selected.[16]

If you want to make the experiment more rigorous, place the illustrations in two sealed, opaque envelopes; some people have acute vision and can determine the identity of an illustration through the covering paper if only one envelope is used. You may also want to apply statistics. If there are four pictures, there is one chance in four that the correct telepathy target will be chosen by chance. A statistician can show you accurate ways to apply statistics to your choices and can tell you if your record of correct "guesses" is above, below, or consistent with the laws of chance.

You might even record the time of year, the phase of the moon, and (with the help of a geomagnetic tracking station) the presence or absence of sunspots and electrical storm activity. There may be environmental influences on telepathic dreaming—such as those identified by Michael Persinger. In view of the provocative nature of this topic, it is not surprising that the Parapsychological Association, an international society of researchers in this field, concluded that "whatever the outcome of this search may be, it cannot help but add to the sum of knowledge about humanity and the human condition."[17]

Clairvoyant Dreams

*M*any native tribes, such as the Mapuche Indians of Chile, believe that dreaming involves a journey of the soul outside the human body, during which the soul can observe distant places and faraway events. When this kind of remote viewing occurs in a dream, it is what parapsychologists term a "clairvoyant" dream. The dream report for a clairvoyant dream accurately corresponds with a remote occurrence or locale about which the dreamer had no ordinary way of knowing.

For the Mapuche, a dream can serve as a channel of communication between the dreamer and other people, as well as the spirit world. What Westerners consider to be anomalous dreams, (such as those felt to be clairvoyant), the Mapuche see as one of many common types of dreams, made possible by the dream's capacity to link the dreamer with other people, other time periods, and distant places. Mapuche shamans use dreams in their work, but in Mapuche society all dreamers are thought to have this potential.

Some contemporary dream practitioners believe that clairvoyant dreams occur rather frequently, without being recalled. According to these writers, when individuals experience déjà-vu (a sense of having been in a location before), it is because they were actually at the location in their clairvoyant dream, but forgot the dream when they awoke. (There are simpler explanations for déjà-vu, most of them involving shifts in attention that provide an illusion of "having been here before.")

The Russian newspaper *Pravda* once printed a letter from a soldier who awakened from a dream about a forthcoming Nazi attack during the Second World War. Indeed, the Nazi troops were advancing, and the soldier was able to rouse his troops and repel the attack. The soldier claimed that his mother, who had died when he was six months of age, had appeared to him in the dream giving him the warning.[1]

David Ryback, a clinical psychologist, has suggested that clairvoyant dreams result from an "intercerebral holographic reflection." He believes that both the brain and the world at large operate in a holographic fashion. The brain acts as a hologram, storing its information throughout the two hemispheres. The world at large also operates in a holographic manner, storing information throughout the universe. In other words, the brain has holographic properties and it perceives a world that also has holographic properties; both store information in a manner that is widely dispersed, not narrowly focused. These storage spaces are uneven, but sometimes information about distant events can be perceived accurately due to the holographic nature of both the brain and its external environment.[2]

An example of this process might be seen in an experience told to us by another clinical psychologist. His sister's eighty-year-old father-in-law was in the hospital after undergoing multiple bypass surgery, and he was not recuperating from the operation. One morning the psychologist awoke and recalled this dream:

> In the dream, I am in a hospital room and see what I believe to be my own outstretched arms, although they do not look like my own. Somehow, I think of my sister's father-in-law. Then I hear a voice call out, "Hey, that man is alive!"

That evening he learned that his sister's father-in-law had responded to external stimulation for the first time in a month. From that time his health improved steadily.

Many explanations have been given for clairvoyant dreams, from the soul leaving the body, to the roaming of the "subtle body," to information obtained from a benevolent spirit. And as the examples cited show, there is no sharp dividing line between clairvoyant dreams and those that are telepathic or precognitive in nature. The dream about the Nazi troops could have been classified as precognitive, as it foreshadowed the Nazi advance. The psychologist's dream could have been classified as telepathic rather than clairvoyant, as he might have obtained information from the patient's mental processes.

In considering dream reports of this type, one must also allow for the strong possibility of chance, coincidence, or inaccurate reporting. People dream several times each night; it is to be expected that at least a few of these dreams will be congruent with waking life events, simply by happenstance. In addition, people who do not record their dreams may embellish their recall (consciously or unconsciously) so that it resembles the waking life event.

The English psychical researcher G. N. M. Tyrrell reported a dream that could be classified as telepathic, clairvoyant, precognitive, or even coincidental. The dreamer, Dudley Walker, simply felt that it was "no ordinary dream":

> I was in an overhead signal-box, extending over a railway-line I had never seen before. It was night, and I saw approaching what I knew was an excursion train, full of people, returning from some big function. I knew it was my duty to signal this train through, which I did, but at the same time I had a feeling that the train was doomed. In my dream I seemed to hover in the air, and follow the express as it slowed to round a loop line. As it approached a station I saw, to my horror, another small train on the same line. Although they seemed both traveling slowly, they met with terrible impact. I saw the express and its coaches pitch and twist in the air, and the noise was terrible. Afterwards, I walked beside the wreckage in the dim light of dawn, viewing with a feeling of terror the huge overturned engine and smashed coaches. I was now amid an indescribable scene of horror with dead and injured people and rescue workers everywhere.
>
> Most of the bodies lying by the side of the track were those of women and girls. As I passed with some unknown person leading me, I saw one man's body in a ghastly state, lifted far away and laid on the side of an overturned coach. . . . On coming home, you can imagine my feelings when I beheld the newspaper headlines announcing the accident.

The train accident had occurred just before midnight of the night that Walker had the dream. A newspaper report contained several details that corresponded with Walker's dream: It was an excursion train: it collided with another train;eight people were killed—a man, six women, and one little girl; an engine was derailed; one gruesome sight was that of a man's body lying on top of one of the carriages.[3]

Another dream, reported by a woman living in the San Francisco Bay area, could also be classified as either telepathic or clairvoyant.

Louise's Dream

An illustrator, Louise, reported a number of psychic experiences in connection with a close friend who lives in Los Angeles, California. One night, Louise had the following dream:

I am racing about in a distant city, trying desperately to reach a friend. The nature of the urgency is unclear; I only know that I must find her. I awake feeling frantic and distraught. I then return to dreaming.

I hear a woman's voice repeating, "It was the worst pain—terrifying. I thought I was dying!" There is no accompanying imagery. I awake confused with the bizarre thought that I am having someone else's dream.

In the morning Louise woke up puzzling over this dream and decided to give her friend in Los Angeles a call. The friend told Louise that her timing was remarkable. The night before, at the time of Louise's dream, the friend had been rushed to the hospital in excruciating pain. Her friend repeated the exact words Louise had heard in her dream. She had thought she was dying, but the doctors had denied Louise's friend any pain reliever until the nature of her condition had been determined.

Louise felt there was now an explanation for the sense of urgency in her dream. She had been looking for her friend who was being rushed to the hospital. This dream not only connected Louise more closely to her friend, but also prepared her for the worst—the possibility of her friend's death. As this dream report shows, clairvoyant and telepathic dreams often occur between family members and friends who share a deep sense of connection.

Research on Clairvoyant Dreams

Jon Tolaas, a Norwegian researcher, interviewed a woman who had dreamed that blue anemones were blooming in her garden. In her dream, she was delighted to find an entire bed of the vivid blue flowers, and bent down to look at them more closely. Actually, it was at least two months too early for blue anemones to sprout. But the morning following her dream, her brother telephoned her quite unexpectedly, saying, "Do you know what I found behind the garage yesterday? The first blue anemones!"

Tolaas suspected that this might have been a clairvoyant dream. On closer inspection, however, he discovered an alternative explanation. In the first place, the woman's brother lived in a warmer part of Norway where the climate is much milder, and where anemones often bloom much earlier. In the second place, the day before the dream, the woman was cleaning the windows of her house, looking down at a bed of blue anemone roots, wondering whether or not they were alive. As a careful researcher, Tolaas considered all possible explanations for the dream, and thought that these two factors outweighed the possibility of clairvoyance.[4]

In the Maimonides studies of anomalous dreams, a similar cautionary attitude was taken. For example, in one of their studies, the group of randomly selected target pictures included *Bijin by a Waterfall*, a painting by Harunobu that portrays a Japanese woman with long hair, dressed in a robe, sitting by a waterfall. The subject for the study one night was a male college student. His first dream contained the following images and associations:

> Right now an association to "Japanese" comes to mind for some reason. . . . Women in kimonos with their hair . . . tied up . . . and the fancy picks or sticks that they put in their hair.[5]

In another nighttime session of the same study, the subject was a female college student. Her first dream report contained the following images:

> Suddenly the whole area is filled with girls, especially in bikinis. . . . Most of them were running around in bathing suits. . . . Somewhere along the line I got to Tokyo. . . . I remember somewhere in the crowd this very, very beautiful Japanese girl, like she was very special. She was in this outfit . . . and she paraded before us.[6]

Although *Bijin by a Waterfall* was a target used in this study, it was not the target selected on the night that either of these two students served as subjects! In other words, it is sometimes easy to find target correspondences in a night of dreams, especially if there have been four or five lengthy dream reports during the session. An apologist can always make the excuse that "displacement" was at work, and that the research participant merely "displaced" his or her clairvoyance, identifying a different target in the pool. But this scenario has no value for serious investigators unless it is hypothesized in advance and worked into the experimental design.

For this reason, elaborate evaluation procedures were used in the Maimonides experiments, both on the parts of outside judges and by the subjects themselves. All potential target pictures were presented and the judges and subjects assigned a number that reflected the correspondences they observed between the dreams and the pictures. They were told the correct identity of the target pictures only after all the evaluations had been made.

In the studies of anomalous dreams at Maimonides Medical Center, there were several dreams that were presumably clairvoyant in nature. The initial experiment, in 1960, involved the famous "psychic sensitive" Eileen Garrett, well known for her work as a medium. One experimenter selected a target pool of three pictures from *Life* magazine, sealed them in envelopes, and gave them to a secretary. The secretary chose one of the envelopes. It included a color photograph of the chariot race in the movie *Ben Hur*. But the secretary misunderstood the directions and did not open the envelope. Therefore, the test actually became one of clairvoyance rather than telepathy.

In the meantime, another experimenter attached electrodes to Eileen Garrett's eyes so that the machine would detect REM sleep. Garrett reported a dream about watching horses furiously running uphill. She remarked that the scene reminded her of the chariot race in *Ben Hur*, a film she had seen two weeks earlier.[7]

Another clairvoyance test involved Arthur Young, an inventor responsible for designing the Bell helicopter, one of which hung in the Museum of Modern Art in New York City. Young entered the laboratory, and an envelope was randomly selected by a blindfolded assistant in another room. In it was a color photograph of a communication satellite, a metal globe with cross bars, mounted on an oval platform and surrounded by circular mirrors. Young reported the following dream:

> Some kind of optical instrument like a hunk of glass that had cross bars on it. A view of a circular room with a lot of things on the floor, including a round stool.

The next morning, he added:

> A globe of glass. I was looking down on an oval room. I said round, but it was oval and had a lot of objects in it. . . . This was very clear and precise.[8]

Young's most accurate information concerning the target took the form of hypnagogic imagery and was reported just before he fell asleep.

Even though the Maimonides researchers conducted no experimental series that focused exclusively on clairvoyance, these pilot studies yielded provocative results. Indeed, they stimulated an English researcher, Trevor Harley, to design a study in which he served as the single subject in a twenty-night study of clairvoyant dreams. His task was to dream about a colorful picture that had been randomly selected from a collection of two hundred pictures. In the morning, he was shown four pictures and asked to select the one that had actually been used. Outside judges also compared his dream imagery to the four pictures, only one of which was the correct target. In this study, Harley's dreams rarely matched the picture. In fact, there were so many "misses" and so few "hits," that the error rate was actually significant when evaluated with statistics.[9] This is the first study of anomalous dreams where "psi missing," indicating a statistically significant number of "misses," was reported. Because the significant error rate was not predicted in advance, more research studies with the same subject would have to be conducted before any definite conclusions could be reached from this study.

Not all work with possibly clairvoyant dreams has a happy ending. In October, 1980, Steve Linscott was awakened by a dream in which a man approached a girl with a blunt object in his hand. In a second dream, this man "was beating her on the head. . . . She was on her hands and knees . . . and didn't resist . . . blood flying everywhere." Linscott went back to sleep, but later that day he noticed police cars two doors away. A young woman had been brutally beaten and murdered in a nearby apartment building. He told the dream to his wife and two colleagues at the Christian halfway house where he worked, in a suburb of Chicago; they all persuaded Linscott to tell his dream to the police. A few weeks later, he was charged with the murder of the young woman; the dream, according to the police, included too many accurate details to be coincidental. Linscott was convicted and sentenced to forty years in prison.[10] Only after several successful appeals by defense attorneys did the prosecution drop the case. Krippner, in his article "A Psychic Dream? Be Careful Who You Tell!" warns us to be cautious of with whom we share our dreams.[11] Not everyone accepts the occurrence of extraordinary dreams.

The Mapuche Indians of Chile, who hold the notion that clairvoyant dreams involve a nighttime journey of the soul, work with dreams on three levels. The first of these is the intratextual level, in which dream imagery is studied. The second is the intertextual level, where dreams are interpreted according to their relationship to past dreams and the dreams of family members. The third is the contextual level, where dreams are interpreted according to the dreamer's social and emotional situation. The latter two methods allow family members to participate directly in the dream interpretation process. They can even relate their own dreams to those of the dreamer.[12]

What Westerners call anomalous dreams (e.g., clairvoyant, telepathic, and precognitive dreams) are considered perfectly normal by the Mapuche Indians. Witchcraft, possession, and the visitation of spirits in dreams are quite common, and become an ordinary part of the dream interpretation process. In other words, where anomalous dreams are looked upon in most Western cultures with suspicion, skepticism, and antagonism, in various native cultures these dreams are honored and welcomed. Only time will tell which cultural mythology is the more useful and functional in dealing with this type of extraordinary dream.

Working with Clairvoyant Dreams

Loyd Auerbach suggests that dreamworkers who are interested in this topic conduct a home experiment, using the following steps to assess their potential for clairvoyant dreaming:

1. Have a friend or acquaintance secretly select a location somewhere in your geographic vicinity that you have never visited. Even though you don't know its identity, think about visiting this locale in your dreams. Use dream incubation techniques every night to focus your attempts at clairvoyance.

2. Record your dreams for at least one month. Make a copy of each dream that seems to be related to that location. On the basis of these dreams, make a guess as to what that location looks like, and note any unusual features of that location as depicted in your dreams.

3. Take the pertinent dreams with you when you visit the location. On a scale from one to ten, record how closely you think you described the location in your dreams.

4. Repeat the experiment, and record your success on a 10-point scale. After half a dozen or more attempts, you will be able to determine whether or not your score went up, down, or stayed the same·

5. If desired, increase the rigor of this experiment by setting the number of attempts in advance, and paying close attention to the ratings given, then analyzing them statistically if you choose. In addition, you might select a quite distant location; have a friend draw a picture of the Great Pyramid, the Roman Coliseum, an Australian aborigine walkabout, or the changing of the guard at Buckingham Palace in England.[13]

Clairvoyant dreams have several possible explanations; subtle sensory clues and unconscious mental processing are two of them. But even if these ordinary factors are at work, the results are still remarkable because they show how the human psyche is constantly active, especially while dreaming, piecing information together to solve problems and make sense out of the environment.

Chapter 12

Precognitive Dreams

*P*remonitions, especially by means of dreams, have been reported throughout history. Indeed, there are fifteen examples of purportedly precognitive dreams in the Bible. Genesis 41:15–24 presents the first of these, relating how the Pharaoh of Egypt asked for Joseph's advice concerning a dream. In the Pharoah's dream, seven fat cattle were devoured by seven lean cattle, and seven plump ears of corn were eaten by seven withered ears of corn. Joseph correctly interpreted the dream to mean that there would be seven years of plenty in Egypt followed by seven years of famine; he recommended that storehouses of food be built in preparation for the dearth that was to come.

The ancient dreamworker Artemidorous claimed that, as a general rule, a dream of sleeping with one's mother presaged the death of the dreamer; however, there were many exceptions to this rule. An artist who dreamed of intercourse with his mother could be confident of success and steady employment in his craft—but only if his mother was alive at the time of the dream. For a politician, the same dream foretold a gain in power or stature since, symbolically speaking, the mother stood for the politician's motherland.

In more recent history, a student at John F. Kennedy University was responsible for pinpointing the new location for their art department in Berkeley, California. Artist Zahra Almufti, who often recalls precognitive dreams and at the time was attending the school, shared a series of dreams that provided images or "signs" of the department's new location.

Zahra's Dreams

Dream 1:

> I am standing in the snow. I have just given birth to a baby *penguin*. It slides to the ground covered with blood. It moves on its belly leaving a trail of blood in the snow. I follow its movement and then I follow the trail of blood until that, too, disappears from my sight. After a while, I tap the snow with my hands. I then put my right ear to the snow and hear the tapping of many penguin feet in response. I see the baby penguin surrounded by the other penguins. I know they will take care of the baby penguin.

Dream 2:

> I am in a plane with *ice* on the wings and fire in the tail. We land safely next to a *control tower*.

Dream 3:

> I dream about an *architectural motif*, the number twenty-two, and water.

Dream 4:

> I walk into an aircraft *control tower*. *Penguins* greet me and tell me that this will be the new space for the Arts and Consciousness Department.

Zahra shared the dreams with the chair of the art department, Michael Grady. He considered the dream images and symbols while looking for the new space. One day, Grady was visiting Dharma Publishing in the Berkeley Business Center and shared Zahra's dreams with a friend who worked there. The friend told him about a large space on the second floor that was for rent, which would be perfect for his department.

While investigating the building with his friend, Grady discovered that an ice cream factory had originally been located on the first floor of the building; he later learned that the company used a penguin as their logo! They also noticed a water tower on the premises, which Grady believed to have been depicted as a control tower in two of Zahra's dreams. And on the second floor, they saw a model of a Spanish fountain from a palace that had the same architectural motif as the architectural motif in Zahra's third dream.

Zahra was not attending the university when she had her first three dreams; school was not on her mind at all. She did, however, incubate her fourth dream after she realized that the art department was interested in relocating. All four of her dreams contained images that might be seen as clues to the department's new location; and despite several obstacles, the department was able to rent and relocate to the space predicted by Zahra's dreams.

Dreams about Future Events

The central focus of dreams in many classical civilizations was prophecy. There was a widespread tendency in Greece, Rome, and the Near East to regard dreams as omens of one's personal future. Dreamworkers were preoccupied with whether the dream omen should be trusted or not. The dilemma that runs through many ancient writings on dreams reflects this concern. Is the dream message direct and trustworthy, or is it potentially deceptive and of little value? The most poignant example of this question in the classical literature occurs in the *Odyssey* as Penelope describes a dream that she thinks may forecast the return of her husband, Ulysses. As she reflects on the dream, she is concerned that the dream may be untrustworthy and makes the following observation:

> Dreams are very curious and unaccountable things. There are two gates through which these unsubstantial fancies proceed; the one is made of horn, and the other ivory. Those that come through the gate of ivory are fortuous, but those from the gate of horn mean something to those that see them.[1]

In other words, dreams that come through the gate of horn can foretell the future, but dreams that enter through the ivory gate are undependable and may reflect unrealistic wishes and delusions.

Aristotle took a skeptical point of view toward conceptualizing dreams as prophecies. In his essay "On Prophesying by Dreams," he noted that some of the lower animals appear to dream, hence "dreams cannot be sent by God." Instead, Aristotle suggested that dreams might have several functions. Some dreams may anticipate the future; others may directly or indirectly influence future events; or still others may simply match a forthcoming situation by coincidence.[2] Centuries later, the Jewish philosopher Moses Maimonides reaffirmed this concept.

Nevertheless, great significance was given to premonitory dreams in ancient Rome. Calpurnia, the wife of Julius Caesar, supposedly had a dream forecasting her husband's death. Shakespeare worked this dramatic event into a scene in the play, *Julius Caesar*. In the scene, Caesar goes from his house to the Roman Senate (where his assassins are waiting for him) despite his observation: "Nor heaven nor earth have been at peace tonight: Thrice hath Calpurnia in her sleep cried out, 'Help, ho! They murder Caesar!'"[3]

Centuries later, Abraham Lincoln described a dream in which he was walking through the White House in Washington, D.C. In the dream he saw a coffin around which soldiers stood as guards; a throng of people were gazing on the corpse, and some were weeping. Lincoln asked, "Who is dead in the White House?" A soldier answered, "The President. He was killed by an assassin." Lincoln confided that he could not return to sleep that night. Within the week he was dead from an assassin's bullet.[4]

Harriet Tubman was a historical figure who claimed to have anomalous dreams. One of them was said to have predicted her escape from the pre–Civil War plantation where she had been held as a slave. Several dreams directed her movements on the underground railroad, through which she led hundreds of slaves to freedom in the North. Another concerned a three-headed serpent that attempted to speak to her. She recalled that one head resembled John Brown, the abolitionist leader, and the others looked like young men. A crowd rushed in and severed the serpent's heads. Shortly afterwards, John Brown and his two sons were killed at Harper's Ferry—a raid that Tubman had been invited to join, but had declined.[5]

Not all anomalous dreams deal with death. A stockbroker dreamed, "A man was trying to sell me a radio. Someone put poison on the doorknob of my door and urged me to come and touch it. I was terribly frightened. He tried to force me to touch the poisoned knob. Struggling, I woke in a cold sweat." The American "psychic sensitive" Edgar Cayce interpreted the poison in this dream as a warning that the stockbroker should "refrain from investing in stocks, bonds, or anything pertaining to radio work for the next sixteen to twenty days." The 1929 Wall Street crash took place a few weeks later, but the stockbroker had failed to heed Cayce's advice.[6]

When Igor Sikorsky was ten years old, he dreamed of coursing through the skies in the softly lit, walnut-paneled cabin of an enormous flying machine. Sikorsky later became an eminent aircraft designer, and three decades after the dream, he went aboard one of his own four-engine Clippers to inspect a job of interior decorating done by Pan American Airways. He immediately recognized the cabin as identical to the one in his boyhood dream.[7]

On 25 May 1941, U.S. President Franklin Delano Roosevelt dreamed that the Japanese were bombing New York City while he was in his home in Hyde Park, New York. The psychoanalyst Paul Elovitz proposed that Roosevelt's unconscious was giving him an important message: not only was Japan capable of striking the United States directly (as it did at Pearl Harbor, Hawaii, on 7 December 1941), but the country could withstand the danger (which is why the setting of the dream was Roosevelt's home). Elovitz also cited Lyndon Johnson's recurring dreams that he should not run for re-election in 1968 as examples of "precognitive dreams—that is, dreams drawing on knowledge that is not yet fully apparent to the conscious mind."[8] It can be seen that dreams, classified as "precognitive," may actually draw upon unconscious information or may be coincidental.

As these dream reports show, precognitive dreams are provocative and extraordinary, but they are often viewed with skepticism. Not only might they be seen as coincidental, but they may also be seen as distortions of memory, confused time sequencing, unknown sensory cues, or even deliberate falsification. From this point of view—determining the amount of precognition involved—dreams and other accurate premonitions about a future event may be divided into five general categories: (1) coincidental; (2) inferential, in which the dreamer intuitively puts together data (often perceived outside of waking awareness) that congeal into a correct assessment of a forthcoming event in a dream; (3) self-fulfilling prophecies, in which the dreamer unconsciously behaves in such a way that the dream comes true; (4) pseudo-anomalous, in which the dreamer deliberately lies or unconsciously fabricates or distorts the facts; and (5) apparently anomalous, in the sense that at the time of the dream there was no available information—conscious or unconscious—that could explain the accuracy of their forecast.

Research on Precognitive Dreams

A precognitive dream may represent a premonition; it may give one a chance to actually change the future, as if the dreamed events do not have to happen or can be modified in some way. In other words, some precognitive dreams appear to represent mutable premonitions (warnings) rather than immutable "destiny," over which one does not seem to have much control. Some evidence does point to a possibility of the dreamer's intervention to prevent the event he or she was "forewarned" about. For example, Louisa Rhine, one of the founders of modern parapsychology, selected 191 apparently precognitive experiences in which people attempted to prevent a foreseen event from taking place. In 131 cases (69 percent) people were successful in taking steps to avoid the undesirable consequences of whatever appeared to have been "foretold" in their dreams.[9]

Rhine spent several decades reading and cataloging the thousands of reports sent to her describing presumptive psi experiences. By 1963, she had placed 10,066 experiences into four categories. The "intuitive" category was responsible for 30 percent of the reports, while 13 percent were termed "hallu-cinatory," 18 percent "unrealistic dreams," and 39 percent "realistic dreams." Hallucinations are more spectacular than intuitive hunches, but there were fewer of them than intuitions. Unrealistic dreams might be thought to be more dramatic than realistic dreams, but they were outnumbered by dreams that seemed life-like. Apparently, the unconscious has its own framework, one that may differ radically from conscious logic and reasoning.

Rhine discovered that three out of four reports of precognition occurred in dreams, even though one would think that an experience about a future event could occur at any time of the day or night—especially as people spend more time awake than asleep. She conjectured that the dreaming unconscious might run ahead in the future more often than during waking awareness.[10]

In 1927, the remarkable book *An Experiment with Time*, by J. W. Dunne (a British airplane designer), was published. In it Dunne reported an investiga-tion that seemed to validate the occurrence of future elements in his own dreams. He also made suggestions for undertaking more rigorous studies.[11] These studies were carried out at Maimonides Medical Center as part of its project on anomalous dreams. To study precognition in dreams, the laboratory obtained the cooperation of Malcolm Bessent, a British "psychic sensitive" who was well known for his purported dreams about the future. In 1969, the Maimonides team attempted to explore whether or not Bessent could dream about a waking life experience that would be arranged for him after he had completed his night of dreaming. Bessent spent eight nights at the Maimonides Dream Laboratory; his dreams were monitored and recorded. When Bessent was awakened after his final period of REM sleep, a different experimenter (one who had not been present during the night) selected a ran-dom number by tossing dice. This number directed him to a list of dream images appearing in a book written by Calvin Hall and Robert Van de Castle.[12] An experience was created by the experimenter to match the randomly selected image.

One morning the image "parka hood" was randomly chosen by a toss of dice, and the experimenter had one hour to prepare a post-sleep experience based on the image. When Bessent left the soundproof sleep room, he was taken to an office draped with sheets (to resemble snow). As he inspected a photograph of an Eskimo wearing a parka hood, an ice cube was dropped down his back. Several hours earlier, Bessent had dreamed about ice, a room in which everything was white, and a man with white hair. His dreams on each of the other seven nights of the study also were congruent with the following morning's experience, and outside judges were able to match the correct dream with the correct post-sleep experience with an accuracy that was statistically significant.[13]

Bessent returned the following summer for a similar experiment, but one in which the controls were even tighter. For example, a dozen experiences were "packaged" by an experimenter who left for Europe shortly after he selected the props and wrote the instructions. Again, a team of experimenters put Bessent to bed, monitored his sleep, and collected his dreams. In the morning, another experimenter selected a number randomly, and picked the sealed container to which it corresponded. Outside judges (without knowing the correct match) were able to detect traces of the post-sleep experiences in Bessent's pre-experience dreams, and their judgments again yielded statistically significant results, indicating that coincidence was highly unlikely.[14]

One night Bessent had several dreams about birds, one of which he reported as:

> Just water. . . . A few ducks and things. It's fairly misty, but there are quite a lot of mandrake geese and various birds of some kind swimming around in rushes or reeds. . . . I just have a feeling that the next target material will be about birds.

The following morning, Bessent was taken into a darkened room, sat before a screen, and watched several dozen slides of birds—birds in the water, birds in the air, birds on the land—while an accompanying tape played bird calls. His dreams closely matched the event that had been randomly selected after Bessent had awakened.

What was the reaction of mainstream science to these two experiments? A book entitled *Anomalistic Psychology* dismissed the experimental results, stating that Bessent had been "primed" before going to sleep with pictures and music. It concluded, "The receiver was an English 'sensitive,' but it is obvious that no psychic sensitivity was required to figure out the general content of the picture and to produce an appropriate report."[15] The psychologist Irvin Child remarked, "The correct sequence of events was quite clearly stated in the . . . original research report . . . This erroneous reading . . . could easily have been corrected by a more careful rereading."[16] The authors in question, however, never apologized for their mistake, nor was it mentioned in the reviews of their book written by mainstream psychologists.

In another experiment, the English investigator Keith Hearne encouraged one subject to systematically record her presumptive precognitive dreams with him. Later, judges compared her dreams with events in newspapers, both for the periods of time when she was recording her dreams and for "control" time periods when she did not have dream notebooks. The study did not produce significant results, but did include some remarkable correspondences. For example, there was a premonition about an attempted assassination of the Pope three days before an attempted attack on him at Fatima, Portugal in 1982.[17]

Another investigation was carried out by David Ryback in the United States. Ryback estimated that about 9 percent of the population have reported one or more precognitive dreams. To Ryback, a precognitive dream must include the following: (1) detailed information that clearly corresponds with details of the event in waking life; (2) the unlikelihood of the frequent occurrence of the event in waking life; (3) proof of precognition (e.g., that the dreamer told someone about the dream, or recorded it, before the waking life event took place).

One example that met Ryback's criteria was a dream that a man described to a friend shortly after waking up. In the dream, he found himself opening a checking account in a bank. Two armed robbers came into the bank and one robber put a gun in the dreamer's mouth. The robbers went to the teller's cage, obtained a great deal of money, and escaped. Later that day, while the dreamer was in a bank opening a checking account, two robbers rushed in and held up the bank, confronting the tellers with guns. The robbers took the exact same position they had in his dream, and threatened the customers with their weapons. The robbers did not place a gun in the dreamer's mouth, but otherwise the events corresponded exactly.[18]

Some skeptics criticize the study of anomalous dreams, stating that these accounts support "magical thinking" and "irrationality." However, the Maimonides team, as well as most other parapsychologists, rigorously employ the experimental method in their studies. They consider these dreams natural, not "supernatural," and normal, not "paranormal." However, little experimental work has been conducted with anomalous dreams that the mechanisms of their operation remain unknown. At least a dozen possible explanations have been proposed, ranging from models based on quantum physics to those evoking geomagnetic fields.[19]

Anomalous Dreams between Parents and Children

The frequency of anomalous dreams between mothers and their children is thought by some investigators to originate in the intrauterine period of mother-fetus symbiosis. If so, it may have developed in the early postnatal period as an emergency channel of communication.[20] This point of view was most forcefully stated by the psychoanalyst Jan Ehrenwald, who noted that symbiosis is a physiologically reciprocal dependent relationship between two different organisms, but beneficial for both. For several months after birth, the baby is a direct extension of the mother's body image, and the baby perceives the mother as part of him- or herself.[21]

The following dream by Caroline, points out the strength of the bond that can exist between mothers and daughters:

> I enter the den of my childhood home and see my mother lying on the sofa. I slowly approach her and feel somewhat startled. To my surprise, she has a new hairstyle that is identical to mine. She is also wearing youthful clothing that is similar to mine. Overall, she appears to be much younger and more vibrant. I'm still feeling confused because she is a mirror image of myself. I tell her that she looks good and she smiles knowingly.

Caroline awoke from her dream, startled by its imagery. She quickly wrote down a description of her dream in her dream journal and forgot it until two months later when she traveled to Arizona to visit her mother. She walked through the airport terminal and immediately saw her mother. Both she and her mother stared in amazement: they had the same hairstyle and similar clothing. Neither Caroline nor her mother had mentioned their new hairstyles to one another previous to their encounter at the airport. Caroline realized that she had had a precognitive dream and discussed it with her mother. For Caroline, her precognitive dream implied that her mother was trying to recapture her youth and independence. During her visit with her mother, Caroline noticed that her mother started to search for a part-time job and that she identified with Caroline's single lifestyle. For her mother, Caroline's precognitive dream highlighted the genetic similarities that continue to express themselves as both women grow older.

This symbiosis also holds true for fathers who assume parenting functions. Parents feed babies when they are hungry, give them warmth when they are cold, lift the covers when they are too warm, change their diapers when they are wet, and monitor the immediate environment to produce comfort and stimulation. Ehrenwald, Tolaas, and others have suggested that this interaction can include anomalous phenomena that may persist as the children grow into adolescence and even adulthood.

Carl Jung called the parent-child relationship an archetypal situation in which "synchronicities," or anomalous coincidences, could occur.[22] One researcher reported that when there are anomalous communications within the family, parent-child interactions account for one out of three.[23] Moises Tractenberg concluded that some dreams have a premonitory aspect, preparing the dreamer for future events or containing insights useful in future experiences.[24] Many of these dreams, perhaps like the one reported by Caroline, may have parent-child interactions at their root.

Another precognitive dream was reported by a student, Robert.

Robert's Dream

I dream that I am in a car with my family driving north towards the coast. We are driving through steep hills and winding roads. Suddenly, the car goes out of control and crashes into the side of a mountain. The back door flies open and my sister and I are thrown out of the car with no harm. My parents remain inside the car and within moments they are killed.

Two weeks after this dream, some relatives were coordinating a holiday trip to the sea and invited Robert's family to join them. Robert's father decided the family should not go because the dates conflicted with Robert's academic work. On the way to the coast, his relatives collided head on with a truck and the parents died immediately. Their son and daughter, however, survived the horrible car accident.

Robert was not aware that his dream was precognitive, but he did tell his dreamworker that the dream had an unusual sense to it and disturbed him. He did not make a connection between his relatives' trip to the coast and his dream until after the accident.

Once a person recognizes a precognitive dream that is tragic in nature, it may sometimes be possible to prevent the event from occurring in waking life. Precognitive dreams can be literal or metaphorical. A plane crash may simply be a metaphor for a sudden change, or a breakthrough into a major problem or issue. To prevent the events from an ominous precognitive dream from really occurring, it is important to study the dream very carefully from every possible perspective. In addition, it is extremely important to examine the possible events in one's waking life that might correspond to the dream content.

If Robert had sensed that his dream was precognitive, then he could have shared the content of his dream and his concern with his relatives before they embarked on their trip. In other words, if the driver had been aware of a possible car accident, he might have driven more defensively or he may have decided to take a different route.

Working with Precognitive Dreams

There are some simple procedures you can follow if you think one of your dreams might be precognitive:

1. Record the dream as soon as you wake up. Dreams are often forgotten very quickly, even when you think you have them clearly in mind. Recalling the specific details is important if the dream is later judged to be precognitive.

2. Prepare yourself mentally and emotionally for the possibility that the dream may come true. Some people have an intuitive hunch that a particular dream is precognitive. If you have such a hunch, spend a few minutes thinking and feeling your way through the content of the dream, asking yourself how the events would influence your life if they were actually to occur. Sometimes a dream can prepare the dreamer for the serious illness of a loved one or a surprising turn of events.

3. Take preventive measures if the dream event is unpleasant or unfavorable. If you dream about an automobile accident, ask yourself if you have been ignoring any unwarranted noises or problems with your car. Dream content that may be precognitive merely foreshadows a possible future event, one that is often amenable to change.

4. Plan what you would do during and after the dream event to minimize its negative impact and maximize its positive impact. Anticipating action is one of the best ways of ensuring the least harm and the most benefit from the unfolding of potentially psychic dreams.[25]

You might want to pay special attention to the date of your dream, and the date in which an event in waking life took place that seemed to match your dream content. Alan Vaughan kept a record of his apparently precognitive dreams between 1968 and 1977, later turning them over to James Spottiswoode, a specialist in environmental interactions. Spottiswoode checked the geomagnetic conditions on each of those nights, finding that there was significantly lower geomagnetic activity in the environment at the times of the dreams when compared with nights in which no presumptively precognitive dreams were recorded by Vaughan. For Vaughan to label a dream "precognitive," it had to contain three or more specific items that corresponded to the future event. In a dream that preceded the assassination of Robert Kennedy in 1968, there were eleven correspondences between the dream and the tragic event, for example: "A party is planned. Many people come, including Senator Robert Kennedy, suprisingly." "A murder has been committed. . . . The killer . . . was a person people did not suspect."[26]

Do not be unduly concerned over the correct category for anomalous dreams; such classifications are somewhat arbitrary. For example, here is a dream reported by Milton, one of our friends:

> I am with Lucia, a maid who worked for my family about two years earlier but with whom we had lost contact. In the dream, I am having breakfast with my family when the doorman rings the apartment phone. I answer the phone and hear Lucia's voice. She says she is going to come for a visit. I discussed the dream with my family at breakfast that morning. Just then, the doorman of the building rang us. It was Lucia. She was in the neighborhood and had decided to drop by for a visit.

Assuming the dream was correctly related and was not coincidental, it could be either telepathic (in which case Milton and Lucia had some type of mind-to-mind contact), clairvoyant (in which case Milton sensed that Lucia was on her way to his family's apartment), or precognitive (in which case Milton had a premonition that she would have the doorman phone the apartment). Human beings often make divisions of phenomena that do not accurately reflect natural processes; some anomalous dreams can be examples of this situation.

The Society for Psychical Research was the first major organization to attempt the scientific study of experiences that are not easily explained by existing psychological models. Among the topics the society investigated, at the end of the nineteenth century, were hypnosis, multiple personalities, out-of-body experiences, near-death experiences, lucid dreaming, and such parapsychological phenomena as precognitive dreams.[27] One by one, most of these topics have passed into the scientific mainstream. It is quite likely that someday the scientific study of anomalous dreams will be granted respect and recognition as well.

Past Life Dreams

*T*he doctrine of reincarnation is basic to the religions and philosophies of most Asians, Australian aborigines, tribal Africans, Pacific Islanders, and many American Indian tribes. This concept is immensely appealing. It satisfies the hope for immortality, and it assures eventual justice for everyone because it proposes that the incidents in one's present life are, to some extent, the results of actions in previous lives.

The doctrine of reincarnation has been incorporated into the procedures of a number of Western psychotherapists who often refer to themselves as "past life therapists," and who have formed an organization, the Association for Past Life Therapy and Research. One of these therapists, Phoebe McDonald, has written extensively on the topic of dreams that contain episodes of her clients' purported former lives. She advises that other psychotherapists examine their clients' dreams with this point of view in mind, especially if the dreams "seem to bear no relation to the dreamer's present life."[1] Some of these practitioners choose to refer to their work as "past life report therapy," noting that the alleged past life experience might be a metaphor for contemporary problems in living.

Dreams That "Announce"

French anthropologist Andre Pinart reported on the belief in reincarnation among the Alaskan Tlingits (or Koloches) in 1872. He drew attention to the fact that although the Tlingits chiefly expect an incarnation into another human form, they also believe in transmigration from one animal species to another. He observed that if a pregnant woman sees a deceased relative in a dream, she will declare that the same relative has returned in her body and that he or she will come back into the world in the form of her child.[2] This practice can be found in some other tribes as well, many of whom give the newborn baby the name of the deceased person.

James G. Matlock, another anthropologist, has found that in many cultures the return of a deceased person is "announced" in a dream that usually is reported by a pregnant woman. In some cases, the "announcing dream" comes to the father, a relative, or a friend of the mother. In some of these instances, the expectant woman will have cravings for food preferred by the deceased person, who, presumably, she is carrying in her womb. Announcing dreams are rarely reported in Lebanon, consistent with the Druse doctrine of immediate rebirth. However, they are frequently reported in Myanmar (Burma), among the Alevi people in Turkey, among Eskimo tribes of Alaska and British Columbia as well as among the American Indian tribes in that area (such as the Tlingit, Haida, Kutchin, Beaver, Gitskan, and Carrier tribes).[3]

There is considerable variation in the prevalence, timing, and character of announcing dreams between cultures. The dreams tend to occur in the last month of pregnancy among the Tlingit, but shortly before conception among the Burmese tribe. Tlingit announcing dreams generally take symbolic forms; for example, the figure may appear at the garden gate carrying suitcases. In Sri Lanka, announcing dreams are even more symbolic. In Myanmar, by contrast, the dreams are polite and petitionary; rather than announcing their intention to come to the family, the figures request permission to be reborn there.[4]

Renée Haynes, an English investigator, found that accounts of past lives often contain specific information that the dreamer would have no ordinary way of knowing. However, she suggests several alternatives to reincarnation, such as the "collective unconscious" that Carl Jung hypothesized.[5] But Haynes also observes that one woman recalled being so poor in her life in thirteenth-century England that she had nothing to eat but potatoes. Haynes conducted research and discovered that potatoes were unknown in England until the fifteenth century!

Research on Past Life Dreams

Research on reincarnation has focused on children who spontaneously recall their purported past lives. Typically, the child will begin to speak of a previous existence before the fifth year of age. Such memories do not seem to be much different from the child's regular recollections and are incorporated unobtrusively. Some children, as well as adults, report dreams in which past life recall occurs. The English investigator, Edward Ryall, reported four characteristics of dreams about supposed former lifetimes:

1. The dream is accompanied by emotions unlike those usually experienced in regular dreams.

2. The dreamer has some awareness that the dream content relates to a former life.

3. The dream does not fade away as quickly as ordinary dreams.

4. If the dreamer is an adult, it often has an impact upon the person's world view, for example, changing his or her viewpoint regarding death or dying.[6]

Scott Rogo, another investigator of past life dreams, also identified four characteristic elements of adult dream reports he examined:

1. The dreamer usually links the dreams to a past life, often on the basis of their vividness or related subjective factors.

2. The experience often concerns the dreamer's death in the former life.

3. Anomalous details are sometimes communicated through the dream (for example, information that only the deceased person would have known).

4. Even if the dreamer is not interested in reincarnation before the dream, he or she reports a peculiar quality to the dream that supports the notion of a past life.[7]

Rogo reported a recurring dream that was reported to him by a man living in Texas:

There was a suspension bridge high above a wide expanse of water. It was a narrow walkway, swaying in the wind, with nothing to hold onto and floor boards spaced so one could see the water below the cracks. The bridge was reached by a ladder. Here my dreams varied. Sometimes I would mount the ladder and turn back as soon as I reached the top; other times I would creep out on to the bridge on hands and knees; and a few other times I would go out on to it a short distance walking erect. Never did I reach the other side. About twenty-five or thirty years ago I picked up a copy of *Life* magazine and what should I find but a half page picture of my bridge. And what is more, it was taken from the same angle [from which I had] always approached the bridge in my dreams. The article accompanying the picture identified it as the first catwalk thrown across the East River preparatory to building the Brooklyn Bridge back in the 1870s; it also stated that a number of persons, both men and women, had fallen to their deaths from the bridge. I am convinced that I was one of those because I have never had that particular dream again.[8]

Psychiatrist Ian Stevenson has conducted the most systematic research on past life reports. He has focused on cases where individuals produce information about the previous personality which could not have been easily obtained through ordinary means. Sometimes these past life reports come from the waking state and sometimes from dreams. When this information comes from dreams, the dreamers visually experience themselves as participating in a scene during some earlier time before their present lives. At other times, the dreamers simply observe the scene in the dream. In either case, the dreamers claim that they cannot account for these images by events in their present life situation. According to Stevenson:

> Such images usually occur briefly, sometimes in the waking state and sometimes in dreams. The percipient experiences himself as participating (occasionally only watching) a scene of some other earlier time before his present life. And he cannot account for the images by recalling any source of them in his present life.[9]

The children who Stevenson interviewed often remarked, "Such a thing happened to me when I was big." They did not usually relive the past as if it were happening at the present time, except in dreams. Characteristically, in those dreams, the children experienced themselves with a different identity living a scene in some past time and different place. For the duration of the dream, and sometime a little longer, they experienced themselves as a different personality. Dreamers, both children and adults, experiencing these different personalities sometimes examined themselves in a mirror upon awakening to make certain of their appearance.[10] Stevenson also has stated that it is possible that some of his subjects acquired their information in dreams, but only later communicated it to others, after they had resumed their ordinary personalities.

The following dream from one of our students, Lita, describes a past life experience consistent with Stevenson's data.

> I am a small boy of Indian and English parentage living in India sometime during the nineteenth century. I am wandering alone fearfully through our village and I sense rioting in the nearby streets. I walk down a back alley and enter a door through a familiar wall. I am in a garden that is also familiar to me, but it is now overgrown and abandoned. I feel extremely sad; the Englishman who lived here was my father. I walk up to the back of the house and push the door so that it slowly opens. Silently, I look up and see the dark, colossal furniture. I climb the staircase and enter the

master bedroom. A very old monkey is sitting in the center of the bed. I remember him as our household pet. Now, he, too, has been abandoned. I climb onto the bed and sit with him as we hold one another.

Lita reflected upon the story line of her dream after awakening. She intuited that her mother was a young Indian servant living in an Englishman's estate. Her mother fell in love with the married Englishman and had a baby boy (i.e., Lita). Shortly before the uprising she and her three-year-old boy were banished from the estate and her mother died soon afterwards. The young Indian boy was abandoned, unable to find acceptance in either culture because he obviously had a mixture of English and Indian blood.

The story line had a sensory quality that paralleled her experience of waking reality; Lita felt that she had relived a memory. Inspired by the sensory details of her dream (traditional Victorian furniture) and her knowledge of history, she decided to research the time period of her dream. She gathered several Eastern history books at the library and discovered that the time period of her dream coincided with the Sepoy Uprising of 1857. This uprising between the British and the Indians occurred in northern and central India and lasted well over a year.

While reading about this uprising, Lita felt a sense of confirmation that enabled her to reflect upon the possible connection between her past life experience and her present life. In her present life, Lita's parents had divorced when she was three years old and she had lived with her mother. Like the Indian boy, her abandonment by her father at a young age caused her to feel intense sorrow, fear, and anger. However, in her current lifetime she was able to locate her father after twenty-one years and reunite with him. Their reunion occurred in her father's garden and Lita gained a sense of resolution - both from her present life and her past life.

Working with Past Life Dreams

There were six past life dream reports in Krippner's study of cross-cultural dream reports, half of them from Brazil and Russia. However, a Japanese woman reported,

In this dream I was a young beggar somewhere in Europe. Two other beggars and I came back from begging on the street. We had no food or money. My clothes were dirty and I had long, curly, brown hair. I had not bathed in a long time. I opened a heavy wooden door at a gate of a thick stone fortress. In the fortress there was an area for miserable beggars to sleep. An ugly old woman found me and other beggars trying to keep warm by a fire. She hit one of us and dashed a container of liquid on the head of the other one. Nobody tried to stop her, or to help us. I think it was the tenth or eleventh century. I was not Japanese. It might have been a former lifetime.[11]

If you have actually lived before, and if experiences from these past lives appear in your dreams, it is likely that you need to work with the dreams in ways similar to those you would use with ordinary dreams. You simply need to make a few modifications to accommodate the purported past life aspects of the dream report. One system that is particularly useful has been outlined by David Ryback.[12]

1. Record the dream in your dream notebook. Try not to let the act of writing interfere with the flow of your dream recall. Include the dream mood as well as details, expressions, and humor.

2. Identify the most salient elements of the dream and underline them.

3. Apply the word association technique to each of these elements. Write each important element on top of a piece of paper and write any associations that come to your mind.

4. Imagine that the dream is a play. What would the scenes of the play be? Divide the dream into dramatic scenes in this manner.

5. Place your associations into the proper places so that they match the dramatic scenes.

6. Interpret each scene according to its word associations to find the situation, the conflict, the climax, and the resolution—if there is one.

7. Make a positive response to the dream. How can you apply the lesson of the dream to your waking life?

Antonia's Dream

Antonia, who had recurring neck pains, recalled the following dream and related it to her psychotherapist:

I am a seamstress in France, and a revolution has just taken place. I am taken before a tribunal and am called an enemy of the people because I worked for a countess. I protest my innocence, but to no avail. I am condemned to death, and taken to the guillotine where I am beheaded.

Antonia and her therapist identified the most salient dream elements as "seamstress," "France," "revolution," "tribunal," "enemy," "countess," "protest," "innocence," "condemned," "death," "guillotine," and "beheaded." Some of Antonia's associations were:

> Seamstress: hard worker, detailed effort, mending things, feminine occupation, producing something to wear.
> France: a country with civilized, elegant, but temperamental people.
> Revolution: sudden change, challenging authority, an invitation to bloodshed.
> Tribunal: judges, people in authority, older men who have power.
> Enemy: adversary, antagonist, competitor, rival, opponent.
> Countess: a woman of elegance and power.
> Protest: assert, challenge, demand to be heard.
> Innocence: not guilty, righteous, virtuous.
> Condemned: convicted, culpable, guilty.
> Death: the end of it all, destruction, bloodshed.
> Guillotine: beheading, bloodshed, technology for death.
> Beheaded: losing one's head, death, bloodshed, getting it in the neck.

Antonia found it was quite easy to divide her dream into scenes. In the first scene, she is a seamstress in France when a revolution takes place. In the second scene, she is taken before a tribunal and accused. She protests her innocence, but she is found guilty of being the people's enemy. In the third scene, Antonia is taken to the guillotine and beheaded.

Her associations to the first scene were: hard worker, detailed effort, mending things, feminine occupation, producing something to wear in a country with civilized, elegant, but temperamental people at a time of sudden change when authority is challenged leading to bloodshed. Her associations to the second scene were: Being judged by older males in authority who have power; being called an adversary, antagonist, competitor, rival, and opponent because of working for a woman of elegance and power; demanding to be heard and asserting that she is not guilty, but righteous and virtuous. Her challenge does not work and she is convicted, being declared culpable and guilty. Antonia's associations to the third scene were: the end of it all—destruction and bloodshed by technology for losing her head and getting it in the neck.

Antonia and her psychotherapist observed the obvious connections between her neck pain in this life and her death in the past life. In the first scene, she is a hard worker engaged in a feminine occupation where she does detailed work, mending and making clothes. However, she does all of this at a time of momentous challenge and in a setting that is imperious. In the second scene, neither her employer's power or her own protest is a match for the male tribunal that condemns her. In the third scene, she gets it in the neck, and everything comes to an end.

Antonia applied this lesson to her daily life. She worked very hard as a housewife, providing basic necessities for her family and mediating disputes, especially those between her husband and her children. But her husband, despite his high-paying job and education as an engineer, often would come home drunk and throw the house into disarray. Her feminine skills were no match for his demands and accusations. His abuse was verbal rather than physical, but she would still suffer neck pains after his outbursts of temper.

According to Antonia's psychotherapist, her home situation resembled her life in the days of the French Revolution when she had been unjustly accused and executed. Even though she was innocent at the present time, as she had been two hundred years earlier, her innocence did not prevent her from suffering malediction. The psychotherapist urged her to find resources of her own to counterbalance her husband's power. This was very difficult, because Antonia's culture believed that a husband could not be upbraided for his actions, even if he was inebriated at the time. Nor could Antonia leave her husband, as she had no way to support herself and her children. Nevertheless, Antonia's neck pain stopped once she accepted the past life report as valid. And within a few years, her husband finally began to see a psychotherapist himself and reduced both his alcohol consumption and his abusive behavior.

Did Antonia's dream actually refer to a past life? Or, was the dream a metaphor for her current situation? Or, was the dream a combination of both, as suggested by her psychotherapist? The important achievement in this case was Antonia's acceptance of a new personal myth. Once she accepted the past life event as real, she had an explanation for her neck pain. The explanation by itself was empowering, and the neck pain disappeared. Antonia's personal myth was so substantial that it sustained her until her husband's behavior changed.

Did the dream reflect reality or create reality? Did it uncover a personal myth, or construct a personal myth? Some therapists who work with their clients' purported past lives claim that it makes little difference. An explanatory narrative of this nature can provide hope and comfort with profound therapeutic effects.

Initiation Dreams

*Initiation dreams, in which the dreamer is approached by a deity, spirit, or ancestor, are prominent in the *Iliad* and the *Odyssey*. These dreams were later institutionalized as part of the mystery schools. In these visitation dreams, the spirits and deities travel to the actual sleep setting of the dreamer, rather than having the dreamer go to the spiritual realm.

Initiatory dreams were accepted as direct contacts with the supernatural entities who affected the destiny of the clan, the tribe, or the community. These deities, spirits, or guardians could instruct the dreamer in the lore and wisdom of his or her people, ordain him or her as their messenger, and confer various powers, privileges, and duties. The Ojibway culture used dreams for initiation into adulthood. Boys between the ages of ten and fifteen years fasted for six or seven days. This period of time prepared them for dreams of spirit guides that gave them personal power.

Among many contemporary native people, initiation dreams are still viewed as important. It is believed that they can be elicited by prayer, by fasting, or by vigils. Some aspirants prepare themselves for a "vision quest" in which they leave the community, go to an isolated area, and wait for a dream in which their totem animal or guardian spirit will reveal itself. Sometimes the initiation is from childhood into adulthood, while at other times it is a "call" for special service to the community.

Dreams That "Call" the Dreamer

Shamans were the first dreamworkers and were often called to their profession by dreams. In some tribes it was believed that everyone who dreamt made contact with the world of shamanism.¹ As tribal practitioners who entered the spirit world, they emerged in hunting, gathering, and fishing societies. When tribes settled down and developed agriculture, many of the shaman's roles were assumed by other practitioners such as priests, sorcerers, diviners, and healers.² However, shamanic influences can still be found in traditional native medicine as it is practiced today.

Shamans are men and women who use altered states of consciousness to travel into "dreamtime," obtaining power and knowledge to help and heal members of their community. In psychological terms, shamans regulate their attention, obtaining information not available to their peers, using it to reduce stress and improve the living conditions of members of their society. Shamans are able to self-regulate many bodily functions and achieve a degree of concentration that surpasses the ability of their peers. They master a complex body of knowledge through instruction and direct experience, and they are able to apply this wisdom to individual situations in appropriate ways. Dreamwork is an integral part of most shamanic traditions. An Arctic explorer once inquired of an Eskimo acquaintance if he were a shaman. The man responded that he had never been ill and had not recalled dreams, therefore he could not possibly be a shaman.³ This sentiment is echoed in one way or another by inhabitants of many other tribal societies, as is another key concept in shamanic dreamworking—that if someone could imagine or dream an event, that action was considered to be, in some sense, "real."

Shamans enter their vocations in several ways: through heredity, unusual birth conditions or markings, spirit-mediated recovery from illness, vision quests and other rituals, or by means of an initiatory dream. In Okinawa, spirits notify the future shaman through visions and dreams; many of the recipients who are "called" try to ignore their summons, but eventually succumb to the spirits' directives. Most shamanic traditions take the position that refusal to follow the "call" will result in a terrible accident, a life-threatening sickness, or insanity.

Common themes in initiatory dreams are dismemberment, death, and rebirth. In one instance, an Eskimo candidate for shamanism went into the hills to sleep. He dreamt that he was swallowed by a monstrous bear, chewed up, and spat out. Eskimo tradition held that this was a call to become a shaman. The initiation of a shaman in western Australia consists of dreaming of being swallowed by a serpent, vomited out, cut into pieces by older shamans, and revived by their songs.

A Mexican Huichol shaman, don Hilario, was called to his profession in a boyhood dream. Kauyumarie, the patron of shamans, appeared in the dream as a newborn deer who brought the message from Tatewari, or Grandfather Fire. Once this visitation had taken place, don Hilario embarked on the arduous apprenticeship required by Huichol tradition—meditations in the mountains, pilgrimages to sacred places, days of ceremonial chanting, prolonged periods of sexual abstinence, and engagement in further visitations both in dreams and sacred peyote cactus sessions.[4]

Fred Swinney, a Canadian psychotherapist, was camping in an Ontario forest when he dreamed about animal predators emerging from the woods and devouring him. Awakening in terror, Swinney cast his gaze toward the coals of the campfire. Just beyond, he discerned two piercing eyes and the large gray form of a wolf. Surprisingly, fear gave way to total surrender, just as if Swinney had been transformed into a wolf himself. Initially resisting the call, Swinney eventually took the name Graywolf and began working with his clients from a shamanic perspective.

Among several Native American tribes, initiatory dreams contain birds and animals, such as eagles, owls, bears, and deer. The dream creature (who often becomes the shaman's "power animal" or "totem") typically enables the dreamer to incorporate its wisdom into his or her own and to begin shamanic training. Among the Inuit Eskimos, a shaman is "called" by dreaming about an animal spirit who then "possesses" the dreamer. Upon awakening, the dreamer withdraws from society and wanders naked through the land. Eventually, the initiate gains control over the spirit, celebrating this victory by making a drum. Among the Wintu and Shasta tribes of California, dreams about deceased relatives are said to mark one's call. For some Australian aboriginies, the call to heal frequently comes through the dreams of the neophyte's father or grandfather.

In California's Diegueno and Luisano tribes, future shamans can be selected in childhood on the basis of their dreams. Choctaw Indians believe that sick children's dreams should be observed for signs of shamanic calling. Spirits will often seize the souls of these children in the dreams and take them to caves, offering them a knife, a bundle of noxious herbs, or a bundle of medicinal herbs. If the child selects the medicinal herbs, this is an indication that the child has been called to heal.

Sometimes the training period for the initiate takes several years, but in other traditions it is quite brief. In the Washo tribe of Nevada and California, the initiates receive power during their dreams and are awakened by a whistle. The initiate follows the whistle, which changes to a whisper that dictates instructions. For example, it might give the command to bathe on four successive mornings and treat a sick person on four successive nights. If the client recovers from the illness, the initiate's status as a shaman is confirmed.

Among the Naskapi, a group of Algonquin Indians in Labrador, dreams are actively sought by the entire tribe through fasting, dancing, singing, drumming, rattling, sweating, and drug-taking. The Cashinahua Indian shamans of eastern Peru also pursue dreams, believing that the more dreams they have each night, the greater the power that will accrue them. Other members of the Cashinahua tribe, however, attempt to reduce the frequency of their dreams because it is held that dreaming interferes with skill in hunting. As a result, the hunters may request an herbal preparation that will "calm the dream spirits."

In Africa, Zambian shamans believe that they can derive powers of diagnosis in dreams, obtaining accurate information about an illness without examining the client. The Siberian Chuckchee, who "channel" spirits during altered states of consciousness, consider dreams to be a useful way to communicate with these entities. Anthropologists Larry Peters and Douglass Price-Williams found that "channeling" spirits and out-of-body "journeying" are the two major shamanic states of consciousness.[5]

The North American Navajos have a set of standard procedures they use for treating the victims of distressing dreams. Navajo shamans believe that unremembered dreams are unimportant, but those that are recalled represent the traveling of the dreamer's spirit outside the body. The spirit can travel through both space and time, sometimes encountering good fortune. In such an event, no intervention by the shaman is necessary. However, if a future event is potentially dangerous, or if a past action has negatively affected the dreamer's relationship with the spirit world, dream time will take the form of a nightmare. In this instance, the dreamer should reveal the nightmare to a shaman as soon as possible. The shaman will explain the dream's meaning and will prescribe either a major ceremony or a protection prayer. Because the misfortune might involve other members of the tribe as well as the dreamer, there is considerable pressure placed upon the dreamer to perform the recommended ceremony or prayer.[6]

Native American Iroquois posit that dreams contain symbols that can be interpreted by shamans through a technique resembling free association. The Iroquois believe that the "unfulfilled natural desires of the soul" (i.e., the unconscious) are expressed through dreams, but that frustration of these dream wishes can result in illness.[7] Such dreams provide clues to the Iroquois shaman as to what can be done to restore a client's health. Sometimes the client is encouraged to act upon these desires in ways that society at large would otherwise consider disruptive behavior. Such activities are formalized during a dream festival, held annually for three or four days. The psychological anthropologist Geza Roheim has presented a vivid description of this festival:

> Men, women, and children would rush about almost naked. Sometimes they would have masks or paint. In a state of frenzy, they ran from hut to hut smashing and upsetting everything and pouring hot water or cold ashes on the people. Each of them had dreamed of something and he would not leave the house till somebody had guessed his dream and carried it out in practice. The person in question was bound to present the dreamer with the thing he had dreamed of, for his life depended on obtaining it. But he would not state it in simple words, he would hint at it or indicate it by gestures.[8]

The dream festival also encourages children to ascertain their guiding spirits. A man or woman is appointed by each clan to hear children's dreams. These dreams are then related to tribal practitioners whose duty it is to determine the guardian spirits for each dreamer. The Hurons and the Eskimos, who also believe that dreams can be influenced by the conflicts and wishes of waking life, hold similar dream festivals.

In many societies, an important function of the shaman is dream interpretation. The Taulipang shamans of the Caribbean are considered to be experts in explaining their own dreams and dreams of others. Australian aborigine shamans move into "dreamtime" with great facility to assist tribal hunting activities. Shamans among the Northern Yakuts in Siberia conduct an evening ceremony using the shoulderblade of a deer, and then they ask the group members to pay attention to their dreams. The next morning, the Yakut shaman uses these dreams for divinatory purposes, not only for the dreamer but also for other members of the tribe. Diegueno Indian shamans make frequent use of dream interpretation to treat their clients; dreams concerning incest are seen as especially critical. These shamans chew Jimson weed (a mind-altering plant) to enhance their dreams. If they dream of putting their hands around the world, this is felt to signify all-embracing knowledge—the highest degree of wisdom that a dream can symbolize.[9]

Kelly's Dream

It is not only shamans who claim to receive initiatory calls through their dreams. A young woman named Kelly (one of our students) was debating whether to major in creative writing or psychology, and could not make a decision. While taking a psychology course, she began reading about dream interpretation, and one night she recalled a vivid dream:

> I am back in Louisiana where I used to spend my summers at my grandmother's house. I am out on a wooden pier on the river. . . . I am building a new section of the pier, hammering and doing all the work. I have a leather belt with tools hooked on it and I am working away. My older sister, Lucy, comes over and I am talking to her about her relationship with her husband. It is almost as if I am counseling her about her marriage.

When she awoke from her dream, Kelly had a sense of confidence that she had rarely experienced in her life. Two days later, someone told Kelly about opportunities for women in trades. She needed a summer job and decided to enroll in a new apprenticeship program for young women. Within one week of her dream, she had taken a six-month leave from school. She never returned to college. Within a few years, Kelly had become a licensed contractor with a thriving cabinet-making and remodeling business.

As Kelly thought back upon her dream, she recalled the summers with her grandmother as the happiest times of her life, especially the days she played on the pier. When she counseled her older sister, she recalled how much Lucy reminded her of their mother. Kelly had always observed how much her father had dominated her mother, and that he would not let her express any opinions or pursue any interests of her own. Perhaps the dream represented a "call" to be something her mother never could be—a woman who was competent and expressive, both physically and verbally. Being able to work for herself reminded her of the freedom she had felt during those precious summers with her grandmother.[10]

In 1992, Alessandra Mussolini claimed that she was called to enter politics by her grandmother in a dream. The first of Benito Mussolini's grandchildren to seek election for a political office, Alessandra's dream concerned Rachele Mussolini, the wife of the former Italian dictator. In the dream, Rachele supposedly told Alessandra not to worry about her family lineage because it was time to shed the burden of history.[11]

In the nineteenth century, Thérèse of Lisieux, a Carmelite nun, was experiencing inner turmoil regarding her desire to adjust to the cloistered life of the Carmelite Order and her equal desire to be a missionary. One night she dreamed that she was in a gallery filled with people. Standing near her were three veiled Carmelite nuns she knew were from heaven. She walked over to one of them and pulled the veil from her face. Instantly, she recognized the woman as the founder of the Carmelite Order. The woman's face was filled with a radiant light; she smiled and kissed Thérèse. She then told Thérèse that

God would call for her soon. Thérèsé asked whether God wanted her to do more with her life. The nun answered with an even more radiant smile, embraced Thérèse, and replied that God asked nothing more. When she awoke, she felt an immediate sense of relief; she also felt loved and cared for, and experienced a certainty about her life as a Carmelite nun that she had never known before.[12]

Research with Initiation Dreams

Ethrologist Katherine Ewing has studied dreams of initiation among Pakistani Muslim Sufis. She found that these dreams typically appear during periods of great personal stress, and are interpreted within the belief system that dreams can often call someone to join a Sufi order. Her observations indicated that this type of initiatory dream often led to positive personal transformation on the part of the dreamer.[13]

In a study on addiction, psychoanalyst Sam Naifeh studied the problem from what he considered to be the archetypal level of the psyche. In one case study, a thirty-two-year-old drug-addicted woman showed signs of recovery after attending Alcoholics Anonymous. Working with her dreams was an important aspect of her recovery; she experienced a number of initiation dreams that helped her re-pattern her inner and outer life.[14]

Krippner interviewed forty spiritistic practitioners in Brazil, all of whom claimed to incorporate spirits during their work. All forty also indicated they had been "called" to their work. Krippner reviewed the most important factors in their call. He found that the largest number of mediums had been called in dreams or visions, and a slightly smaller number had become mediums because they were raised by parents or relatives who were active in such spiritistic religions as Umbanda, Candomblé, or Kardecismo. Several entered mediumship through an assimilative process and others through reading spiritistic literature. A few developed mediumship abilities as a part of their own therapeutic program; they had come to a spiritistic medium because of illness, and were prescribed training as a medium as part of their treatment.

Krippner concluded that Brazilian spiritism is a major social force. Its social service projects are extensive, and it is an important adjunct to medicine and psychotherapy, especially for those individuals who cannot afford to see a private practitioner or go to a clinic. The spiritistic groups serve as resources for those suffering from existential problems, psychosomatic illnesses, and ailments for which medication and traditional therapy have been ineffective.

Spiritistic mediumship is exercised under the Biblical motto, "Give freely what you have received freely" (Matthew 10:8). There are no entrance fees, no charges for healing, and no financial requests, but donations are always welcomed. Dreams play an important part in Brazilian spiritism, especially in the mediums' initiatory call.[15]

Dreamers from each of the countries (except Japan) included in Krippner's collection of 1,666 dreams contributed initiation dream reports, for a total of fifteen. For example, a Russian man recalled,

> I dreamed about some deities who told me that I needed to transform myself to become a healer. It seemed as if I had died and then was reborn again. The deities told me that I needed to advance one more level, to learn about external kindness but also to be kind to myself. Once I learned this lesson, I would be able to start healing people. I went through three cycles of death and rebirth, and when I awakened, I felt that my initiation was complete.

Brazilians contributed the most initiation dream reports, followed by Russians and the Americans.[16]

Working with Initiation Dreams

A Canadian psychologist, Pamela Biele, has developed a method for working with initiation dreams. She asks people who recall this type of dream to record it as completely as they can, and then answer a series of questions (either orally or in writing):

1. What was it about the dream that made you feel certain that it was important to you?

2. Is there any one part of the dream that stands out in particular?

3. How was this dream different from your ordinary dreams?

4. How did the dream change your life?

5. Has the change lasted?

6. How do you view the dream experience now, especially in terms of how you now view your life and your world?

Biele has observed a remarkable series of changes that have been attributed to initiatory dreams. The advent of the initiatory dream appears to create a new reality for the dreamer, as well as a concomitant new personal myth. Before the dream, the dreamer typically feels incomplete, burdened, longing for answers, engaged in a struggle with one's self, and/or blocked in some way.[17]

Linda's Dream

The following dream by one of our students, Linda, demonstrates the life-changing potential of an initiatory dream. After taking a class entitled, "Sacred Intention, Sacred Manifestation," Linda began to paint artistically and had the following dream:

> I am at the mouth of a huge cave. The entrance is pitch black. There is a river that flows both in and out of the cave. I lay down in the water on my belly; my arms extend and my feet move toward the entrance to the cave. The water pulls me deep into the belly of the cave and then pushes me out again with great force. This process continues a few more times.
>
> I leap out into the opening of the cave and wade in the waters. I see a double-headed eel. It is dead. I pick it up and hold each head within my palms. I take care to feel the eyes and mouth of each head. There are still some stinger-type hairs on the mouth of one. It looks as though it could still sting, but I know that it is dead and does not have any more power. I gently lay it down on a rock.
>
> Then this very light male being and I are walking in a pasture. The grass is sweet and there is a house up on the hill; it's where I live. I sense that a newcomer is arriving, so I start to hurry toward the house in anxious anticipation—excitement for her/his arrival. The male being says, "Don't rush. When someone comes, take your time. Let them get comfortable with where they are and let them orient themselves. Then greet them. Go slow." I relax and we continue to walk. In the silence, we look at the next five or six years of my life. I can feel that what we are really looking at is my death. I turn to him and say, "I would just like to give my children something." He knows what I mean—not material things, but some inner experience that they can pass on. He rests his hand on my back, behind my heart. His words come from the purest compassion: "You can do anything you want." With these words, all decisions are left up to me: my life and my death, the "where" and the "how." On the deepest level, I feel that heaven also trusts me.

When Linda awoke from this dream, she wrote in her journal:

> I have taken refuge at the spring waters of my soul. It is my sacred intention to remain here. It is here that I live a life of continual renewal. For now, the particular intention that I have to manifest is sacred art.

Linda was forty-four years old at the time of the dream and had never considered herself to be an artist. Since her dream, she has been exploring the inner realities of the spiritual realm through painting for the first time in her life. This dream seemed to tell Linda that she wanted to give something of herself that was a deep expression of her true essence. Listening to her dream's profound message, she changed her major to painting and art. Her dream became an intention to enter a new world; the death of the eel became the renewal of herself as a creative woman. She later wrote:

> I have been painting for almost one year now. My life completely supports my creative process. Personal and financial problems have virtually disappeared. I sleep peacefully at night and wake up with enthusiasm. A constant level of anxiety no longer exists. I am not angry and my days are filled with joy and gratitude for the gift of being alive!

Biele has noted several elements that are fairly common to initiation dreams: an encounter with a significant person, intense involvement with the dream activity, vividness and clarity, a feeling of intimacy and closeness, an expression of intense emotionality, relevance to the dreamer's personal life, and a vibrant feeling of reality. If there are dream symbols, they are easily understood. Rather than witnessing the action, the dreamer is fully a part of it.

Biele found that after the dream, her dreamers were aware that something important had happened. The message appeared to be very direct and needed little interpretation. It resolved the personal dilemma, and brought feelings of relief, release, freedom, awe, wonder, insight, understanding, growth, excitement, elation, and/or reassurance. Her dreamers felt a sense of gratitude for the dream as well as a sense of renewed spirituality, even though there was much about it that they could not adequately describe. Although these experiences have long been an integral part of Native American dream tradition,[18] Biele's study indicated that initiation may be a latent potential of other cultural groups as well.

Group Dreamwork

The "dream festivals" of the Iroquois have their modern-day counterparts in dream groups. These groups can provide a safe environment in which to work with initiatory and other extraordinary dreams. Clara Hill has outlined a process for both individual and group dream work in psychotherapy. The therapist puts dreamers back in their dream experience in the "exploration" stage, moves them into the "insight" stage where meanings are developed from what was learned in dream exploration, and ends with the "action" stage, where the insights are applied to daily life. Psychotherapy clients who work with dreams have been found to express greater satisfaction with the therapy sessions than those whose dreams are ignored.[19]

Arthur Clark has provided a model for working with dreams in group counseling. He finds that as group members share their dreams and obtain interest and support from other group members, rapport and acceptance are enhanced. The group leader ensures that clients collaboratively process each others' dreams, and that hostile, insensitive, and demeaning comments are modified or avoided. Clark has noted that "group dreams" are sometimes reported that reveal conflicted issues and that improve relationships among group members.[20]

Montague Ullman has developed a dreamwork procedure in which members of a group respond to each report with the statement, "If this were my dream. . . ." The process ensures a multiplicity of interpretations for the dreamer to consider. The procedure is used internationally; for example, a dream group forum was established in Sweden in 1990. Extraordinary dreams are dealt with in these groups, and Ullman suspects that the safety of this type of dream sharing facilitates initiation and other extraordinary dreams because the dreamers feel a connection to the world at large.[21]

Chapter 15

Spiritual and
Visitation Dreams

*I*n many cultures, dreams have been associated with the spirit world. To the ancient Hebrews, dreams provided an opportunity to receive God's commandments. In the book of Genesis for example, after Jacob was blessed by his father, "he dreamed and, behold, a ladder was set up on the earth, and the top of it reached to heaven; and, behold, the angels of God ascended and descended on it."[1] Centuries later, the Hebrews began to look upon dreams as demonic portents, but the story of Jacob's ladder still retained its potency as a guarantee of God's attention to His "chosen people."[2]

The Egyptians also felt that deities could visit them in dreams. An inscription dating from the thirteenth century B.C.E. in the temple at Karnak relates a dream reported by a Pharaoh who feared an invasion and wanted to prepare a vigorous defense. In the Pharaoh's dream, the god Ptah appeared, extending his sword and commanding, "Take this sword and rid yourself of fear!" The Pharaoh interpreted this dream as guaranteeing divine support; he related it to his troops and they were victorious in their battle.[3]

Cyrus the Great, founder of the Persian Empire, reportedly had a visitation dream near the end of his life. As he slept in his palace, a majestic figure appeared to him in a dream, saying: "Make ready, Cyrus, for you shall soon depart to the gods." Upon awakening, Cyrus knew that his death was at hand. He made a thanksgiving offering to the gods, reviewed his life, arranged for his succession, gave advice to his heirs, and speculated on the immortality of the soul. He proclaimed, "There is nothing in the world more akin to death than is sleep, and the human soul at just such times is revealed in its most divine aspects, and at such times it also looks forward into the future, for then—it seems—it is almost free from its attachment to the flesh."[4]

Vibia Perpetua was a young woman from the Roman provinces who was arrested in the year 203, and charged with being a Christian. Before her execution, she wrote a remarkable autobiographical journal, which has survived and which most scholars accept as authentic. This journal contains four dreams, all of them spiritual in nature. A portion of one dream reads:

> I saw a bronze ladder of astonishing height extending all the way to the heavens, and it was so narrow that only a single person would be able to ascend it. To the sides of the ladder all kinds of iron weapons were fastened. There were swords, lances, hooks, single-edged swords, and javelins, so that if anyone ascended upwards carelessly or without paying attention, he would be lacerated and his flesh would adhere to the iron weapons. Under the ladder itself lay a dragon of great size, which waited in ambush for those who ascended, and frightened them so they would not ascend. . . . And suddenly, as though afraid of me, the dragon stuck its head out slowly from under the ladder itself. And . . . I trod on its head and ascended.

Some psychoanalysts have found sexual metaphors and symbols in Perpetua's climbing of the ladder, the shape of the various weapons, and the presence of the dragon. But to her, the dream foretold the defeat of Satan and the ascent to heaven of Perpetua and other Christian martyrs.[5]

Baha'u'llah, the prophet of the Baha'i faith, had his most important revelation in a dream. Confined in chains in the prison of Syah Chal in Persia because of his religious faith, he had a spiritual call in a dream in which he heard a heavenly voice:

> Grieve Thou not for that which hath befallen Thee, neither be Thou afraid, for Thou art in safety. Ere long will God raise up the treasures of the earth—men who will aid Thee through Thyself and through Thy name, wherewith God hath revived the hearts of such as have recognized Him.[6]

The prophet was not executed but was exiled from his home country. However, he brought his revelation to people ten years after this dream.

In visitation dreams, a deceased person or an entity from a spiritual realm (or even an "alien" from a UFO) reportedly provides counsel or direction that the dreamer finds of comfort or value. Sometimes the dreamer visits a domain that transcends his or her ordinary reality, learning about matters that involve the most profound aspects of the human psyche. Visitation dreams seem to represent a transpersonal reality only dimly perceived by human beings. They create a way in which the dreamer can be either visited by an inhabitant of this realm, or called to make a journey to this realm, encountering a deceased loved one, an angel, a spirit, or a deity. These dreams are mythic in nature; like myths, they focus on existential human concerns and have consequences for the dreamer's behavior. The message from the otherworldly visitor can change the dreamer's life.

Dreams of the Spirit

Carl Jung was a pioneering psychoanalyst who delved deeply into dreams in different times and places. His theoretical formulations came from an impressive galaxy of sources—mythology, comparative religion, alchemy, esoteric texts, his own dreams, and the dreams of clients who came from around the world. Jung used the term "archetypes" to describe what he felt were universal mythic symbols and metaphors. Among them were common dream characters such as wise old men and women, magical children, heroes, charlatans, and such dream activities as journeys, initiations, and transformations. For Jung, the universality of archetypes was due to the existence of innate neuro-psychological mechanisms that have the capacity to initiate, control, and mediate similar behavior among all humans, irrespective of ethnicity, culture, and creed.[7]

However, the common occurrence of these powerful dream images can be demystified. The psychiatrist Anthony Stevens points out that all cultures, whatever their geographical location or historical era, display a large number of similar social traits due to the fact that human beings share a common genetic code. Human cultures the world over have

> laws about the ownership, inheritance and disposal of property, procedures for settling disputes, rules governing courtship, marriage, adultery, and the adornment of women, taboos relating to food and incest, ceremonies of initiation for young men, associations of men that exclude women, gambling, athletic sports, co-operative labor, trade, the manufacture of tools and weapons, rules of etiquette prescribing forms of greeting, modes of address, use of personal names, visiting, feasting, hospitality, gift-giving, and the performance of funeral rites, status differentiation on the basis of a hierarchical social structure, superstition, belief in the supernatural, religious rituals, soul concepts, myths and legends, dancing, homicide, suicide, homosexuality, mental illness, faith healing, dream interpretation, medicine, surgery, obstetrics, and meteorology.[8]

Rather than posit an unknown universal mental structure, we need merely acknowledge that certain people and activities achieve salience in the dreams of dreamers worldwide because all dreamers share a common humanity and a common physical body.

Even so, the ways in which these archetypes take specific form varies from culture to culture because of historical and social differences. Most early societies venerated an Earth Mother who gave birth to all plants and creatures, but in ancient Egypt all the world's vegetation sprouted from Geb, the Earth God, as he lay prone on his stomach. In Scandinavia, Njord, another male god, personified the earth, while the Incas of Peru worshipped Pilcomayo, Lord of the Earth. The marital archetype appears to be universal, but it takes different forms around the world. In the non-industrialized countries, 68 percent of people practice monogamy, 31 percent polygamy (multiple wives), and 1 percent polyandry (multiple husbands). And half of the "monogamous" societies practice occasional polygamy (plurality of wives and/or mistresses).[9] Some dreamworkers do quite well without recourse to the term "archetype," but those who use it need to consider the wide variation in human behavior. Many life themes are the same, but the way that those themes shine in the galaxy of experience resembles a variegated rainbow rather than a narrow spotlight.

Canadian psychologist Alan Moffitt took the position that "dreams are the biological basis of spirituality and religion because they are the only place where you can meet the dead." He saw dreams as a way in which the "nervous system comes to know itself"; the brain does not have internal receptors, so it must rely on the dreaming process. The creative ability of the dream to represent the deceased, as well as other events not experienced in waking life, "is the biological basis for spirituality." From that recognition, a culture can decide that the deceased still exist in an afterlife. Or, a culture can take a different path, concluding that all experience is illusion. Moffitt's work with Tibetan Buddhists has demonstrated this latter set of concepts, which include the notion that waking life is illusory as well in that it is a set of experiences that each society constructs somewhat differently.[10]

Nevertheless, Jungian psychotherapists have made significant contributions to the study of visitation dreams. Marie-Louise von Franz wrote extensively about dreams of death, using a spiritual perspective. She found that death takes many forms in dreams, among them a gnarled tree about to collapse, a passage through fire or water, and encounters with death's messenger (for example, a burglar, bride, angel, or deceased relative). For von Franz, dreams give frequent hints that death is not the end of existence; her client who dreamed of the gnarled tree reported that its roots slowly detached themselves from the earth, and the tree, once uprooted, did not fall but floated freely.

Von Franz, like her mentor, Carl Jung, took the position that the task of aging is to create a living myth. This can be done through a fusion of personal and cultural symbols, many of which appear in one's dreams. She believed that only in mythic terms can one make sense of death, an assertion supported by the Egyptian and Tibetan books of the dead, early Christian teachings on the resurrection of the body, Western and Taoist alchemy, Tantric yoga, and other spiritual traditions. For von Franz, the final goal of spiritual growth is not to transcend the material world, but to transform the elements of ordinary life into a "philosopher's stone," "diamond vehicle," or other symbolic testament that brings closure to one's personal mythology.[11]

Visitation dreams sometimes assist in the process of mourning the death of a loved one. Margaret Gerne has observed an increase in the appearance of the deceased person in the dreams of the mourner immediately after the death event. After a period of time, appearances by the deceased wane and the appearance of living friends and family members increase. To Gerne, this shift indicates a successful mourning process. The dreamer can be aware of the emotional content of his or her dreams at this time, although there appears to be no predictable pattern. In general, death themes in the dreams increase after the death event, and decrease some time later if the mourning process proceeds in an effective manner. Other signs that the mourning is reaching closure are the appearance of dreams about work and new activities.[12]

Research with Spiritual Dreams

Bogzaran selected a group of lucid dreamers in an attempt to determine the relationship between their waking concept of "the Divine" and their experience of the Divine in lucid dreams. The study consisted of incubating lucid dreams with the intention of exploring the spiritual dimensions. Of the seventy-eight dreamers who participated in the study, thirty-five were able to have a lucid dream and carry out their intention. Two categories emerged based on people's lucid dream experiences: individuals who experienced the Divine as "personal" and those for whom the experience was "impersonal." Twelve individuals indicated that their concept of the Divine was that of a personal God while twenty-three individuals indicated that their concept of the Divine was "all-compassing Energy" or other impersonal forces. When the dreams were examined, it was discovered that 83 percent of the dreamers who believed in the Divine as a person encountered a personal God, while 87 percent of the dreamers who believed in an impersonal form of Divinity experienced it in forms other than that of a person. In other words, people's dream images usually matched the concepts they had of the Divine in waking life.

One dreamer who had a concept of a personal God reported the following lucid dream:

> I was floating and saw the back of a throne. A chair arm, solid and massive, is cut into the side of a marble block. I crept around the side and saw a person's arm on the marble chair arm. The hand was old, but firm and strong, like a carpenter's. The sleeve was white and full. The fingers were curved downward over the edge of the arm—relaxed, but full of life. I couldn't see higher than the elbow from my position slightly behind and below the throne. I knew it was God without any doubt.[13]

A dreamer who had an impersonal concept of the Divine had a very different lucid dream: "Before me appears a moving picture with numerous interwoven cycles—like the workings of a clock. It is also like patterns of pulsating light and shadow moving in cycles. No complete cycle can be seen."

Bogzaran also studied the way in which the dreamers incubated their lucid dreams. Thirteen dreamers formulated their pre-sleep suggestions in ways that actively sought the Divine, while nine dreamers requested an experience of the Divine. The remainder of the dreamers used other incubation techniques that could not be classified as active or passive. When the dreams were examined, it was discovered that 92 percent of the dreamers who decided to "seek" the Divine were actively looking in their dreams for an encounter. Eighty-eight percent of the dreamers who decided to "experience" the Divine had such an experience in their dream. Once again, the dreamers' pre-sleep preparation, expectations and intention had a strong influence upon the reported dream.[14]

Visitation and other spiritual dreams have played an instrumental part in motivating some people to change their religion, adopt a new faith, or lead them to a different spiritual world view. Theologian Kelly Bulkeley has collected case studies in which dreamers changed their religious affiliation because of the spiritual content of their dreams.[15]

Roya's Dream

The following dream is a clear example of a visitation dream in which the dreamer encounters a powerful divine being. Roya is an accupuncturist. Her mother-in-law passed away after a long and painful illness. The last eight hours before she passed away was the most difficult period for her and for everyone around her. The second night after her passing, Roya had the following visitation dream:

> I am standing outdoors. I look up and see a very large bird coming toward me. As the bird comes close to me, I see the face of my mother-in-law in the bird. She is smiling and looks very happy. I ask my winged in-law, "But you were suffering so much and you were in so much pain. What happened?" My mother-in-law smiles and replies, "But do you remember the pain of your birth?" I tell her, "No" then the winged creature begins moving its wings with a great smile and disappears into the horizon.

Roya shared the dream in the family gathering the day after the dream occurred. Everyone in the family was in mourning, remembering in particular the last moments and suffering of the mother-in-law's death. After she shared this visitation dream everyone began talking about what to make of this visitation. One member of the family synthesized the meaning of this visitation dream to be a clear sign that the mother-in-law was no longer attached to the physical realm and that her last eight hours of passing was a "labor of death." She was no longer concerned with the physical world and was born into a new reality.

After this synthesis of the dream was expressed, there was a great sigh of relief in the room. This incredible dream allowed the family to let go of their attachments to the last moments of the suffering body of the deceased and to begin the natural mourning process. This dream was seen as a gift to the family to help them cope with the process of dying; also the dream confirmed the family's belief about the existence of the spirit world.

Sylvia Wright interviewed sixty-one adults who felt that they had experienced contact with the dead. All sixty-one individuals had responded to flyers posted in Eugene, Oregon. There were forty-six women and fifteen men in the group. The most common venue for these contacts was "vivid dreams" (thirty-five people), followed by sense of presence, symbolic events, and purported telepathic communication (thirty-four people each).[16]

Applications of Visitation Dreams

Psychologist Gayle Delaney perceives many dreams as having spiritual messages. Time after time, her clients bring her dream reports infused with metaphors of love and relationships, which she sees as opportunities to practice one's spirituality on a daily basis. One day, a member of her dream group brought a dream report that turned out to be an insightful analysis of the problems she was having with her fiancé. The dreamer accepted the analysis, then sadly commented, "I had hoped this dream would be about my spiritual path, but it was only about my boyfriend." Delaney gently reminded her that it is through relationships that our spiritual path has its greatest opportunity to express itself.

Delaney explains how working with dreams also allows dreamers an opportunity to express their spiritual values and priorities. Dreams seem vitally interested in helping the dreamer be the best scientist, artist, construction worker, homemaker, or teacher that he or she is able to be. Dreams in which dreamers visit their places of work and receive some spiritual insight often direct the dreamer toward action, responsibility, productivity, and conscientiousness on the job.[17]

Several members of the clergy have used visitation dreams in their spiritual counseling sessions. L. T. Howe, a Methodist minister, has pointed out how dreams can disclose spiritual growth as well as revelation. From a religious viewpoint, according to Howe, the most important dreams may be those by which the dreamer gains new insight into himself or herself or about the divine source of the dreamer's present and future existence. Many of these dreams involve visitations from spiritual beings or visits to spiritual places.[18]

In a study involving graduate students in pastoral counseling, Fredrica Halligan and John Shea worked with twelve students who shared their dreams in the group. Archetypal images of life, death, and "internal marriage" became a recurring theme. The dreamwork clearly pointed toward the "individuation process" as explained by Carl Jung, indicating that dreams can be an instrument for psychospiritual development.[19] Halligan and Shea, and many other writers as well, have observed that the dreamer's "internal marriage" can represent a unification of diverse elements of what Jung called the "Self." Moreover, this internal dream journey can actually serve as a sacred venture toward a communion with God. A Jewish perspective has been provided by Samuel Shalev, who argues that dreams can portray an individual's transformation from fearing death to assuming responsibility for personal growth, moving toward authentic self-actualization and integrity.[20]

Jeremy Taylor, a Unitarian-Universalist minister and dream practitioner, adds that sincere seekers of spiritual experience can use their dreams to remove the blocks to their spiritual growth. Visitation dreams, and other types of dreams as well, can be invaluable in pointing out how dreamers deceive themselves, how they repress yearnings and desires that do not conform to their idealized self-image, and how they behave in ways that are false, artificial, and not reflective of their authentic self. According to Taylor, it is only by finding the authentic person, the genuine individual who lives beneath the veneer of artifice, that one has any chance of sensing the energy and presence of the Divine. The love bestowed by God, the spirits, the Earth Mother, and the Cosmic Energy, is directed toward an authentic person, not toward a facade of surface pretense and false identity.[21]

In Krippner's cross-cultural collection of dream reports, 19 were scored as "visitations," that is, dreams in which the dreamer was greeted by ancestors, spirits, or deities, and given messages or counsel by them.[22] When the same collection was examined for the broader category of "spiritual dreams," there were 101 that met the criterion of dreams in which one's focus was on, reverence and/or openness, and connectedness to "something of significance believed to be beyond one's full understanding and/or individual existence." The highest percentage of spiritual dreams came from the Brazilian sample (23 percent), the lowest from the Japanese sample (5 percent).[23]

Working with Spiritual Dreams

Louis Savary, a former Jesuit priest, and his associates have provided five key questions to ask when working with spiritual dreams and other dreams containing visitation elements.

1. How can this dream be a gift to my family, friends, or spiritual community?

2. How can this dream teach me to foster the growth of my family, my friends, or my spiritual community?

3. How can this dream teach me to act responsibly, and with love and compassion, toward my family, friends, or spiritual community?

4. Is there something that my family, friends, or spiritual community is asking of me through this dream? Have I recently experienced conflicts or confrontations with them that need to be resolved?

5. Have I recently received affirmations or signs of esteem for my talents and services from my family, friends, or spiritual community? If so, how can this dream be seen as a confirmation that I have been using these abilities wisely?[24]

Lee Lawson is an artist who collects visitation dreams and other experiences of altered states of consciousness. She emphasizes their potential for healing and observes that these experiences may occur even if the recipient has never been receptive to the notion of spirits or an afterlife. She advises that the people who have these experiences simply accept the visit as a mystery. Instead of trying to fathom the reasons for the visitation intellectually, people might look for the meaning embedded in the visit, and how it can become a catalyst for healing and enhanced appreciation of life.[25]

The interest in seeking meaning in religious or spiritual dreams is growing in the Western world. The question of significance and theoretical background of such growth is widely explored in the book by Kelly Bulkeley, *The Wilderness of Dreams*.[26] What is becoming apparent in the growing literature on dreams is that the experience of spiritual and visitation dreams can be a powerful life-changing event.[27] Whether these dreams are incubated or happen spontaneously, they are worth recording and studying. The meaning of these types of dreams might not be understood immediately, but by working with them, the meaning is slowly unveiled.

Dreams and
Personal Mythology

*E*xtraordinary dreams stand out from ordinary dreams, although both can be useful in illuminating the dreamer's personal myths and personal problems. Personal myths are woven from many strands, including the events of the past, the myths of the culture in which the dreamer was raised and lives, the mandates of genetic programming, and those inspirational moments that allow a person to sense the spiritual essence of the universe and peer into its nature. Personal problems may pertain to relationships, work issues, finances, family matters, spiritual imbalances, and a host of other topics. Personal myths and personal problems are closely connected. Often, personal problems are the result of dysfunctional personal myths.[1]

Since personal mythology often is rooted in the ways the dreamer learned to make sense of the world during childhood, it inevitably lacks balance. We use the term "inevitably" because the mythic worldview that develops during childhood is largely determined by the hopes, fears, strengths, and weaknesses of one's parents and by other circumstances beyond one's control. Nevertheless, that mythology shapes a person's desires, attitudes, and choices just as unconscious psychodynamics shape one's dream life. While personal mythologies continually mature throughout the years and a dreamer may have some conscious access into that process, it is a realm that operates largely below the level of awareness for most people. Nonetheless, people pay a price for its imbalances, limitations, and any disharmony with their actual needs, traits, or potentials.

Personal myths appear to form in a manner that is parallel to the way dreams develop. It is likely that personal myths tie into the brain's propensity for language, narrative, and storytelling. As such, the brain plays an active role in the ongoing revision of the individual's personal mythology. While dreams serve many biological and psychodynamic functions, the function that is most important when working with personal myths involves the dream's role in synthesizing the person's existing mythic structure with the data of a person's ongoing life experiences. As Montague Ullman notes, "Our dreams serve as corrective lenses which, if we learn to use them properly, enable us to see ourselves and the world about us with less distortion and with greater accuracy."[2] We suspect that dreams owe their structure to the inherent self-organizing properties of the brain itself.

Dreams and the Dialectic

A conflict in an individual's personal mythology that affects his or her feelings, thoughts, or behaviors may indicate the presence of a mythic crisis. This crisis occurs when a prevailing myth becomes so outdated or otherwise dysfunctional that the psyche generates a counter-myth to organize perceptions and responses in a different way. When this occurs, the psyche is in conflict, as each myth competes for attention and reinforcement. This conflict between the old myth and the counter-myth is worked out largely outside of conscious awareness. The counter-myth typically becomes crystallized and develops within the individual's cognitive affect system of thoughts and feelings, emerging in response to the old myth's limitations. It challenges the old myth and the two become engaged in a dialectical process. Self-organizing subsystems in the brain compete for salience. The greater the conflict, the more intense the dreams are, and the greater these impacts. Phenomenological research data indicate that intense, impactful dreams are more likely to generate meaningful metaphors and symbols.[3] The mythic dialectic, as a result, reflects the brain's self-organizing and self-creating (or "autopoetic") properties.[4]

Dream workers can develop a categorization system that describes several aspects of dreams in this ongoing dialectic, and any particular dream may involve one or more of them. For people who have learned to understand inner events in terms of personal mythology, this can be a useful framework for understanding their dreams. Of course, we cannot go so far as to say that dreams always reflect personal myths any more than we can claim that a Freudian client's sexual dreams confirm Freudian theory or that a Jungian client's archetypal dreams validate Jungian theory. However, this system has been strikingly effective when used clinically to interpret inner experience from a mythic perspective.

To evaluate dreams in terms of a mythic dialectic, psychologist David Feinstein has considered the meaning of a dream from three possible perspectives.

1. The dream may attempt to strengthen an old, self-limiting myth (particularly when it is challenged) by (a) emphasizing past experiences that provided evidence for the validity of the old myth; (b) resolving conflicts between the old myth and daily experiences through the assimilation of these experiences into the structure of the old myth; (c) providing visions of a future dominated by the old myth or a preview of the future according to the old myth, often with a sense of resignation.

2. Dreams may create or strengthen a counter-myth that has grown out of the old myth's deficiencies by (a) reworking old experiences and interpreting them in a less self-limiting, more affirming manner, thus providing an alternative to the old myth's template of reality; (b) interpreting new experiences in this manner and/or accommodating the old myth to fit new experiences in a manner that corresponds more closely to the counter-myth; (c) by organizing possibilities into a positive future with wish-fulfillment qualities. While inspiration for pursuing these possibilities is often present, instruction for how to translate them into daily life is not evident.

3. The dream may facilitate a cognitive integration between the two myths. As ongoing experiences bring the two toward a centerpoint, they tend to become more compatible, an integration of essential elements of each becomes attainable, and the cognitive forces that work against cognitive dissonance begin to integrate the two. This becomes evident in dreams that (a) highlight experiences from the past in which the mythic conflict was evident and show ways it could be integrated; (b) highlight the conflict as it emerged in recent experiences and show ways of resolving it; (c) portend a future where the conflict is resolved, often instructing the person how to accomplish the resolution.[5]

This system interfaces with other dream theories to some extent. The counter-myth is the psyche's attempt to solve problems around dilemmas caused by the prevailing myth. Freud's theory of wish fulfillment also involves the counter-myth, as does Jung's idea that compensatory dreams express an undeveloped part of the psyche. The Gestalt psychologists' view of dream elements as conflicting parts of the psyche also focuses on the conflictual aspect of this system.

Feeling tone often gives a clue as to the function of the dream. "Old myth" dreams typically feel defeating, hopeless, and draining in terms of energy and vitality. "Counter-myth" dreams typically tend to feel hopeful, optimistic, even exhilarating. "Integration" dreams tend to produce a calm, positive, realistic feeling. Of course, the feeling tone in a dream is highly dependent upon the dreamer's thinking and feeling style. Therapists working with this categorization system report that by identifying the type of dream that has been reported, less attention need be paid to the meaning of every nuance of dream content. Feeling tone takes precedence in the dreamwork. For this reason, the mythic approach—focused as it is on current life issues—can be a useful and practical way of working with dreams.

Are Dreams Meaningful?

If dreams are to be used to identify personal myths, they must be infused with meaning that is useful and appropriate. Nevertheless, there are many individuals, some of them well informed, who claim that dreams are meaningless. If dream content is devoid of meaning, why is it that scientific studies have detected differences when the dreams of two or more groups of dreamers have been compared? Robert Van de Castle reported a striking relationship between the percentage of dreams containing animals and the dreamers' chronological ages. Younger people, especially children, dreamed about animals more frequently than did older dreamers. However, when the focus was shifted from the United States to groups of native peoples, there were cultures in which no difference was found between children and adults regarding animal content, presumably because contact with animals in these societies was common among both age groups. In addition, Van de Castle studied the Cuña Indians in Panama, noting that their dreams included very few acts of aggression against other people, a trait also noticeable in their daily lives.[6]

People in developing countries with dense populations and frequent food shortages have an unusually low frequency of food consumption in their dreams.[7] This correlation appears to contradict Freud's notion of "wish fulfillment"—that we dream about those activities that we most desire. Instead, the data support Alfred Adler's and Calvin Hall's proposal that there is continuity between dream life and waking life. For this reason, dreams provide an excellent pathway to the identification and understanding of personal myths. Activities in a dream may serve as metaphors for a personal myth, and images in the dream may symbolize important aspects of these myths.[8]

Robert Levine studied three groups of male Nigerian students and found that dream content differed in relation to their tribal background. For example, the Ibo culture has a value system and social structure favoring upward mobility of its members. The Hausa culture does not support social mobility and individual achievement, while the Yoruba culture takes an intermediate position. Dream reports from Yoruba students contained more achievement themes than those of Hausa students, but less than those of Ibo students, exactly what one would predict if dream time reflects waking life.[9]

Several studies demonstrate that people undergoing episodes of depression have more dreams that take place in the past than do non-depressed people. Further, depressed dreamers report more content characterized by masochism, dependency, and blandness of emotion. If the depression begins to lift, however, dream content changes; for example, more feeling and emotion begin to appear in their dreams.[10] Other studies have demonstrated how dreams can play an important part in the mastery of new emotional experiences and their assimilation into one's personal repertoire of abilities.[11]

These and dozens of other studies indicate that dreams generally mirror waking activities, and that people's dreams reflect detectable differences in age, gender, and cultural background. Those individuals who denigrate dreams insist that they "are full of sound and fury, signifying nothing." But the next time you hear anyone make this claim, ask how he or she would explain the comparative data collected by Robert Van de Castle, Rosalind Cartwright, and other dream researchers.

The Dreaming Brain

There are many physiological theories about how dreams are produced by the brain, but we consider the neuropsychiatrist J. Allan Hobson's model to be an elegant description that is firmly rooted in laboratory data.[12] Hobson contends that dreams are tales told by the brain to make sense of the images evoked by random neural firings that accompany sleep cycles. Even though few visual or motor messages from the outside world enter during REM sleep, the higher-level neurons in the cortex's visual-motor area are stimulated by messages sent by the brain stem and act as if they are getting those messages from the external environment.

The eyes are closed and the muscles are virtually paralyzed during REM sleep; thus, the ensuing activity must be internally generated rather than externally generated. The brain stem also activates the limbic system, the brain's emotional center, so dreams are often marked by strong feeling tones. The brain's pain, taste, and smell centers are rarely activated, so few dreams are characterized by these sensations.

Hobson's position is not opposed to the search for meaning in dreams. In fact, Hobson maintains that dream metaphors represent high-level associations that infuse a great deal of material into an economical unit. Hobson is skeptical, however, that dreams focus on hidden meanings, because he asserts that the dream begins when signals from the lower brain strike the higher brain, which then tries to produce a more or less continual narrative. Hobson's model suggests that dreams reflect meaning that is already embedded in the dreamer's experiences, memories, and life issues. This stance mandates making sense of experience, including dream experience.

On the other hand, Gordon Globus takes an existential stance. In his seminal book *Dream Life, Wake Life,* Globus sees dreaming and wakefulness as equally viable ways of being. Human existence is, at heart, a creative movement fairly similar across its dreaming and waking phases.[13] Globus's book pays special homage to psychiatrist Medard Boss, a leading existential thinker who once made this wry comment on laboratory sleep research:

> The findings from sleep research are certainly highly interesting in their way, and even necessary. They tell us, however, almost nothing about what they are supposed to represent. Not one of them brings us a single step nearer to an explanation of dreaming as a unique mode of human existence.[14]

Boss suggests that dream images and dream experiences should be accepted in their own right, on their own terms, with respect for their unique feeling tone and with a minimum of translation. He treats dreams as texts or narratives that make dreamers aware of their possible life choices.

Globus also comments on the contributions of David Foulkes, who sees dream texts as cognitive plans for dealing with more or less randomly activated memories. Dreams can be meaningful and symbolic, but they are not preplanned, encoded messages that need to be "translated," in the same way that a linguist would work with a foreign language. Foulkes believes that the dream is knowledge-based and "bound to reflect some of the ways in which the dreamer mentally represents his or her world."[15] Where Globus takes issue with Foulkes is in the extent to which bizarre intrusions in the dream are random or meaningful. Foulkes holds that such intrusions are often random, the result of neurologically evoked memories stimulating a planned scenario. Globus contends that the dream's bizarre shifts and changes are usually meaningful, a case of the planned scenario reaching for the most easily obtainable memories to continue the story.

Although the views of Hobson and Globus differ in several ways, these two share many perspectives. Globus sees the dream process as the fundamental creative action inherent in the human condition. Hobson views the brain as so determined to find meaning that it creates dreams out of random signals. Both take most dreams on their own terms, rather than looking for hidden meanings that represent censored desires that have been festering for years or even decades. However, Globus takes exception to Hobson's assertion that a dreamer simply "makes the best of a bad job," finding those memories that "best match" the sensations evoked by random neural firing and using these images as a giant inkblot into which meaning is injected. Hobson observes that stimulating the neurons chemically can even induce dreams. Once again, the dreamer would insert a meaningful story into the resulting images.

Globus agrees with Hobson to a point: one's dream images are neurologically based. Random neural firing turns on a switch and activates a mechanism. In Globus's view, however, unconscious wishes and fears could well take advantage of this random stimulation and emerge full-blown once the appropriate memory is initiated. Simply because neural firing initiates a dream does not mean that it is necessarily responsible for the continuation of the dream.[16]

From our vantage point, there is a critical difference between these two researchers. For Globus, the essence of dreams is not random but meaningful. In his belief, there is a whole process that enfolds all meanings, and the meaningful dream is unfolded from it in a formative creative act. The debate is basically between randomness and fullness.

Some of the differences between Hobson and Globus stem from the fact that each is working from a different level of the brain/mind system. As a laboratory researcher, Hobson focuses on the mind's brain; as a clinical researcher, Globus focuses on the brain's mind. Both agree that dreams have meaning, but Hobson's "meaning" is more immediate; whereas Globus's "meaning" has deeper roots. Additional research studies will help us decide which emphasis is justified. In the meantime, we can gain satisfaction from the knowledge that dreams are now being taken seriously by scientists and that models of great ingenuity are being advanced to explain their function. Indeed, the quest originally begun by Freud has become increasingly sophisticated and scientific.[17]

David Kahn, an associate of Hobson, worked with Stanley Krippner and Allan Combs in an attempt to reconcile some of these varying perspectives. The result was an article published in the *Journal of Consciousness Studies* that described the brain as a self-organizing system composed of self-organizing subsystems. Brain activity appears to be "chaotic" in nature, exhibiting a "butterfly effect" in which a small stimulation can set into fluctuation all its subsystems. During wakefulness, these fluctuations are constrained by sensory input, a condition also described by Globus. But during sleep, these constraints are loosened, as are capacities for logic and self-reflection.[18] Recent experiences and longstanding issues can be incorporated into the dream narrative; as Globus observes, the dream spontaneously moves toward harmonious self-consistency: its "wisdom" is akin to that of a rubber band that spontaneously relaxes after it has been stretched.[19]

We believe that Hobson's research provides factual support to the innately creative nature of the dream process and that Globus gives dreaming a unique philosophical dimension. Based on these theories, it is apparent that, in addition to everything else, dreams are a royal road to the human condition. As Globus observes, once we make our existential choice and decide to remain in the world (i.e., rather than releasing ourselves from it), we face a challenge to develop the possibilities of our being alive. One of our greatest resources in this task is our potential for imagination and creativity—to see what we are and who we can become and to make wise decisions that will leave our world a better place than it was when we arrived. The role of dream life in articulating these visions and anchoring them in waking life is assuming greater recognition both by scientists and laypeople.

Dreams as an Example of Human Creativity

We agree with Montague Ullman that REM sleep is a natural arena in which creativity is at play. Dreams tend to arrange information in unique and emotionally related ways. They depart from rational thought, grouping images together in bizarre associations and making liberal use of metaphor in constructing the dream story. As a consequence, new relationships emerge that sometimes provide a breakthrough for a waiting and observant mind. Dreams serve a vigilance function, like a sentry alerting the dreamer to whatever may intrude into his or her dream consciousness.[20] This is evident in "false awakenings" or dreams within dreams, when the dream attempts to preserve its continuity by creating a new narrative instead of giving way to wakefulness.

Ullman's "vigilance theory" of dreaming posits that during REM sleep, the dreamer scans not only the internal environment but also those aspects of the external environment that he or she can perceive by anomalous means. During sleep, hunters and gatherers were vulnerable to attack. Contemporary human beings respond to symbolic threats rather than to physical dangers. Yet, vigilance still operates and REM sleep, perhaps because of its linkage to a primordial danger-sensing mechanism, provides a favorable state for anomalous communication such as dream telepathy, clairvoyance, precognition, and collective dreams.

Ullman's theory is not incompatible with Hobson's proposal that, during REM sleep, the brain is activated internally by random neural firing from lower brain centers that stimulate higher brain centers. For Hobson, the dream results from a knitting together of these neurologically evoked memories and images.[21] We would propose that the random nature of this neurological firing provides an opportunity for anomalous effects to operate, either influencing the portions of the cortex that are stimulated or the images that are evoked. The result is a great variety of extraordinary dreams—those felt to be healing dreams, out-of-body dreams, or those related to purported past lives.

In Ullman's vigilance theory, the condition that produces the dream narrative reflects recent emotional residues and explores these residues from an historical perspective, thus connecting them to the past and projecting them into the future. Pregnancy dreams afford an opportunity for this phenomenon, as they typically span past, present, and future aspects of the expected arrival of a new child. Ullman implies that there is a collection of dream stories waiting to be told, while Hobson suggests that dream narratives are created "on the spot." However, anomalies could enter both types of dream production, either finding their niche in a carefully constructed, metaphorical tale that contains an emotional linkage to the anomalous element, or filling a gap in a story that is creatively but haphazardly put together to make sense of a barrage of randomly evoked images.

We have suggested that dreams typically reflect inner and outer reality, but occasionally can create it as well. Charles Tart proposes that, in the conventional view of dreams, all the dreamer's images and activities are constructed from memory. Yet, the dreamer experiences the dream as "perceiving" not "remembering." As a result, it makes sense to consider that dreams are just as "real" as waking experience, a position held thousands of years ago by tribal shamans. The neural patterns that are activated while a person is awake are similar to those activated while that person is asleep. What an individual perceives is thus of equal substance and equally "real" in both states of consciousness. We see this process at work in creative dreams, initiation dreams, and even in visitation dreams, where an entity from another dimensions seems to enter the dream, giving advice or guidance.

In both dreaming and wakefulness, an active, complex world simulation process is going on. The major difference is that in waking, the world simulation process must constantly adapt to and be consistent with a steady inflow of sensory information originating in the external physical world and the physical body. On the other hand, in dreaming there is almost no input from the physical world or physical body with which the world simulation process needs to adapt or be consistent. As a result, the world simulation process can be richer and more varied than it is in the waking state, the only limitation being the images evoked by brain activity on any given night.[22]

The patterns produced by this brain activity can be called "chaotic." Chaos theorists look for the patterns in everything from stock market fluctuations to human moods and emotions. It is uncanny that order is often created out of chaos, and the self-organizing properties of the dream reflect the residues of daily life as well as longstanding personal myths and even deeply rooted spiritual concerns. One chaos theorist, Christine Hardy, describes how dreams can provide "networks of meaning" that reflect the dreamer's "emotional intelligence," helping him or her understand personal issues, emotional states, and even socially oriented concerns. Hardy notes that these "networks" can overlap, accounting for telepathic dreams, shared dreams, and other dreams that we have termed extraordinary.[23] We suspect that chaos theory is an especially appropriate tool for understanding dreams that have been dismissed as "coincidental" or "illusory" by mainstream scientists caught up in linear cause-and-effect models of the brain and the universe. Instead, Montague Ullman's notion of a subtle, underlying order may be on target—an order that is more accessible in dreams than in ordinary wakefulness.[24]

Chaos theorists speak of "chaotic attractors" that organize organic and non-organic material, and even information into a fluctuating whole in a way that resembles magnetic attraction. We suspect that personal myths serve as chaotic attractors in a dream, and their identification can clarify the dream's meaning.[25] Sometimes, data from beyond the dreamers themselves are pulled into the flux, and anomalous elements in dreams (precognitive, clairvoyant, etc.) are drawn to the chaotic attractor, as is the case with extraordinary elements of pregnancy dreams, healing dreams, and initiation dreams. Change and tradition in a person's life can be charted by his or her dreams, especially those that we have termed "extraordinary."

This self-organizing property of dreams allows them to be constructed in a fashion that resembles processes in the external world, because habits of thinking and perceiving occur in both states of consciousness.[26] However, a dream is just as "real" as waking reality at the time it is experienced, even if it is an out-of-body dream, a visitation dream, or another extraordinary dream—the events of which would be considered bizarre if the dreamer were awake. Dream reality is dismissed by Western culture because little effort is made to recall dreams, use dreams, or take them on their own terms.[27] We hope that this review of extraordinary dreams will play a role in redressing this neglect. In affirming the importance of dreams, dreamers may move toward a greater understanding of their creative potentials as well as a greater enjoyment of the dreamworking process.

The creative potential of dreams is apparent to readers of this book who have had extraordinary dreams of their own. It is tempting to ignore or dismiss these dreams when they do not easily "fit in" with one's daily life, one's personal mythology, or with the prevailing cultural mythology. However, extraordinary dreams can become exceptional human experiences, can be woven into the fabric of dreamers' lives, and can serve as the sprout from which a new life story can grow. The Huichol Indians of western Mexico claim that unless you do something with an extraordinary dream, you have the capacity to do little with your life.[28] Finally, Swami Sivananda Radha remarked, dreams can be the vehicle that takes the dreamer to the "world of the unseen."[29] We hope that our readers will glimpse this unseen world and from it, find inspiration for their future extraordinary dreams.

$\mathcal{N}otes$

—— $\mathcal{CO}$ ——

Chapter 1. Introduction

1. Hobson, J. A., *The dreaming brain* (New York: Basic Books, 1988).

2. Cavallero, C., & V. Natale, "Was I dreaming or did it really happen?" *Imagination, Cognition, and Personality* 8 (1989-1990), 10–24.

3. White, R. A. "Dissociation, narrative, and exceptional human experiences," in Broken images, *broken selves: Dissociative narratives in clinical practice*, edited by S. Krippner & S. M. Powers,(Washington, DC: Brunner/Mazel, 1997): 90.

4. Speier, A., *Dreams: Symbolism and therapy* (Buenos Aires: Editora Nueva Visiòn, 1991).

5. Rupprecht, C. S. "Our unacknowledged ancestors: Dream theorists of antiquity, the middle ages, and the Renaissance." *Psychiatric Journal of the University of Ottawa* 15 (1990): 121.

6. Hall, C., & R. L. Van de Castle. *The content analysis of dreams* (New York: Appleton-Century-Crafts, 1966).

7. Krippner, S., & A. Combs, "Self-organizing in the dreaming brain," *Journal of Mind and Behavior*, 21 (2001): 399–412.

Chapter 2. Understanding Dreams and Dreaming

1. Savary, L. M., P. H. Berne, & S. K. Williams, *Dreams and spiritual growth* (New York: Paulist Press, 1984).

2. Stevens, A., *Private myths: Dreams and dreaming* (Cambridge: Harvard University Press, 1995).

3. Freud, S., *The interpretation of dreams* (New York: Avon, 1966). (Original work published in 1900.)

4. Tractenberg, M., "O significado do sonhosam Freud, Garman, Kemper," *Jornal Brasileiro de Psiquiatria* 30 (1981): 317–322.

5. Adler, A., *What life should mean to you* (New York: Capricorn, 1958).

6. Ansbacher, H. L., & R. R. Ansbacher, *The individual psychology of Alfred Adler* (New York: Basic Books, 1956).

7.Jung, C. G., *Dreams* (Princeton: Princeton University Press, 1974).

8. Neisser, U., *Cognition and reality* (San Francisco: W. H. Freeman, 1976).

9. Foulkes, D., *Dreaming: A cognitive-psychological analysis* (Hillsdale, NJ: Erlbaum, 1985).

10. Foulkes, D., *Children's dreaming and the development of consciousness* (Cambridge: Harvard University Press, 1999).

11. Rycroft, C., *The innocence of dreams* (New York: Pantheon, 1979).

12. Hobson, J. A., & R. W. McCarley:, "The brain as a dream state generator," *American Journal of Psychiatry* 134 (1977): 1335–1348.

13. Porte, H. S., & J. A. Hobson, "Bizarreness in REM and non-REM sleep research," *Sleep Research* ,15 (1986): 81.

14. Crick, F., & G. Mitchison, "The function of dream sleep," *Nature*, 304 (1983): 111–114.

15. Hobson, J. A., *The dreaming brain* (New York: Basic Books 1988): 18.

16. Antrobus, J., "The neurocognition of sleep mentation: Rapid eye movements, visual imagery and dreaming," in *Sleep and cognition*, edited by R. Bootzin, J. Kihlstorm, & D. Schacter (Washington, DC: American Psychological Association, 1990): 4–21.

17. Solms, M., *The neuropsychology of dreams: A clinico-anatomical study.* (Mahwak, NJ: Lawrence Erlbaum, 1997).

18. Solms, M., "Dreaming and REM sleep are controlled by different brain mechanisms," *Behavioral and Brain Science*, 23 (2000): 843–850.

19. Boss, M., & B. Kenny, in *Phenomenological or dasienanalytic approach in dream interpretation: A comparative study*, edited by J. L. Fossage, & C. A. Loew (New York: Spectrum, 1978): 149–189.

20. Boss, M., *I dreamt last night* (New York: Gardner Press, 1977): 5.

21. Ullman, M., & C. Limmer, editors, *The variety of dream experience* (New York: State University of New York Press, 1999).

22. Globus, G., *Dream life, wake life: The human condition through dreams* (Albany: State University of New York Press, 1987): 61.

23. Arden, J. B., *Consciousness, dreams and self: A transdisciplinary approach* (Madison, CT: Psychological Press, 1996): 7.

24. Ibid., p. 75.

25. Ibid., p. 74.

26. Wolf, F. A., *The dreaming universe* (New York: Simon & Schuster, 1994).

27. Baylor, G. W., & D. Deslauriers, "Dreams as problem solving: A method of study. Part II. A detailed analysis," *Imagination, Cognition and Personality* 7, no. 2 (1988): 23–45.

28. Feinstein, D., & S. Krippner, *Personal mythology: The psychology of your evolving self* (Los Angeles: Tarcher, 1989).

29. Deslauriers, D., & J. Cordts, "Dreams and current concerns: A narrative co-constitutive approach," *Dreaming*, 4 (1995): 250.

30. Hunt, H. T., *The Multiplicity of Dreams* (New Haven: Yale University Press, 1989): 95.

31. Ibid., p. x.

32. Foulkes, D., *Children's dreaming and the development of consciousness* (Cambridge: Harvard University Press, 1999).

33. Hartmann, E., *Dreams and nightmares: The new theory on the origin and meaning of dreams* (New York: Plenum Press, 1999).

34. Kilroe, P. A., "The dream as text, the dream as narrative," *Dreaming* 10 (2000): 125–137.

Chapter 3. Creative Dreams

1. Torrance, E. P., *Guiding creative talent* (Englewood Cliffs, NJ: Prentice-Hall, 1962).

2. Weisberg, R. W., *Creativity: Genius and other myths* (New York: W. H. Freeman, 1988).

3. Hall, J. A., "The use of dreams and dream interpretation in analysis." In *Jungian analysis*, edited by M. Stein (La Salle, IL: Open Court, 1982): 151–152.

4. Kaempffert, W. A., *A popular history of American invention*, vol. 2 (New York: Scribners, 1924).

5. Ullman, M., "Discussion: Dreaming—a creative process," *American Journal of Psychoanalysis* 24 (1964): 10–12.

6. Arieti, S, *Creativity: The magic synthesis* (New York: Basic Books, 1976): 10.

7. Ellis, H, *The world of dreams* (Boston: Houghton-Mifflin, 1911): 276.

8. de Becker, *The understanding of dreams and their influence on the history of man* (New York: Hawthorn Books, 1968).

9. Davé, R., "Effects of hypnotically induced dreams on creative problem solving," *Journal of Abnormal Psychology* 88 (1979): 293–302.

10. Barrios, M. V., & J. L. Singer, "The treatment of creative blocks: A comparison of waking imagery, hypnotic dream, and rational discussion techniques," *Imagination, Cognition and Personality* 1 (1981–1982): 89–109.

11. Evans, C., *Landscapes of the night* (New York: Washington Square Press, 1985): 234.

12. Krippner, S., & L. Faith, "Exotic dreams: A cross-cultural survey," *Dreaming* 11 (2001), 73–82.

13. Webb, W. B., "A historical perspective of dreams," in *Handbook of dreams: Research, theories and applications,* edited by B. B. Wolman (New York: Van Nostrand Reinhold, 1979): 3–19, 4.

14. Delaney, G., *Living your dreams,* revised edition (New York: Harper and Row, 1988): 23–26.

15. Schredl, M., "Creativity and dream recall," *Journal of Creative Behavior,* 29 (1995): 16–24.

16. Tonay, V., *The art of dreaming: Using your dreams to unlock your creativity* (Berkeley: Celestial Arts, 1995).

17. Krippner, S., & J. Dillard, *Dreamworking* (New York: Bearly Limited, 1988).

18. Barrett, D., *The committee of sleep* (New York: Crown Publishers, 2001).

Chapter 4. Lucid Dreams

1. Van Eeden, F. W., "A study of dreams," in *Altered states of consciousness: A book of readings,* edited by C. T.Tart (New York: John Wiley, 1969), 145–158.

2. Aristotle, "On dreams," in *Aristotle* vol. 1: edited by R. M. Hutchins, 702–706. (Chicago: Encyclopedia Britannica, 1952): 706.

3. de Saint Denys, H., *Dreams and how to guide them.* (London: Duckworth, 1982). (Originally published in 1867): 62.

4. Freud, S. *The interpretation of dreams,* 2nd ed., (New York: Avon, 1965. Original work published 1909): 611

5. Garfield, P., *Pathway to ecstasy: The way of the dream mandala* (New York: Holt, Rinehart and Winston, 1979).

6. Thurston, M., *How to interpret your dreams—practical techniques based on the Edgar Cayce readings* (Virginia Beach, VA: Association for Research and Enlightment Press, 1978).

7. Sechrist, E., *Dreams: Your magic mirror* (New York: Cowles, 1968).

8. Garfield, P., *Creative dreaming* (New York: Simon and Schuster, 1974).

9. LaBerge, S., *Lucid dreaming* (New York: Ballantine, 1985). Gackenbach, J. & J. Bosveld, *Control your dreams* (New York: Harper and Row, 1989). Godwin, M., *The lucid dreamer* (New York: Simon and Schuster, 1994).

10. Galvin, F., & E. Hartmann, "Nightmares: Terrors of the night," in *Dreamtime and dreamwork*, edited by S. Krippner (Los Angeles: J. P. Tarcher, 1990): 233–245.

11. LaBerge, S., "Exploring the world of lucid dreaming," *NightLight* 2, no. 3 (Summer 1990): 2.

12. Worsley, A., "Personal experiences of lucid dream," in *Conscious mind, sleeping brain*, edited by J. Gackenbach & S. LaBerge (New York: Plenum, 1988): 321–341

13. LaBerge, S., "The psychophysiology of lucid dreaming," in *Conscious Mind, Sleeping Brain*, edited by J. Gackenbach, & S. LaBerge (New York: Plenum Press, 1988): 135–153.

14. Gackenbach, J., "Women and meditators as gifted lucid dreamers," in *Dreamtime and dreamwork*, edited by S. Krippner (Los Angeles: J. P. Tarcher, 1990): 244–251.

15. Snyder, T. J., & J. Gackenbach, "Individual differences associated with lucid dreaming," in *Conscious Mind, Sleeping Brain* edited by J. Gackenbach & S. LaBerge (New York: Plenum Press, 1988): 221–259.

16. Gackenbach, J., "Psychological content of lucid versus nonlucid dreams," in *Conscious Mind, Sleeping Brain,* edited by J. Gackenbach & S. LaBerge (New York: Plenum Press, 1988): 181–218.

17. Weil, P., "Tibetan dream yoga," in *The transpersonal revolution in dreams* edited by M. A. Descamps, C. M. Bouchet, & P. Weil (Paris: Editions Trismegiste, 1988): 61–97.

18. Sparrow, S., *Lucid dreaming: Dawning of the clear light.* (Virginia Beach: ARE Press, 1974).

19. Bogzaran, F., "Experiencing the Divine in the lucid dream state," *Lucidity* 10, no. 1 & 2 (1991): 169–176.

20. Gillespie, G., "Lucid dreaming and mysticism: A personal observation," *Lucidity Letter,* no. 3 (1983): 2.

21. Gackenbach, J., & J. Bosveld, *Control your dreams* (New York: Harper and Row, 1989): 184.

22. Bogzaran, F., *Images of the lucid mind: A phenomenological study of lucid dreaming and modern painting* (Michigan: U.M.I., 1996): 209–213.

23. Ibid., 186.

24. Bogzaran, F., *Through the light: An exploration into consciousness* (San Francisco: Dream Creations, 1997): 26.

25. Tart, C. T., "From spontaneous event to lucidity," in *Conscious mind, sleeping brain,* edited by J. Gackenbach & S. LaBerge (New York: Plenum Press, 1988): 67–103.

26. Castaneda, C., *Tales of power* (New York: Simon and Schuster, 1974).

27. Stewart, K., "Dream theory in Malaysia," *Complex* 9 (1953–1954): 3–30.

28. Tart, op. cit., 97–99.

29. Price, R., & D. B. Cohen, "Lucid dream induction: An empirical observation.," in *Conscious mind, sleeping brain,* edited by J. Gackenbach & S. LaBerge (New York: Plenum Press, 1988): 105–134.

30. Price & Cohen, op. cit., 115–117.

31. Bogzaran, F., *Images of the lucid mind: A phenomenological study of lucid dreaming and modern painting* (Michigan U.M.I., 1996).

32. Levitan, L., "Sleep on the right, as a lion doth...," *NightLight* 3, no.3 (1991): 4.

33. LaBerge, S., & J. Gackenbach, "Lucid dreaming," in *Varieties of anomalous experience: Examining the scientific evidence,* edited by S. J. Lynn, E. Cardeña, & S. Krippner (Washington, DC: American Pscyhological Association, 2000): 151–182.

34. Krippner, S., & L. Faith "Exotic dreams: A cross-cultural survey, *Dreaming,* 11 (2001): 73–82.

35. Kelzer, K., *The sun and the shadow* (Virginia Beach, VA: A.R.E. Press, 1987): 220.

36. Blagrove, M., & S. J. Hartnell, "Lucid dreaming: Associations with internal locus of control for cognition and creativity," *Personality and Individual Differences* 28 (2000): 41–47.

Chapter 5. Out-of-Body Dreams

1. Greenhouse, H. B., *The astral journey* (Garden City, NY: Doubleday, 1975).

2. Tedlock, B., *Dreaming: Anthropological and psychological interpretations* (Melbourne, Australia: Cambridge University Press, 1987).

3. Basso, E. B., "The implications of a progressive theory of dreaming," in *Dreaming: Anthropological and psychological interpretations,* edited by B. Tedlock (Melbourne, Australia: Cambridge University Press, 1987): 89.

4. Blackmore, S., "A postal survey of OBEs and other experiences." *Journal of the Society for Psychical Research* 52 (1984): 227–244.

5. Green, C. E., *Out-of-the-body experiences* (London: Hamish Hamilton, 1968).

6. Blackmore, S., "Have you ever had an OBE? The wording of the question," *Journal of the Society for Psychical Research* 51 (1984): 292–302.

7. Levitan, L., & S. LaBerge, "In the mind and out-of-body," *NightLight* 3, no. 2 (1991): 1–4, 9.

8. Gabbard, G. O., & S. W. Twemlow, *With the eyes of the mind* (New York: Praeger, 1984).

9. Krippner, S., & L. Faith, "Exotic dreams: A cross-cultural survey," *Dreaming* 11 (2001): 73–82.

10. Blackmore, S., "Near-death experiences: In or out of the body?" *Skeptical Inquirer* (Fall, 1991): 34–45.

11. Levitan, L., & S. LaBerge, "Questions and answers," *NightLight* 2 (1990): 13.

12. Levitan, L., & S. LaBerge, "Mind in body or body in mind?" *NightLight* 3 no. 3 (1991): 1–3.

13. Garfield, P., *Creative dreaming* (New York: Simon and Schuster, 1974).

14. Mindell, A., *Working with the dreaming body.* (London: Routledge and Kegan Paul, 1985).

15. Gendlin, E., *Let your body interpret your dreams* (Wilmette, IL: Chiron, 1986).

16. Alvarado, C., "Out-of-body experiences," in *Varieties of anomalous experience: Examining the scientific evidence,* S. J. Lynn, E. Cardeña, & S. Krippner (Washington, DC. American Psychological Association, 2000): 183–218.

Chapter 6. Pregnancy Dreams

1. Pinart, A., "Notes sur les Koloches," *Bulletins de la Societe d'Anthropologie de Paris,* 7 (1872): 788–811.

2. Maybruck, P., "Pregnancy and dreams," in *Dreamtime and dreamwork,* edited by S. Krippner (Los Angeles: J. P. Tarcher, 1990): 143–151.

3. Freud, S. *The Interpretation of Dreams* (New York: Avon Books, 1966): 437.

4. Van de Castle, R. L., & P. Kinder, "Dream content during pregnancy," *Psychophysiology* 4 (1968): 375.

5. Garfield, P., *Woman's bodies, women's dreams* (New York: Ballantine Books, 1988): 178–181.

6. Van de Castle, R. L., *The psychology of dreaming* (Morristown, NJ: General Learning Press, 1991): 40–43.

7. Krippner, S., N. Posner, W. Pomerance, & S. Fischer, "An investigation of dream content during pregnancy," *Journal of the Society of Psychosomatic Dentistry and Medicine* 21, (1974): 111–123.

8. Maybruck, P., *Pregnancy and dreams*(Los Angeles: Jeremy P. Tarcher, 1989).

9. Winget, C., & F. Kapp, "The relationship of the manifest content of dreams to duration of childbirth in primiparae," *Psychosomatic Medicine*, 34 (1972): 313–320.

10. Albon, S. L., "The usefulness of dreams during pregnancy," *International Journal of Pscyho-Analysis* 75, (1994): 291–299.

11. Sered, S., "Pregnant dreaming: Search for a typology of a proposed dream genre, *Social Science and Medicine* 34 (1992): 1405–1411.

12. Siegel, A. B., *Dreams that can change your life* (Los Angeles: Jeremy P. Tarcher, 1991): 72–73.

13. Zayas, L. H., "Thematic features in the manifest dreams of expectant fathers," *Clinical and Social Work Journal* 16 (1988): 282–296.

14. Zayas, L. H., "As son becomes father: Reflections of expectant fathers on their fathers in dreams," *Psychoanalytic Review* 74 (1987): 443–464.

15. Harkness, S., "The cultural mediation of postpartum depression," *Medical Anthropology Quarterly* 1 (1987): 194–209.

16. Seligson, F. J., *Oriental birth dreams*(Elizabeth, NJ: Hollym, 1989).

17. Stukane, E., *The dream worlds of pregnancy*. (New York: Quill, 1985).

18. Maybruck, P. *Pregnancy and dreams* (Los Angeles: Jeremy P. Tarcher, 1989).

19. "Dreaming of a Baby," *Time* (26 June 2000): 82.

20. Krippner, S., & L. Faith, "Exotic dreams: A cross-cultural survey," *Dreaming*, 11 (2001): 73–82.

21. Trad, P., "Adaptation to developmental transformation during the various phases of motherhood," *Journal of the American Academy of Psychoanalysis* 19 (1991): 403–421.

Chapter 7. Healing Dreams

1. Owsei, T., *Hippocrates in a world of Pagans and Christians* (Baltimore: John Hopkins University Press, 1991): 188.

2. Ross, W.D., *The works of Aristotle*, vol. 3 (Oxford, England: Clarendon): 454–458, 463.

3. Gray, L., "Healing among Native American Indians," *Psi Research* 3 (September–December 1984): 141–149.

4. Hobbes, T., "Dreams caused by 'distemper of inward parts,'" in *The world of dreams* edited by R. L. Woods (New York: Random House, 1947): 214–216.

5. Kasatkin, V. N., *Theory of dreams*(Leningrad: Meditsina, 1967).

6. Sacks, O., "How dreams reflect neurological disorders," in *Dreamscaping*, edited by S. Krippner & M. R. Waldman (Los Angeles: Lowell House, 1999): 259–265.

7. Krippner, S., & L. Faith, "Exotic dreams: A cross-cultural survey,' *Dreaming* 11 (2001): 73–82.

8. Dement, W., "Experimental dream studies," in *Science and Psychoanalysis* edited by H. Masserman (New York: Grune and Stratton, 1964): 129–162.

9. Lamberg, L., "Night pilot," *Psychology Today* (July/August 1988): 35–42.

10. Barasch, M. I., *Healing Dreams: Exploring the dreams that can transform your life,* (New York: Riverhead Books, 2000): 2–3.

11. Simonton, O. C., S. Matthews-Simonton, & J. Creighton, *Getting well again* (Los Angeles: Jeremy P. Tarcher, 1978).

12. Smith, R. C., "A possible biological role of dreaming," *Psychotherapy and Psychosomatics* 41 (1984): 167–176.

13. Smith, R. C., "Traumatic dreams as an early warning of health problems," in *Dreamtime and dreamwork*, edited by S. Krippner (Los Angeles: Jeremy P. Tarcher, 1990): 226–227.

14. Smith, R. C., "Do dreams reflect a biological state?" *Journal of Nervous and Mental Disease* 147 (1987): 587–604.

15. Boersma, F. J., "Dreamwork with a cancer patient: The emergence of transpersonal healing," *Medical Hypnoanalysis Journal* 5 (1990): 3–23.

16. Wilmer, H. A., "Combat nightmares: Toward a theory of violence," *Spring* 32 (1986): 120–139.

17. Kellogg E. W. III, "A personal experience in lucid dream healing," *Lucidity Letter* 8, no. 1 (1989): 6–7.

18. Moss, R., *Conscious dreaming* (New York: Crown Trade Paperbacks, 1996).

19. Moss, R. *Dreaming true* (New York: Pocket Books, 2000): 304–305.

20. Garfield, P., *The healing power of dreams* (New York: Simon and Schuster, 1991): 25–29.

21. Aristotle, "On prophesying by dreams," in *Aristotle*, vol. 1, edited by R. M. Hutchins, (Chicago: Encyclopedia Britannica, 1952): 707–709.

22. Moss, R., *Dreaming true* (New York: Pocket Books, 2000): 259.

23. Rocca, R., "The analytic cure mediated by the vivid dream," *Acta Psiquiatrica y Psicologica de America Latina* 3 (1985): 284–290.

24. Ullman, M., "Group dream work and healing," *Contemporary Psychoanalysis* 20 (1984): 120–130.

Chapter 8. Dreams within Dreams

1. Karacan, I., "Uterine activity during sleep," *Sleep* 9 (1986): 393–397.

2. Fisher, C., "Cycle of penile erection synchronous with dreaming (REM) sleep," *Archives of General Psychiatry* 12 (1965): 29–45.

3. Garfield, P., *The healing power of dreams* (New York: Simon and Schuster, 1991).

4. Berman, L. E., "Primal scene significance of a dream within a dream," *International Journal of Psycho-Analysis* 66 (1985): 75–76.

5. Silber, A., "A significant dream within a dream," *Journal of the American Psychoanalytic Association* 31 (1983): 899–915.

6. Lipschitz, F., "The dream within a dream: Proflection vs. reflection," *Contemporary Psychoanalysis* 26 (1990): 716–731.

7. Tractenberg, M., "O significado dos sonhos em Freud, Garman & Kemper," *Jornal Brasileiro de Psiquiatria* 30 (1981): 317–322.

8. Krippner, S., & L. Faith, "Exotic dreams: A cross-cultural survey." *Dreaming* 11 (2001): 73–82.

9. Baylor G. W., & D. Deslauriers, *Le rêve, sa nature, sa fonction et une méthode d'analyse.* (Silléry, Québec: Presses de l'université du Québec, 1987).

10. Feinstein, D., & S. Krippner, *The mythic path* (New York: Putnam/Jeremy P. Tarcher, 1997): 290.

Chapter 9. Collective Dreams

1. Van de Castle, R. L., *Our dreaming mind* (New York: Ballantine 1994): 49.

2. Magallón, L. L., *Mutual dreaming* (New York: Simon and Schuster, 1997).

3. Krippner, S., & L. Faith, "Exotic dreams: A cross-cultural survey," *Dreaming,* 11 (2000): 72–83.

4. Hart, H., *The enigma of survival* (London: Rider, 1959).

5. Faraday, A., *The dream game* (New York: Harper and Row, 1974).

6. Reed, H., *Getting help from your dreams* (Virginia Beach: Inner Vision, 1985).

7. Ibid., pp. 82–83.

8. Thurston, M., "An investigation of behavior and personality correlates of psi incorporating a humanistic research approach (Unpublished doctoral dissertation, Saybrook Institute 1978).

9. Magallón L. L., *Mutual dreaming.* (New York: Simon and Schuster, 1997).

10. Shohet, R., *Dream sharing* (Wellingborough, Northamptonshire, England: Turnstone Press, 1985).

11. Magallón, L. L., & B. Shor, "Shared dreaming: Joining together in dream-time," in *Dreamtime and dreamwork*, edited by S. Krippner (Los Angeles: Jeremy P. Tarcher, 1990), 252–260.

12. Ibid., pp. 257–259.

13. Bogzaran, F., personal correspondence with L. L. Magallón, 1996.

14. Castaneda, C., *The art of dreaming* (New York: Harper Collins, 1993).

15. du Maurier, G., *Peter Ibbetson* (New York: Harper & Brothers, 1892).

16. Lessing, D., *The making of the representative for planet eight* (New York: Vintage Books, 1983).

Chapter 10. Telepathic Dreams

1. Cicero, M. T., "Argument against taking dreams seriously" in *The World of Dreams*, edited by R. L. Woods (New York: Random House, 1947), 203–204.

2. Sidgwick, H. E. Sidgwick & A. Johnson, "Report on the census of hallucinations," *Proceedings of the Society for Psychical Research* 10 (1894): 25–422.

3. Marks, D., & P. McKellar, "The nature and function of eidetic imagery," *Journal of Mental Imagery* 6 (1982): 1–124.

4. Posey, T. B. & M. E. Losch, "Auditory hallucinations of hearing voices in 375 subjects." *Imagination, Cognition and Personality* 3 (1983–1984): 99–113.

5. Palmer, J. A., "Community mail survey of psychic experiences," *Journal of the American Society for Psychical Research* 73 (1979): 221–251.

6. Ibid.

7. Myers, F. W. H., *Human personality and its survival of bodily death* (London: Longmans, Green, 1903).

8. Gurney, E., F. W. H. Myers, & F. Podmore, *Phantasms of the living* (London: Trubner, 1886).

9. Krippner, S., & M. Ullman, "Telepathy and dreams: A controlled experiment with electro-encephalogram-electro-oculogram monitoring," *Journal of Nervous and Mental Disease* 151 (1970): 394–403.

10. Krippner, S., "An experimental approach to the anomalous dream," in *Dream images: A call to mental arms*, edited by J. Gackenbach & A. A. Sheikh (Amityville, NY: Baywood Publishing, 1991): 31–54.

11. See Globus, G. G., et al., "An appraisal of telepathic communication in dreams," *Psychophysiology* 4 (1968): 365; Hall, C. S., "Experimente zor telepathischen Boein-flussung von Traümen," *Zeitschrift fur Parapsychologie und Grenzgebiete der*

Psychologie 10 (1967): 18–47; Van de Castle, R. L., "The study of GESP in a group setting by means of dreams," *Journal of Parapsychology* 35 (1971): 312; and Hearne, K., "A dream-telepathy study using a home 'dream machine,'" *Journal of the Society for Psychical Research* 54 (1987): 139–142.

12. Ullman, M., S. Krippner, & A. Vaughan, *Dream telepathy: Experiments in nocturnal ESP*, second edition (Jefferson, NC: McFarland, 1989).

13. Persinger, M. A. & S. Krippner, "Dream ESP experiments and geomagnetic activity," *Journal of the American Society for Psychical Research* 83 (1989): 101–116.

14. Krippner, S., & M. Persinger, "Evidence for enhanced congruence between dreams and distant target material during periods of decreased geomagnetic activity," *Journal for Scientific Exploration* 10 (1996): 487–493.

15. Krippner, S., & L. Faith, "Exotic dreams: A cross-cultural survey," in *Dreaming* 11 (2001): 72–83.

16. Auerbach, L., "Working with psychic dreams," *Fate* (February 1992): 19–22, 27, 29, 32–34.

17. Parapsychological Association, "Terms and methods in parapsychological research," *Journal of Humanistic Psychology* 29 (1989): 394–399.

Chapter 11. Clairvoyant Dreams

1. Vilenskaya, L., "In the pages of the Soviet press," *Psi Research* 5, no. 1–2 (1985–1986): 11–15.

2. Ryback, D., "Future memory as holographic process: A scientific model for psychic dreams," *Journal of Creative Behavior* 20 (1985): 283–295.

3. Tyrrell, G. N. M., *Science and psychical phenomena* (New Hyde Park: University Books, 1961): 24–25.

4. Tolaas, J., "The puzzle of psychic dreams," in *Dreamtime and dreamwork*, edited by S. Krippner (Los Angeles: J. P. Tarcher, 1990): 261–270.

5. Krippner, S. "An experimental approach to the anomalous dream," in *Dream images: A call to mental arms*, edited by J. Gackenbach & A. A. Sheik (Amityville, NY: Baywood Publishing, 1991): 31–54.

6. Ibid., p. 38–39.

7. Ullman, M., S. Krippner, & and A. Vaughan, *Dream telepathy: Experiments in nocturnal ESP*, second edition (Jefferson, NC McFarland, 1989): 67–68.

8. Ibid., p. 121.

9. Harley, T., "Psi missing in a dream clairvoyance experiment," *Journal of the Society for Psychical Research* 56 (1989): 1–7.

10. Wagner-Pacifici, R., & H. J. Bershady, "Portents or Confessions: Authoritative Readings of a dream text," *Symbolic Interaction* 16 (1990):129–143.

11. Krippner, S., "A psychic dream? Be careful who you tell!" *Dream Network* 14 no. 3 (1995): 35–36.

12. Krippner, S., "The dream models of the Mapuche of Chile," *Dream Time* 14–15, no. 2 (1996): 5.

13. Auerbach, L., *Psychic dreams* (New York: Warner Books, 1991).

Chapter 12. Precognitive Dreams

1. Homer, *The Odyssey*, in *The Iliad of Homer; The Odyssey* edited by R. M. Hutchins (Encyclopedia Britannica, 1952): 181–322.

2. Aristotle. "On prophesying by dreams," in *Aristotle* vol. 1, edited by R. M. Hutchins (Chicago: Encyclopedia Britannica, 1952): 707–709.

3. Shakespeare, W. *Julius Caesar*, in *Shakespeare*, vol. 1, edited by R. M. Hutchins (Chicago: Encyclopedia Britannica, 1952): 568–596.

4. Brook, S., *The Oxford book of dreams* (Oxford, England: Oxford University Press, 1983): 143–144.

5. Bradford, S., *Harriet Tubman: The Moses of her people* (Gloucester, MA: Peter Smith, 1981). (Original work published 1869).

6. Sechrist, E., *Dreams: your magic mirror* (New York: Coales, 1968): 43.

7. Krippner, S. F., and J. Dillard, *Dreamworking* (Buffalo NY: Bearly, 1988): 99.

8. Elovitz, P. (1988). "Dreams as a psychohistorical source," *Journal of Psychohistory* 16 (1988): 289–296.

9. Rhine, L. E., "Precognition and intervention" *Journal of Parapsychology* 19 (1955): 1–34.

10. Rhine, L. E., *ESP in life and lab: Tracing hidden channels.* (New York: Macmillan 1967).

11. Dunne, J. W. *An experiment with time* (New York: Hillary, 1958). (Original work published in 1927).

12. Hall, C. S., & R. L. Van de Castle, *The content analysis of dreams* (New York: Appleton-Century-Crofts, 1966).

13. Krippner, S., M. Ullman, & C. Honorton, "A precognitive dream study with a single subject," *Journal of the American Society for Psychical Research*, 65 (1971): 192–203.

14. Krippner, S., C. Honorton, & M. Ullman, "A second precognitive dream study with Malcolm Bessent," *Journal of the American Society for Psychical Research* 66 (1972): 269–279.

15. Zusne, L., & W. H. Jones, *Anomalistic psychology: A study of extraordinary phenomena of behavior and experience.* (Hillsdale, NJ: Lawrence Erlbaum, 1982): 260–261.

16. Child, I. L., "Psychology and anomalous observations: The question of ESP in dreams," *American Psychologist* 4 (1985): 1219–1230.

17. Hearne, K., *Visions of the future: An investigation of premonitions* (London: Aquarian/Harper Collins, 1989).

18. Ryback, D., & L. Sweitzer, *Dreams that come true: Their psychic and transformative powers* (New York: Doubleday, 1988).

19. Stokes, D. M., "Theoretical parapsychology," in *Advances in Parapsychological Research* vol. 5, edited by S. Krippner (Jefferson, NC: McFarland, 1987): 77–189.

20. Tolaas, J., "Vigilance theory and psi," *Journal of the American Society for Psychical Research,* 80 (1986): 357–373.

21. Ehrenwald, J., *The ESP experience: A psychiatric validation* (New York: Basic Books, 1978).

22. Jaffé, A., *From the life and work of C.G. Jung* (New York: Harper Colophon, 1971).

23. Stevenson, I., *Telepathic impressions* (Charlottesville: University Press of Virginia, 1970).

24. Tractenberg, M., "O significado do sanhas em Freud, Garman, and Kemper," *Jornal Brasileiro de Psiquiatria* 30 (1981): 317–322.

25. Ryback and Sweitzer, op. cit.; Eppinger, R., & T. R. Pallo, *Sonhos, parapsicologia e aconselhamento* (Curitiba, Brazil: Pestalozzi, 1997).

26. Krippner, S., A. Vaughan, & J. Spottiswoode, "Geomagnetic factors in subjective precognitive dream experiences," *Journal of the Society for Psychical Research* 64 (2000): 109–118.

27. Stowell, M. S. "Researching precognitive dreams," *Journal of the American Society for Psychical Research* 89 (1995): 117–151.

Chapter 13. *Past Life Dreams*

1. McDonald, P., *Dreams: Night language of the soul* (Baton Rouge, LA: Mosaic Books, 1985): 9.

2. Pinart, A., "Escrits en les Koloches," *Bulletins de la Société d'Anthropologie de Paris,* 7 (1972): 788–811.

3. Matlock, J. G., "Past life memory case studies," *Advances in Parapsychological Research,* volume 6, edited by S. Krippner (Jefferson, NC: McFarland, 1990): 184–267.

4. Ibid., p. 222.

5. Haynes, R., "Why I do not accept the theory of reincarnation" in *Reincarnation: Fact or fable?* edited by A. Berger & J. Berger (London: Aquarian/Harper Collins, 1991): 131–142.

6. Ryall, E.W., *Born twice: Total recall of a seventeenth-century life* (New York: Harper & Row, 1974).

7. Rogo, D. S., "States of consciousness factors in reincarnation cases," in *Reincarnation: Fact or fable?* edited by A. Berger & J. Berger (London: Aquarian/Harper Collins, 1991): 16–30.

8. Ibid., pp. 19–20.

9. Stevenson, I., *Twenty cases suggestive of reincarnation* second edition (Charlottesville, VA: University Press of Virginia, 1974): 21.

10. Ibid., pp. 350–351.

11. Krippner, S., & L. Faith, "Exotic dreams: A cross-cultural survey," *Dreaming* (2001): 11: 73–82.

12. Ryback, D., & L. Sweitzer, *Dreams that come true: Their psychic and transformative powers* (New York: Doubleday, 1988).

Chapter 14. Initiation Dreams

1. Kracke, W. H., "Everyone who dreams has a bit of Shaman": Cultural and personal meanings of dreams: Evidence from the Amazon," *Psychiatric Journal of the University of Ottawa* 12 (1991): 65–72.

2. Winkelman, M., *Shamanism: The neural ecology of consciousness and healing* (Westport, CT: Bergin & Garvey, 2000).

3. Halifax, J., *Shaman: The wounded healer* (New York: Crossroad, 1982): 72.

4. Norman, J., "Mexico's people of myth and magic," *National Geographic,* (June, 1997): 832–853.

5. Peters, L. G. & D. Price-Williams, "Towards an experiential analysis of shamanism," *American Ethnologist* 7 (1981): 398–418.

6. Topper, M. D., "The traditional Navajo medicine man: Therapist, counselor, and community leader," *Journal of Psychoanalytic Anthropology* 10 (1987): 217–249.

7. Wallace, A. F. C., "Dreams and the wishes of the soul: A type of psychoanalytic theory among the seventeenth century Iroquois," *American Anthropologist* 60 (1958): 234–248.

8. Roheim, G.,*The gates of the dream* (New York: International University Press, 1952): 193.

9. Krippner, S., "Tribal shamans and their travels into dreamtime," in *Dreamtime and dreamwork*, edited by S. Krippner (Los Angeles: Jeremy P. Tarcher, 1990): 185–193.

10. Siegel, A. B., *Dreams that can change your life* (Los Angeles: Jeremy P. Tarcher, 1990): 128–130.

11. Cowell, A., "Politics are turning volatile: Enter a Mussolini," *New York Times International* (24February 1992): 8.

12. Marjasch, S., "On the dream psychology of C. G. Jung," in *The dream and human societies*, edited by G. E. Grunebaum & R. Callois (Berkeley: University of California Press, 1966): 145–161.

13. Ewing, K. P., "The dream of spiritual initiation and the organization of self representations among Pakistani Sufis," *American Ethnologist*, 17 (1990): 56–74.

14. Naifeh, S., "Archetypal foundations of addiction and recovery," *Journal of Analytical Psychology* 40 (1995): 133–159.

15. Krippner, S., "A call to heal: Entry patterns in Brazilian mediumship," in *Altered states of consciousness and mental health: A cross-cultural perspective*, edited by C. A. Ward (Los Angeles: Sage, 1989): 186–206.

16. Krippner, S., & L. Faith, "Exotic dreams: A cross-cultural survey," *Dreaming* 11(2001): 73–82.

17. Biele, P., "A phenomenological investigation of a breakthrough dream experience," (Unpublished masters thesis, University of British Columbia, 1986).

18. Krippner, S., & A. Thompson, "A 10-facet model of dreaming applied to dream practices of sixteen Native American cultural groups," *Dreaming* 6 (1997): 71–96.

19. Hill, C. E., *Working with dreams in psychotherapy* (New York: Guilford, 1996).

20. Clark, A. J., "Working with dreams in group counseling: Advantages and disadvantages," *Journal of Counseling and Development* 73 (1994): 141–143.

21. Ullman, M., "The enduring mystery of dreams," *Dream Appreciation* 5, no. 3 (2000): 1–4, 6.

Chapter 15. *Spiritual and Visitation Dreams*

1. Genesis (28: 12). *Bible*, King James Version, (American Bible Society, New York, 1816:27.

2. Hunt, H., *The multiplicity of dreams: Memory, imagination, and consciousness* (New Haven: Yale University Press 1989): 9.

3. Knapp, B. L., *Dream and image* (Troy, NY: Whitson 1979): 7.

4. Hughes, J. D., "The dreams of Xenophon the Athenian," *Journal of Psychohistory* 14 (1987): 271–282.

5. Rousselle, R., "The dreams of Vibia Perpetua: Analysis of a female Christian martyr," *Journal of Psychohistory* 14 (19870): 193–206.

6. Baha'u'llah, *The seven valleys and the four valleys* (Evanston, IL: Baha'i Publishing Trust, 1945).

7. Jung, C. G., *The integration of the personality* (London: Kegan Paul, 1940).

8. Stevens, A., *Archetypes: A natural history of the self* (New York: William Morrow, 23, 1982).

9. Murdock, G. P., & D. R. White, "Standard cross cultural sample," *Ethnology* 8 (1969): 329–369.

10. Nielsen, T., "Reflections on dreaming, computers, and growth: An interview with Alan Moffitt," *Association for the Study of Dreams Newsletter* (March/April 1989): 7–9.

11. von Franz, M.-L., *On dreams and death: A Jungian interpretation* (London: Shambhala, 1986).

12. Gerne, M., *Problem-solving in dreams concerning the mourning process* (Unpublished doctoral dissertation: University of Zurich, 1982).

13. Bogzaran, F., *Experiencing the Divine in the lucid dream state*, (Michigan, U.M.I, 1990): 26.

14. Ibid., pp. 13–39.

15. Bulkeley, K., "Conversion dreams," *Pastoral Psychology* 44, no.1 (1995): 3–11.

16. Wright, S. H., "Paranormal contact with the dying: Fourteen contemporary death coincidences," *Journal of the Society for Psychical Research* 63 *(1999):* 258–267.

17. Delaney, G., "The spiritual dimension of dreams," *Venture Inward* (January/February 1992): 37.

18. Howe, L. T., "Dream interpretation in spiritual guidance," *Journal of Pastoral Care* 40 (1986): 262–272.

19. Halligan, F., & J. Shea, "Sacred images in dreamwork: The journey into self as journey into God," *Pastoral Psychology* 40, no.1 (1991): 29–38.

20. Shalev, S., "Individuation as freedom," *Israel Journal of Psychiatry and Related Sciences* 22 (1985): 61–69.

21. Taylor, J., *Where people fly and water runs uphill: Using dreams to tap the wisdom of the unconscious* (New York: Warner Books, 1992).

22. Krippner, S., & L. Faith, "Exotic dreams: A cross-cultural survey," *Dreaming* 11 (2001): 73–82.

23. Krippner, S., C. Jaeger, & L. Faith, "Identifying and utilizing spiritual content in dreams," *Dreaming* 11 (2001): 121–134.

24. Savary, L. M., P. H. Berne, & S. K. Williams, *Dreams and spiritual growth: A Christian approach to dreamwork* (New York: Paulist Press, 1984): 179–180.

25. Lawson, L., *Visitations from the afterlife* (San Francisco: Harper San Francisco, 2000).

26. Bulkeley, K., *The wilderness of dreams: Exploring the religious meaning of dreams in modern Western culture* (Albany: State University of New York Press, 1994): 205–214.

27. Bulkeley, K., *Spiritual dreams: A cross-cultural and historical journey* (New York: Paulist Press, 1995).

Chapter 16. *Dreams and Personal Mythology*

1. Feinstein, D., & S. Krippner, *The mythic path* (New York: Penguin/Jeremy P. Tarcher, 1997).

2. Ullman, M., "The experiential dream group," in *Handbook of dreams: Research, theories and applications,* edited by B. B. Wolman (New York: Van Nostrand Reinhold, 1979): 410.

3. Kuiken, D., & L. Smith, "Impactful dreams and metaphor generation," *Dreaming* 1 (1991):135–145.

4. Krippner, S., & A. Combs, "Self-organization in the dreaming brain," *Journal of Mind and Behavior* 21: 399–412; 401–402.

5. Feinstein, D., "The dream as a window on your evolving mythology," in *Dreamtime and dreamwork,* edited by S. Krippner (New York: Tarcher/Putnam): 21–33.

6. Van de Castle, R. L., *Our dreaming mind* (New York: Ballantine books, 1994): xviii.

7. Munroe, R. L., S. B. Nerlove, R. H. Munroe, & R. E. Daniels, "Effects of population density on food concerns in three East African societies," *Journal of Health and Social Behavior* 10 (1969): 161–171.

8. Mauron, C., *Des mètaphores obsèdantes au mythe personnel: Introduction à la psychocritique* (Paris: Librarie J. Corti, 1962).

9. Levine, R., *Dreams and deeds: Achievement motivation in Nigeria* (Chicago: University of Chicago Press, 1966).

10. Cartwright, R., "Affect and dream work from an information processing point of view," *Journal of Mind and Behavior* 7 (1986): 411–428.

11. Tedlock, B.,"The new anthropology of dreaming," *Dreaming* 1 (1991): 161–178.

12. Hobson, J. A., *Dreaming as delerium: How the brain goes out of its mind* (Cambridge, MA: MIT Press, 1999).

13. Globus, G. G., *Dream life, wake life* (Albany: State University of New York Press, 1987).

14. Boss, M., *"I dreamt last night..."* (New York: Gardner Press, 1977): 10.

15. Foulkes, D., *Dreaming: A cognitive-psychological analysis* (Hillsdale, NJ: Lawrence Erlbaum, 1985): 46–47.

16. Farrell, B., "What dreams are made of," *New York Review of Books* (15 June (1989): 28–29.

17. Valadez, A. A., *Historia de la investigación de los sueños* (Mexico City: Centro de Investigación y Estudio de los Suenos, 1956).

18. Kahn, D., S. Krippner, & A. Combs, "Dreaming and the self-organizing brain," *Journal of Consciousness Studies* 7 (2000):4–11.

19. Globus, G., *The postmodern brain* (Amsterdam: John Benjamin's, 1999).

20. Ullman, M., "Dreaming, altered states of consciousness and the problem of vigilance," *Journal of Nervous and Mental Disease* 133 (1961): 529–535.

21. McCarley, R. W., & J. A., Hobson."The form of dreams and the biology of sleep," in *Handbook of Dreams: Research, Theories and Applications*, edited by B. B. Wolman (New York: Van Nostrand Reinhold, 1979).

22. Tart, C. T., "World simulation in waking and dreaming," *Journal of Mental Imagery* 11 (1987): 145–158.

23. Hardy, C., *Networks of meaning: A bridge between mind and matter* (Westport, CT: Praeger, 1998).

24. Ullman, M., "Dreaming consciousness: More than a bit player in the search for answers to the mind/body problem," *Journal of Scientific Exploration* 13 (1999): 91–112.

25. Krippner, S., "From chaos to telepathy: New models for understanding dreams," in *Dreamscaping* edited by S. Krippner & M. R. Waldman (Los Angeles: Lowell House, 1999): 265–269.

26. Combs, A., & S. Krippner, "Dream, sleep and waking reality: A dynamical view of two states of consciousness," in *Toward a science of consciousness: The second Tucson discussions and Debates* edited by S. Hameroff, A. W. Kaszniak, & A. C. Scott in (Cambridge, MA: MIT Press, 1996): 487–493.

27. Krippner, S., "Dreams and the development of a personal mythology," *Journal of Mind and Behavior* 7 (1986):449–461.

28. Krippner, S., Personal communication with Huichol shaman don José Rios (1977).

29. Radha, S. *Realities of the dreaming mind* (Spokane, WA: Timeless Books, 1994).

Glossary

This glossary presents our definitions of the key terms used in dream research.

Dream interpretation is an attempt by someone (often the dreamer) to attribute meaning to the content of dream reports for purposes of counseling, psychotherapy, and/or personal growth. A great variety of approaches to dream interpretation exists. Some approaches are contradictory, and some investigators insist that dream content is essentially meaningless.

Dreams are series of images, typically emotionally-toned and reported in narrative form, that occur during sleep. They can be recalled spontaneously upon (or somewhat after) awakening, or can be evoked if someone is awakened from REM sleep. On some occasions they are evoked following an awakening from non-REM sleep.

An *EEG* (or electroencephalogram) is a graphic depiction (voltage vs. time) of the brain's electrical potentials recorded by scalp electrodes and usually delineated by ink tracings (as are the EMG and EOG).

An *EMG* (or electromyogram) is a graphic depiction of muscle potentials that measures the amount and nature of muscle activity at the site from which the recording is taken.

An *EOG* (or electrooculogram) is a graphic depiction of eye movement potentials that measures the amount and nature of muscle activity around the eyes.

Hypnagogia is the condition immediately preceding sleep. Hypnagogic reports typically include imagery (such as visual, auditory, kinesthetic), but little narrative.

Hypnopompia is the condition immediately preceding awakening. Hypnopompic reports typically include imagery (such as visual, auditory, kinesthetic), but little narrative.

Nightmares are reports of anxiety-provoking dreams marked by confusion, fear, and/or horror.

Non-REM mentation reports, given after awakening from non-REM sleep, are characterized by narrative but little or no imagery. Similar reports are sometimes, but infrequently, evoked after awakening from REM sleep, in which case they are often called *non-dream mentation reports.*

Non-REM sleep consists of four sleep stages that occur in a cyclical pattern. Stage One sleep occurs immediately after sleep begins, with a pattern of low-amplitude and rapid-frequency EEG tracings; Stage Two sleep has characteristic EEG tracings of twelve to sixteen cycles per second, known as *sleep spindles*; Stages Three and Four have progressive further slowing of EEG tracings and an increase in their amplitude. Over a period of about ninety minutes after sleep begins, most people have passed through the four stages of non-REM sleep and emerge from Stages one to four into the first period of REM sleep. Non-REM sleep is also referred to as *orthodox sleep* or *S-sleep* (because of its characteristic synchronized EEG tracings).

Rapid eye movements (REMs) are conjugate, coordinated horizontal and/or vertical eye movements, occurring rapidly during sleep and less frequently during napping, daydreaming, "hypnotic dreaming," and other times when one's attention is turned inward.

REM sleep is a recurring stage of sleep, characterized by rapidly occurring conjugate eye movements, loss of muscle tonus, and desynchronized EEG brain wave activity. REM sleep is also referred to as *Stage One REM sleep, Stage REM, D-sleep* (because of its characteristic desynchronized EEG tracings), and *paradoxical sleep* (because its EEG tracings resemble wakefulness). REM sleep recurs in approximately ninety or one hundred minute intervals in humans; it also occurs in non-human sleep (among most mammals and—in short intervals—among birds).

Sleep terrors (or *night terrors*) are episodic conditions usually occurring during Stage Four sleep, marked by panic, confusion, and poor recall. Characteristically, the reports of sleep terrors do not include imagery or narrative. They occur developmentally, peaking by two years of age.

Sleepwalking is an episodic condition usually occurring during non-REM sleep, marked by motor activity such as walking. The reports of sleepwalking rarely involve imagery or narrative. Sleepwalking peaks in early adolescence.

Tonic and phasic events in REM sleep have been observed by dream researchers. Tonic events are those long-lasting changes that are, for the most part, continuously maintained throughout the duration of REM sleep (for example, low-voltage and irregular EEG patterns, EMG suppression, the elevation of brain temperature). Phasic events are short-lasting and discontinuous (for example, rapid eye movements as measured by the EOG, muscular twitching, higher but irregular breathing and pulse rates, bursts of sharp EEG brain wave patterns ["spikes"] from the pontine-geniculate-occipital region of the brain).

Sleep is the recurring period of relative physical and psychological disengagement from one's environment characterized by a lack of conscious awareness.

Wakefulness is the recurring period of relative physical and psychological engagement with one's environment characterized by the presence of various types of conscious awareness.

Author Index

Thurston, Mark, 87
Tolaas, Jon, 110, 123
Tonay, Veronica, 31
Torrance, E. Paul, 23
Tractenberg, Moises, 80, 124
Trad, Paul, 65
Tyrrell, G.N.M., 109

Ullman, Montague, 18, 24, 76, 97,
    145, 158, 164–166

Van de Castle, Robert L., 8, 59, 84,
    98, 102, 120, 160–161

Van Eeden, F.W., 33
Vaughan, Alan, 125
von Franz, Marie-Louise, 150–151

Weil, Pierre, 38
Weisberg, R.W., 24
White, Rhea, 4
Wilmer, Harry A., 73
Wolf, Fred Alan, 21
Wright, Sylvia, 153

Zayas, Luis, 61

Subject / Name Index

aborigines, Australian, 127, 137, 139
abortion dreams. *See* dreams
African, tribes, 127
Aguaruna tribe, 46
Alevi, 128
Alexander the Great, 57
Algonquin Indians, 138
Almufti, Zahra, 115–117
altered states of consciousness, 7, 43,
    136, 138, 155
ambular, 9
American Indian tribes, 68, 127–128,
    137
Ammon, 57
amplification, 13
ancestor. *See* deceased, dreams of
animus, 4
announcing dreams. *See* dreams
Anomalistic Psychology (Zusne and
    Jones), 121
anomalous: communication, 96–97,
    123, 165; dreams, 96, 102, 104,
    112, 118, 126, 145; dreams between
    parent and child, 122–124; occur-

rences, 93, 123; research on,
    111–113, 120, 122–123. *See also*
    telepathic, precognitive and
    clairvoyant dreams
archetype, 123, 149–150, 154, 158
Art of Dreaming, The (Tonay), 31
Artemidorous, 115
Asclepius, 67
Asian, philosophy, 127
Assurbanipal, King of Assyria, 83
Assyrian dreamers, 9
Australia, 136. *See also* aborigines

Ba, 45
Babylonian: dreamers, 9; folktales,
    Epic of Gilgamesh, The, 23; Gods, 1,
    8
Baha'i Faith, 148
Bartholomew, Brother, 68
Beaver, 128
Besa, 29
Bessent, Malcolm, 120–121
Bible, the, 10, 96, 115, 142
brain: activity during dreaming, 24,
    37, 150, 161–166; activity during